SPEAKING INTELLIGENTLY
For Business and Other Professions

Joann Brown
Florida International University

Brian Schriner
Florida International University

KENDALL/HUNT PUBLISHING COMPANY
4050 Westmark Drive   Dubuque, Iowa 52002

CONTENTS
IN BRIEF

CONTENTS
IN DETAIL

Part Three   **Persuasive Speeches   271**

Part Four   **Special Occasion Speeches   337**

PREFACE

You have decided to enroll in a public speaking course. Your decision may not have been completely voluntary. Maybe your major requires a course in public speaking as a requirement. Your decision is, nevertheless, a wise one. The speaking skills you will learn in a public speaking class will last you a lifetime.

This text is designed to take you step-by-step through the speech-making process. By the completion of the term you will understand how to organize various types of public presentations for almost any occasion. Whether you have been asked by your professor to give an oral report, asked by a club to which you belong to speak at its next banquet, or you would like to persuade your boss to give you a raise, you will be prepared.

The goal of this text is to develop your awareness of not only how to present a public presentation, but why each element in a presentation is important.

This text can be used at any level of higher education and by most any instructor. It is also useful to professionals who may need to brush up on their speech-making skills. Perhaps the most important benefit of this text is that it will help you develop confidence in yourself. You will gain confidence in the fact you know how to:

- Organize a public presentation.
- Research it thoroughly.
- Deliver it effectively.

We wish you the best of luck in this course and encourage you to do your best. With the proper know-how and a little practice you too can look like a professional.

Joann Brown
Florida International University

Brian Schriner
Florida International University

APPRECIATION FOR SUPPORT

This text is the result of the efforts of not just its authors, but those who comprise the Speech Communication Program at Florida International University.

Our heartfelt appreciation goes to Alice Contreras, Lydia Hoadley, Norma Jean P. Perez, and Victoria Vinas for their editing and formatting. Their countless hours made this text a reality. We would also like to thank our colleagues for their ideas and support. We appreciate all the help we have received from: Elaine Cichon, Edward Fischer, Ellen Karsh and Kathleen Watson.

Many of the examples and sample outlines in this text were provided by students from Florida International University who have successfully completed a course in public speaking. We are grateful to all of the students for their hard work, but special thanks are in order for Elizabeth Auer, Evelyn Jones, Joselle Galis-Menendez, Phuoc Nguyen, Michelle Reyes, and Jorge Rodriguez.

PART ONE

GETTING
STARTED

CHAPTER 1
The Communication Process

"The most important thing I learned in school was how to communicate . . . You can have brilliant ideas, but if you can't get them across, your brains won't get you anywhere."

Lee Iacocca

The ability to communicate is the one skill employers are looking for in college graduates. Employers are looking for individuals who have the ability to formulate rational thoughts, articulate those ideas in a meaningful and concise manner, and listen critically. You will develop these skills in this course.

In a survey of business personnel managers, it was determined that "oral communications and listening were ranked number one and number two in importance".[1] Employers even ranked the ability to speak well and listen intelligently over an applicant's technical knowledge of the job! In another survey conducted by *Engineering Education* magazine, 500 leaders in engineering concluded that, "even in a highly technical field like engineering, the most important skill to possess was the ability to communicate".[2]

The Communication Process

We hear the word *communication* used almost everyday. However, despite how frequently the term is used, many communication scholars still have difficulty defining the word.

- Communication is the process of sharing thoughts, ideas, and feelings with each other in commonly understandable ways.[3]
- Communication is the process of sending and receiving verbal and nonverbal messages to create shared meaning.[4]
- Communication is a two-way process of exchanging information.[5]

Communications
The process of sharing thoughts, ideas, and feelings with each other in commonly understandable ways.

3

- Communication is an interactive process in which people exchange and interpret messages with one another.[6]
- Communication is a transactional process of skillfully sharing, selecting, and sorting ideas, symbols, and signs in such a way as to help listeners elicit from their own minds a meaning or construction similar to that intended by the speaker.[7]
- Communication is the creation of shared meaning through symbolic processes.[8]

As you can see from these six examples each definition of communication is similar. Each discusses the concept of *"sharing and/or creating meaning,"* but each is worded differently. The fact that each definition is worded differently, yet they all attempt to convey the same meaning, is indicative of communication. Each definition is different because the ways in which an individual can share or create meaning with another is infinite. What's more, we all have different perceptions and interpretations. In communication terminology, this is known as your frame of reference.

Frame of Reference
An individual's perceptions and/or interpretations

Each person's **frame of reference** consists of his/her educational background, race, gender, religion, personality, beliefs, attitudes, values, language, income, social status, past experiences, expectations, and cultural customs. The participant's frame of reference influences how each individual communicates. Quickly consider all of the elements that compose your frame of reference. Do you think anyone in your class has your identical frame of reference? Do you think anyone in your city (state, country, or the world) has your identical frame of reference? The answer is "No!" There are no two individuals in the world who share identical frames of reference. Each of us is unique in some way. Given the fact that we are all different, and these differences influence how we communicate, 100% successful communication is an impossibility.

For instance, look out the window and describe what you see. The words you choose to describe what you see will be different than those of another person who has the exact same view. The organization of these words and the method you use to organize them will also be different from one another's.

Delivery
The way an individual presents their speech

Audience Analysis
Knowing what the interests/needs of the audience are

To be an effective communicator you first need to understand how the communication process works. If you want to be able to speak to a group of people clearly and with confidence, you need to be able to organize your thoughts and **deliver** this information in such a way that your audience is able to clearly understand your thoughts as they are intended. In other words, you need to have an idea of your audiences' frame of reference. This is known as **audience analysis** and will be discussed in Chapter Three.

Seven Elements of Communication

As we have stated, communication is a process. The word **process,** according to the *American Heritage Dictionary* is "a series of actions, changes or functions that bring about an end or result." Communication does just that. Perhaps communication results in imparting knowledge/information. Communication can also persuade someone to take action, or it can also be used to entertain. Whatever the end result of the communication the process is made up of seven elements.

The first element is the **source** or the sender. The source is responsible for **encoding** a message. To encode a message means to create a message. You have some sort of thought or feeling that you wish to convey to someone else; you need to encode it. In other words, you need to create it and put it in some type of message system.

The second element is the **receiver.** The receiver is responsible for **decoding** a message. To decode a message means to interpret it, to understand it, to give meaning to it. It does not mean to answer. When a classmate asks you what your major is, that classmate is the sender; you are the receiver. Since you are decoding or interpreting the message, you are the receiver. When you answer the question and say "biology," "accounting," or "pharmacy," then you are encoding/creating a message, and that makes you the source.

The third element is the **message.** The message can be *verbal* (oral or written) or *nonverbal*. Your nonverbal messages consist of eye contact, fidgeting, tone of voice, posture, gestures, and volume of voice. Although your tone and volume are related to your voice, they are still considered nonverbal communication. Verbal communication consists solely of words. If it cannot be looked up in the dictionary, then it is considered nonverbal communication. The importance of nonverbal communication cannot be overstated. Anthropologist R.L. Birdwhistell, considered one of the originators of the study of nonverbal communication, has reported that 65–70% of meaning assigned is the result of the interpretation of nonverbal communication (in the United States).

Process
A series of actions, changes, or functions that bring about an end or a result.

Source
The originator of a message

Encoding
To put an idea into a message system

Receiver
The receptor of a message

Decoding
To interpret, to understand, to give meaning to a message

Verbal Messages
Are oral or written

Message
May be verbal or nonverbal
Verbal Messages are oral or written

Nonverbal Messages
Consists of: eye contact, fidgeting, tone, volume, gestures, and posture

---

Nonverbal Communication and Culture

"Nonverbal communication is considered to be all aspects of communication other than the words themselves." Just like verbal symbols are culturally determined, so are nonverbal symbols. There are several categories of nonverbal communication. Here we will examine the relationship between culture and body movements, which is known as Kinetics. Because body movements are culturally specific, an innocent gesture in one culture can be interpreted as an insult in another culture. For reference, the U.S. American "OK" symbol when it is inverted is seen as an obscene gesture in Brazil. So imagine how Richard Nixon felt when he got off of a plane in Brazil and when asked by a reporter about his trip he signaled, "OK." In Japan, this symbol has yet another meaning, money.

Emblems are gestures that have a direct verbal counterpart. You occasionally use these types of gestures in public speaking to quiet an audience. When you place your index finger to your lips, it means shhhh. You could use the same gesture to quiet an audience of Ethiopians but only if the audience was comprised of children. You see, in Ethiopia, to motion silence to adults, one would use four fingers to the lips. Emblems can also be used to complement your verbal message. A signal displaying your middle and index finger upward with a clenched fist is a peace sign in the United States. In Great Britain, Winston Churchill used this sign to represent victory at the end of World War II.

Illustrators, on the other hand, are nonverbal behaviors that are only understood by the context of the verbal message. Unlike emblems, they do not have a meaning apart from the verbal message. If someone were to ask you if you speak Spanish and you reply "un poquito" while displaying with your thumb and index finger the distance of about an inch, that "inch" has no meaning (in U.S. American culture) when it is not accompanied by the verbal message. However, that is not to say that illustrators cannot have meaning in another culture. Remember, body movements have meaning that are culturally specific.

Lastly, there are adapters. Adapters are personal body movements that occur as a reaction to your physical or psychological state. In public speaking, we call it fidgeting. Adapters are usually performed unintentionally, yet it is possible to convey meaning through your nervous fidgeting and this can have dramatic effects. Imagine a nervous speaker who places an index finger to his lips and then rubs it over their eyebrow. In the United States, one would probably think the speaker is very nervous. In Japan, the speaker just accused someone of being a liar. When giving a speech, you are sending a message. It is important to understand that you may be sending a message, you do not wish to send, with one of your gestures.

Ray Birdwhistell. (1970) Kinesics and Context: Essays on Body Motion Communication. (p. 34). Philadelphia: University of Pennsylvania.

Feedback
A response to a message that is decoded by the source

The fourth element is **feedback.** Upon decoding a message, the receiver encodes a response to the sender to indicate that he/she has received the message. This verbal and/or nonverbal response by the receiver to the sender's message is called feedback.

If the receiver perceives he or she has understood the sender's intended message, the feedback will be positive. **Positive feedback** can be in the form of nodding the head, or responding, "Yes, I understand." As you might have guessed, verbal feedback is always easier for a sender to decode.

If the receiver perceives he or she has not understood the sender's message, the feedback will be negative. **Negative feedback** may take the form of shaking the head back and forth or responding, "No, I do not understand." Negative feedback may be the result of: (1) the receiver not agreeing with the sender's message; or (2) the receiver's perception is such that he or she does not understand the concept the sender wishes the receiver to recreate.

Remember, a receiver assigns meaning to the sender's verbal and/or nonverbal messages and indicates to the sender the feeling that he/she has clearly understood the sender's intent. The receiver may or may not be correct when interpreting the message; however, the receiver responds positively, negatively, or with a combination of positive and negative feedback.

The sender of the message must then decode the receiver's feedback. Once again this feedback may be positive or negative, verbal or nonverbal, or a combination of each. The sender then, just as the receiver did, must decode the receiver's feedback and assign meaning to the message. This makes the communication process circular.

Positive Feedback
Suggests agreement or an understanding of the message

Negative Feedback
Suggests disagreement or confusion with the message

Model of Communication

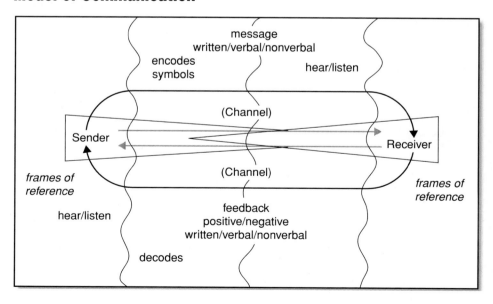

Delivery
The way an individual presents their speech

If the speaker perceives the receiver's feedback to be positive, and the receiver believes to have understood the sender's intent, the sender should not alter the original message. The sender should encode a message that is very similar to the original message. If the sender perceives the receiver's feedback to be negative and the receiver feels he/she has not understood the sender's intent, the sender should alter the original message. The alteration may be through changes in the verbal and/or nonverbal portion of the message.

When **delivering** a speech you will undoubtedly encounter both positive and negative feedback. This is one of the difficulties of public speaking. Unlike a conversation with another person, you do not have the luxury of stopping and asking your audience if they understand your intent, nor will your audience be asking, probing, or clarifying questions while you are speaking.

Unfortunately, when you present a speech to an audience, most if not all of your feedback will be in the form of nonverbal communication. If you are not used to recognizing and reacting to nonverbal feedback this may present a unique problem. An effective speaker must be able to correctly answer the following five questions with respect to feedback:

1. Is the feedback verbal, nonverbal, or a combination of each?
2. Is the feedback positive, negative, or a combination of each?
3. If the feedback is both positive and negative, which components of the message is the audience responding to negatively?
4. If the feedback is both positive and negative, which components of the message is the audience responding to positively?
5. Is the receiver's feedback genuine? (As in the example of nodding your head in the affirmative but questioning if you really understood the message of the sender.)

By identifying and reacting appropriately to feedback you increase your chances of being a successful speaker. Many people who have not been successful failed because they were unable to accurately recognize feedback and react accordingly. For these reasons, your instructor will undoubtedly stress the necessity of maintaining **eye contact** with your audience. If you are not looking at the audience, how can you recognize if the feedback is positive or negative?

In addition, your instructor will probably require you to deliver your presentations in a conversational manner. You will not be permitted to read or memorize your speech word for word. If the words you are using during the presentation are all predetermined, how can you react to feedback? Obviously, you cannot, and your chances for success are greatly diminished.

Eye Contact
Important because it supports a speaker's credibility with the audience

The fifth element in the communication process is the **channel** in which you encode and decode your messages. Your channels are your five senses: sight, sound, smell, taste, and touch. In the United States, individuals primarily rely on the channels of seeing and hearing to decode messages. However, other cultures rely on smell, taste, and touch as much as they do on seeing or hearing.

Channel
The means in which a message is transmitted

Communication and Culture

Whether you live in a city or small town in the United States, a Kibbutz in Israel, a village in Thailand, the jungles of Colombia, or the plains of Kenya, you employ the seven elements of the communication process. The methods will be different but the process remains the same. For example, a Japanese Geisha and a Michigan schoolteacher send and receive messages using different channels with varying amounts of feedback, yet all seven channels of the process are present.

Culture is an important aspect of communication because it is one's culture that determines the formation and content of messages, as well as which messages are noticed and which ones are interpreted. According to Edward T. Hall, "Nothing in our lives is free from cultural influences. It is the keystone in civilizations arch and is the medium through which all of life's events must flow."

Edward T. Hall. *Beyond Culture*. (p.14). Garden City, NY: Anchor Doubleday.

The sixth element in the communication process is **noise.** Noise interferes or inhibits the communication process. There are two types of noise: *internal* and *external*. Internal noise is something that is going on inside of the individual. It can be something simple, such as daydreaming, or more complex, such as cultural differences. External noise is related to the environment. It may be auditory, such as a loud air conditioner, or it can be visual. Perhaps the room in which you are speaking has windows, and something is happening outside. The fact that your audience may be looking out those windows wondering what is happening is considered noise because they are no longer paying attention to you.

The last element is **location** or context. The communication process does not take place in a vacuum. There are both internal and external

Noise
Interference with encoding and decoding of a message; there are two types: internal noise and external noise

Location
Context in which communication is taking place

Encoding
To put an idea into
a message system

Decoding
To interpret, to
understand, to give
meaning to a mes-
sage

factors that contribute to the **encoding** and **decoding** of messages. The context of the communication process, the time, place, and physical and social surroundings may all influence the communication process.

- For instance, the **time** at which your presentation is scheduled will affect both you and your audience. Is your presentation before or after lunch? Is it first thing in the morning? Is it the last speech Friday afternoon?
- The **place** where communication happens also influences the participants. Are you indoors? Are you conducting business at a social gathering? Are you arguing with your friend in a public place?
- The **physical surroundings** also influence the communication process. Are you speaking in a large room? Is the room too cold? Is the person you are speaking with standing too close to you?
- Finally, the social relationships between participants or the **social surroundings** influence the communication process. Are you speaking to your friend? Someone you do not trust? Your parents?

All four factors—time, place, and physical and social surroundings—may contribute to the encoding and decoding of messages. Each influences the process of communication.

Symbols

Symbols
Language or
gestures that are
used to convey
meaning to
another.

In order to communicate, you need to use *symbols*. Messages are sent between the sender and the receiver through symbols. Verbal symbols are words, while nonverbal symbols are gestures, eye contact, posture, facial expressions, tone, and volume of voice.

Words are not objects or things. According to Hamilton Gregory, "If you give someone an apple, you transfer a solid object from your hand to theirs. But if you're making a speech and you mention the word apple, you are no longer transferring a concrete thing. You are transferring a symbol, which may be interpreted by your listeners in ways that are quite different from what you had in your mind. When you say apple, one listener may think of a small green fruit, while another conjures an image of a big red fruit. One listener might think of crisp tartness, while another thinks of juicy sweetness."[9]

**Frame of
Reference**
An individual's
perception and/or
interpretations

As you can see from this example, symbols are ambiguous; they mean different things to different individuals based upon their **frame of reference.** In addition, symbols are arbitrary; they are randomly assigned. The spelling of a-p-p-l-e and the pronunciation ap´ple does not give you any idea of what an apple is or does. That is why when learning to read or studying a foreign language individuals need to learn which words represent which objects. There is no inherent connection between an actual object and the word that symbolizes that particular object. Therefore, a formal definition of symbols is as follows: "Symbols used to create language and nonverbal gestures are arbitrary and ambiguous, yet communication is the process of exchanging mutually agreed upon symbols to stimulate meaning in another."[10]

All in all, the communication process involves sending symbols that represent your message through a channel to your waiting listener(s). Be aware of your audience's reactions, in the form of feedback, and be prepared to face barriers in your quest to make this process easier and provide for better communication.

Listening

As a speaker (a sender) you need to be aware of how your audience (the receiver) receives a message and the problems your audience may experience when receiving your message. A distinction first needs to be made between hearing and listening. **Hearing** is a physical process; the sound waves vibrate your eardrum and your nerves send a message to your brain. **Listening** is a cognitive process. Listening involves the physical energy of your eardrum and nerve endings and the cognitive energy of your brain for perception and interpretation of the message. Your brain decodes the sender's message and assigns meaning and understanding. This is the cognitive process of listening.

After listening intently to a lecture for an hour you probably feel tired. This is an indication that you were indeed listening and not just hearing the lecture. You exerted physical energy to hear the message and cognitive energy to interpret and assign meaning to the lecture. Can you recall a conversation or discussion where you were hearing what the person was saying but you were not really listening? You were physically present and you heard the message, but the message never seemed to register with your brain. You were not listening.

It is difficult not to hear a message. You can hold your hands over your ears or leave the room but you cannot decide not to hear. You cannot keep your eardrums from functioning. Of course, there are exceptions. Sometimes a loud noise may interfere with your ability to hear a conversation or you may have a physical ailment that limits your hearing ability.

Barriers to Listening

There are many obstacles that prevent a person from listening to a message despite being able to hear the message. These obstacles to listening are known as noise. Noise was discussed as the seventh element of the communication process. The following are examples of **noise** and how each affects the listening process.

Hearing
A physical process

Listening
A cognitive process

Noise
Interference with encoding and decoding of a message; there are two types: internal and external noise

No Reward of Listening
A message is not important to the receiver

■ *No Reward for Listening*
Listeners often perceive a message as irrelevant to them. As such, they have trouble listening to the message. When you as the listener determine that you will not benefit from the information or the information doesn't interest you, you may find it difficult to listen. Attending a boring lecture, hearing the same message over and over again, or realizing the information is not relevant to your life are all examples that make listening difficult.

Environmental
Physical and social surroundings distract from message

■ *Environmental*
Other barriers to listening include environmental conditions. Sometimes your chair is uncomfortable, you may not be feeling well, the room may be too hot, or the air conditioner may be making a distracting noise. All of these environmental reasons may inhibit a receiver's ability to listen to a message.

Controversial Information
Causes receivers to question the message

■ *Controversial Information*
Often a speaker will say something that you find puzzling or controversial. In these instances, you may ask yourself silent questions such as, "Is that really true?" or "What do they mean by that?" The speaker, unaware that you are questioning the information in your mind, will continue speaking. Your ear is still hearing the information but you may no longer be listening to the message.

Response Formulation
Causes receivers to think of an immediate reply

■ *Response Formulation*
Another common problem people have when they listen is that they often formulate a response of some kind while a person is still speaking. Your friend may be telling you about a recent vacation to Europe and you may be thinking, "Oh, I have to tell him/her about my trip last summer." While you are formulating a response you may not be listening to the speaker's message.

Trigger Effect
Causes receivers to think of something else

■ *Trigger Effect*
A common barrier to listening occurs when a speaker says something that reminds a listener of a related event or person. If someone were to tell you about his or her childhood in Pennsylvania, you may begin thinking of your friend. You may remember a funny incident. As a result, you may try to recall your friend's phone number. What is the speaker doing during this time? Still talking. You are physically hearing the information but you are not listening to the message.

Psychological
Personal distractions that cause receiver not to listen in the first place

■ *Psychological*
Psychological barriers to listening are personal distractions a listener may be experiencing. You may be worried about your midterm exam or a recent disagreement with a boyfriend or girlfriend. These psychological distractions (personal problems) may

interfere with a person's ability to concentrate on the message and become barriers to listening.

■ *Attitudinal*
Attitudinal biases against a speaker result in a person having trouble listening to a message. You may have trouble listening to people of the opposite sex, people who are younger or older than you, people you feel are unattractive, people you feel are less intelligent than you, or perhaps people from a different ethnicity or race. In each case you may have trouble listening to the speaker's message.

■ *Semantics*
When a person has trouble understanding a person's accent or the use of words this is referred to as a semantic barrier to listening. You may have had trouble understanding a speaker's use of terms or a person's pronunciation of words. If so, you may have had trouble listening to the speaker's message.

Types of Listening

There are different reasons why people listen. Different circumstances (contexts) require a person to listen more or less intently. Do you listen with equal amounts of energy when you are listening to the radio and when you are listening to a lecture in class? As you can see, each type of listening requires a varying amount of energy. The four basic types of listening with respect to the amount of energy required are listening for entertainment, listening for information, listening for judgment, and critical listening.

■ *Entertainment*
This type of listening is for pure enjoyment. Your goal is not complete comprehension or retention of the message but simply to enjoy the message. Listening to music or watching television are examples of listening for entertainment.

■ *Information*
The goal of this type of listening is to retain information. Listening for traffic directions or a friend's telephone number are two examples.

■ *Judgment*
When listeners make value judgments regarding a subject's correctness or a speaker's attributes such as credibility or trustworthiness, they are using more physical energy than when listening for entertainment or for information.

■ *Critical*
Listeners who listen for what is said, how it is said, why it was said, what was not said, and why something was not said are using even

Attitudinal
Personal biases receivers may have towards the speaker

Semantics
Not being able to understand the message due to sender's accent/pronunciation

Entertainment
Listening for enjoyment

Information
Listening to retain information

Judgment
Perceptions made by the recivers about a sender's delivery and/or message

Critical
Listening so as to intently analyze the message

Empathetic
Listening to
understand
another's situation

more physical energy. This is the most difficult type of listening because it requires the most cognitive and physical energy.

■ *Empathetic*

This type of listening occurs most often in interpersonal relationships. When you listen to a friend discuss a problem or concern that he/she is having you are listening to lend support.

With all the various types of listening and the potential barriers to listening, how can you become a better listener? The first thing you need to do is be aware that listening takes cognitive energy. You cannot just sit back and let the information flow into your head. Depending on the type of listening that is required, you will need to actively make decisions while listening. Is this information correct? Is the speaker knowledgeable? What does this information really mean?

Secondly, as an active listener it is not enough to simply ask appropriate questions regarding the sender's intent. You also need to be able to continue listening to the speaker and not let the questions raised by the sender's intent create internal **noise.** This process takes practice.

The best way to become a better listener is to begin practicing. This may sound unusual; however, you can practice listening by being mentally aware of the barriers and stop yourself from falling into one or more of the listening traps. Like any other activity, once you train yourself to listen correctly, it will become increasingly easier.

Noise
Interference with
encoding and
decoding of a message; there are two
types: internal noise
and external noise

Endnotes

1. Cohen, R., A. & Bradsford L. (1990). *Influence without authority.* New York: Wiley.
2. Kimel, R., W. & Monsees E. (1979). Engineering graduates: How good are they? *Engineering Education,* 210.
3. Hamilton, C. (1993). *Communicating for results* (p. 5). Belmont, CA: Wadsworth Publishing Company.
4. Sellnow, D. (2002). *Public speaking: A process approach* (p. 6). New York: Harcourt.
5. Mayer, R. K. (1988). *Well spoken: Oral communication skills* (p. 20). New York: Harcourt Brace Jovanovich.
6. O'Hair, D. (1999). *Public speaking challenges and choice* (p. 15). New York: St. Martin's Press.
7. Ross, R. (1998). *The speech making process* (p. 9). Boston: Allyn and Bacon.
8. Makay, J. (1995). *Public speaking theory into practice* (p. 12). New York: Harcourt Brace.
9. Gregory, H. (1993). *Public speaking: For college and career* (p. 7). New York: McGraw Hill.
10. Hamilton, C. (1993). *Communicating for results* (p. 9). Belmont, CA: Wadsworth Publishing Company.

Chapter One
KEY TERMS

Channel: _____
_____

Communication: _____
_____

Decode: _____
_____

Encode: _____
_____

Feedback: _____
_____

Frames of Reference: _____
_____

Hearing: _____
_____

Listening: _____
_____

Location: _____
_____

Message: _____
_____

Negative Feedback: _____
_____

Noise: _____
_____

Positive Feedback: _____

_____

Receiver: _____

_____

Source: _____

_____

Symbol: _____

_____

Types of Listening: _____

_____

Chapter One
EXERCISES

Use the following terms to draw a model. Some words may be used more than once in the model.

Noise	Context	Encode	Written/Verbal/Nonverbal
Message	Receiver	Sender	Frames of Reference
Hear/Listen	Feedback	Channel	Positive/Negative
Symbols	Decode		

Chapter One
REVIEW QUESTIONS

1. Why are the definitions of communication so varied?

    _____

    _____

    _____

2. Why are the definitions of communication so similar?

    _____

    _____

    _____

3. What is the goal of all communication?

    _____

    _____

    _____

4. Why is communication considered a process?

    _____

    _____

    _____

5. Define the following terms:

    Sender: _____

    Encode: _____

    Decode: _____

    Message: _____

    Receiver: _____

    Symbols: _____

    Feedback: _____

    Verbal Communication: _____

    Nonverbal Communication: _____

    Context: _____

Frames of Reference: _____

Noise: _____

Channel: _____

6. Why is 100% communication considered an impossibility?

_____

_____

_____

7. Why does the burden of communication ultimately rest with the sender?

_____

_____

_____

8. What is the difference between hearing and listening?

_____

_____

_____

9. List and explain the four types of listening in order of the amount of energy each requires.

a. _____ : _____

b. _____ : _____

c. _____ : _____

d. _____ : _____

10. Match the barrier to listening with its appropriate description.

Barrier

_____ No Reward for Listening

_____ Environmental

_____ Controversial Information

_____ Response Formulation

_____ Trigger Effect

_____ Psychological

_____ Attitudinal

_____ Semantic

Description

A. Heavy accent, improper pronunciation of words.

B. "That reminds me of the time. . . ."

C. "I am so tired I can hardly stay awake."

D. "How many times is he/she going to say the same thing?"

E. "I wonder if that is true . . . ?"

F. "Yeah, yeah, whatever . . . Guess what I did!"

G. "What time is it? I need to be at the dentist shortly."

H. "This guy is too young to know what he is talking about!"

Chapter One
POWERPOINT SLIDES

- Definition of communication
- Elements of communication
- Definition of symbols
- Barriers of listening
- Types of listening

COMMUNICATION

The process of people sharing thoughts, ideas, and feelings with each other in commonly understandable ways.

22

ELEMENTS
OF COMMUNICATION

- Sender

- Receiver

- Message

- Channel

- Feedback

- Noise

- Location

SYMBOLS

Used to create language and nonverbal gestures, are arbitrary and ambiguous, yet communication is the process of exchanging mutually understood symbols to stimulate meaning in another.

BARRIERS TO LISTENING

- No reward for listening
- Environmental
- Controversial information
- Response formulation
- Trigger effect
- Psychological
- Attitudinal
- Semantic

TYPES OF LISTENING

- **Entertainment**

- **Information**

- **Judgment**

- **Critical**

- **Empathetic**

CHAPTER 2
Delivery and Anxiety

If something is wrong, fix it if you can. But train yourself not to worry. Worry never fixes anything.

Mary Hemingway, American Journalist

Your worst nightmare is coming true. You have been asked to speak in front of an audience. To you it is irrelevant if the audience consists of 20 people or 100 people. You picture yourself on the stage behind a lectern; your palms begin to sweat, you feel sick to your stomach, your knees are shaking, and you are perspiring from your brow. You open your mouth and for one moment nothing comes out. Your throat is as tense as a piano string. All of a sudden you blurt out "uurbuughthh . . ." You feel like you are about to faint. You have never been so embarrassed in your whole life.

Anyone who has ever given a public presentation has probably experienced some, if not all, of these pre-speech anxiety symptoms. For some of you this may actually be comforting. As they say, "Misery loves company." However, others may be asking, "What can I do? Help me!"

Communication Apprehension

Communication apprehension is experienced by everyone. Approximately 3,000 Americans of all ages and professions were asked, "What are you most afraid of?" The most common response, "speaking before a group." This answer was more prevalent than individuals' fear of snakes, heights, or even death. Clearly you are not alone in your nervousness about speaking to an audience. Consider some of these statements by famous individuals:

> Barbara Streisand: "I suffer from terrible stage fright."

> Katie Couric: "I still get nervous after all these years."

Communication Apprehension
Nervousness everyone has about speaking in public

James Taylor: "Me nervous? Sure—before every time I go out there to perform."

Joe Montana: (concerning a television commercial) "It's a nervous time for me."

Before you try to deal with your anxiety about speaking in front of others, you first need to understand it. James McCroskey defines communication apprehension as "an individual's level of fear or anxiety associated either with real or anticipated communication with another person or persons."[1] This definition has three key components to it. First it touches upon an individual's **level of anxiety.** Some people are more nervous than others. You may be terrified of this class, while a classmate experiences only a mild case of jitters. The point is, everyone gets nervous to some degree. Secondly, McCroskey's definition takes into account **real** or **anticipated communication.** Some people panic for days leading up to a speech. These individuals dwell for days about all the things that could go wrong during their speech, while others are most nervous during the actual speech. These individuals feel confident until the moment they lift their head and see the audience in front of them. Finally, McCroskey's definition recognizes the **number of people** involved. A person can feel nervous talking to another person or to a group of persons. We have all felt a twinge of butterflies when talking to that special girl/guy who has caught our eye and we are sure that most of you are concerned about getting up in front of your class to deliver a speech.

This chapter is designed to help you overcome pre-speech anxiety and deliver a clear, concise, effective presentation. Reading this chapter in no way ensures you perfect **delivery** skills, but it will provide you with the information you need to begin **practicing** and improving your oral communication skills.

Overcoming Speech Anxiety

Everyone experiences pre-speech anxiety to some degree. It is perfectly natural to feel anxious before delivering a public presentation.

There is no magic formula for eliminating speech anxiety. Nobody can guarantee you that all your nervousness will be eliminated prior to speaking; however, there are proven techniques that will reduce your pre-speech jitters.

Level of Anxiety
Degree of nervousness

Anticipated Communication
Thinking about what will happen in the future

Number of People
May affect a speaker's degree of nervousness

Delivery
The way an individual presents their speech

Practice
This is a key component of speech-making. Speakers must feel comfortable with presentation

Proven Ways to Prevent and Deal with Speech Nerves
Joan Detz

"I'm afraid I'll be nervous." That's a common feeling people have when asked to give a speech—and in some ways it's healthy. It shows you care about getting your message across to the audience. You really do want to look and sound good.

But it's important to understand what nervousness is. Nervousness is simply energy. If you channel that energy, you can turn it into a positive force. You can make it work for you. You can use the extra energy to your advantage.

But if you allow that energy to go unchecked—if you allow it to control you—then you're going to have problems. A dry mouth. Perhaps a cracking voice. Lots of rocking back and forth on your feet, or lots of "uh's" and "um's." Maybe even forgetfulness.

How can you channel your nervous energy?

Learn to direct your extra energy into eye contact, body language, and vocal enthusiasm. These physical activities provide an outlet for your nervousness. They offer a way to use up some of that extra energy.

What's more, good eye contact, strong body language, and vocal enthusiasm will build your confidence. It's hard to feel insecure when you look directly at your listeners and see the responsiveness in their faces.

Pre-speech Tricks that Work
There are tricks to every trade, and public speaking is no exception. Do what the pros do to keep their nervousness in check:

Try Physical Exercises
Just before you speak, go off by yourself (to the restroom or to quiet corner) and concentrate on the part of your body that feels most tense. Your face? Your hands? Your stomach? Deliberately tighten those muscles until they start to quiver; then let go. You will feel an enormous sense of relief. Repeat this a few times.

Drop your head. Let your cheek muscles go loose and let your mouth go slack.

Make funny faces. Puff up your cheeks, then let the air escape. Or open your mouth and your eyes wide, then close them tightly. Alternate a few times.

Yawn a few times to loosen your jaw and your mucous membranes.

Pretend you're an opera singer. Try "mi, mi, mi" a few times. Wave your arms as you do it.

Try Mental Exercises

Picture something that's given you pleasant memories: Sailing on a blue-green ocean. Swimming in a mountain lake. Walking on a beach. Feeling the sand between your toes. (Think of something other than your impending speech.)

Try a Rational Approach

Say to yourself, "I'm prepared. I know what I'm talking about." Or, "I've spent a year working on this project. Nobody knows as much about this project as I do." Or, "I'm glad I can talk to these people. It will help my career." Convince yourself that speaking to an audience is not that big of a deal.

I know someone who repeats to herself, "This is better than death, this is better than death." That may sound extreme, but it works for her. And, she's right. Giving a speech is better than death.

If you're scared to give a speech, try to think of something that's really frightening. The speech should seem appealing by comparison.

Try a Test Run

Visualize exactly what will happen after you're introduced. You'll get out of your chair, you'll hold the folder in your left hand, you'll walk confidently across the stage, you'll hold your head high, you'll look directly at the person who introduced you, you'll shake his or her hand, you'll . . .

If you see yourself as confident and successful in your mental test run, you'll be confident and successful in your delivery. Above all, never say that you're nervous. If you do, you'll make yourself more nervous. And you'll make the audience nervous, too.

During-the-Speech Tricks to Use

OK. You've prepared your speech carefully. You've done the pre-speech exercises. Now you're at the lectern and—can it be?—your mouth goes a little dry.

Don't panic. Just intensify your eye contact. Looking at the audience will take away your self-preoccupation and reduce the dryness.

Persistent dryness? Help yourself to the glass of water that you've wisely placed at the lectern. Don't be embarrassed. Say to yourself, "It's my speech, and I can damned well drink water if I want to."

What else can go wrong because of misplaced nervous energy? I once found that my teeth got so dry, my lip actually stuck to them. An actor friend later told me to rub a light coating of Vaseline over my teeth. It's a good tip.

Other mini traumas?

Sweat Rolling Off Your Forehead

Wipe it away with the cotton handkerchief that you placed at the lectern. Don't hesitate to really wipe. Little dabs are ineffectual, and you'll have to dap repeatedly. Do it right the first time and get it over with. Also, avoid using tissues. They can shred and get stuck to your face—not a terribly impressive sight.

A Quavery Voice

Again, intensify your eye contact. Focus on your audience. Then lower your pitch and control your breath as you begin to speak. Concentrate on speaking distinctly and slowly.

Trembling Hands

Take heart. The audience probably can't see your trembling hands, but if they're distracting you, then use some body movement to diffuse that nervous energy. Change your foot position. Lean forward to make a point. Walk out from behind the lectern, if possible. Move your arms. (If your body is in a frozen position, your shaking will only grow worse.)

A Pounding Heart

Your going to have one, but the audience cannot see the rising and falling of your chest.

Throat Clearing

If you have to cough, cough away from the microphone. Drink some water, or pop a cough drop into your mouth. Again, the well-prepared speaker has an unwrapped cough drop handy at all times and ready to use.

Runny Nose, Watery Eyes

Bright lights can trigger this type of reaction. Simply pause, say "Excuse me," blow your nose or wipe your eyes, and get on with it. Don't make a big deal over it by apologizing. A simple "Excuse me" is just fine.

Nausea

You come down with a viral infection two days before your speech and you're afraid of throwing up in the middle of it. Well, that's why they make anti-nausea drugs. Ask your doctor about a prescription.

For actors, the show must always go on . . . even with serious viral infections. Many actors place a trash can backstage so they can throw up between acts. But you are not an actor, and you really don't have to put yourself through this test of will power.

If you are terribly ill—as opposed to being just mildly nervous—cancel your engagement. Since you've prepared a complete manuscript, perhaps a colleague could substitute for you. If substitution is not possible, offer to speak at a later date.

Burping

Some people feel they have to burp when they get nervous. If you are one of these people, do plenty of physical relaxation exercises before you speak. Don't drink any carbonated beverages that day, and eat only a light lunch.

Fumbled Words

Professional speakers, radio announcers, and television anchor people fumble words fairly often. Someone once introduced President Reagan with this slip of the tongue: "Everyone who is for abortion was at one time a feces [sic]." So, why should you expect to be perfect?

If it's a minor fumble, just ignore it and keep going.

If it's a big one, fix it. Simply repeat the correct word with a smile, to show you're human.

Continue with your speech, but slow down a little bit. Once you've had a slip of the tongue, chances are high that you'll have another. A fumble is a sort of symptom that you're focusing more on yourself than on your message. Relax and slow down.

Forgetfulness

Some people look at an audience and forget what they want to say. Aren't you glad you made the effort to prepare an outline? It's all right there, so you have one less thing to worry about.

Ways to Prevent Anxiety

In addition to the ways Joan Detz discussed, we want to emphasize some others because it is very unlikely that you will not experience some *anxiety* about speaking in public. Therefore, it is essential that you know how to channel your nervous energy. We believe there are four ways that will help reduce your anxiety.

Anxiety
Nervousness everyone has about speaking in public

Preparation
The best way to deal with nervousness

Introductions/ Conclusions
Gives a first impression/gives a lasting impression

Be Prepared

The best way to deal with your anxiety is to *be prepared*. The more familiar you are with the subject the less likely you will be overanxious about discussing it. Being prepared means that you have researched your topic thoroughly and practiced your speech before delivering it.

Know Your Introduction and Conclusion

Knowing your *introduction* and *conclusion* will help you as a speaker, as well as your audience. The introduction of your speech is when you are probably going to feel the most nervous. If you know your introduction well, and can make it through the entire introduction without too many mistakes, your butterflies will subside and you will gain confidence. Your speech will then progress smoothly from there. If on the other hand, you make a lot of mistakes in the introduction, chances are you will be thinking about these mistakes and not concentrating on your speech and before you know it, more mistakes will occur. Another reason for knowing your introduction really well is to gain your audience's attention and draw them into your speech. If you do not have an interesting, well-delivered introduction chances are your audience will not be interested in your speech.

Just as important as the introduction is the conclusion. You want to know the conclusion of your speech well in case something happens during the course of your speech and you blank out. If this occurs and you know your conclusion well, you can make a graceful exit and there is a possibility that your audience will not realize that you have left something out. Another reason for knowing the conclusion is that audiences remember most what they heard last. Therefore, by having an interesting, well-delivered conclusion that wraps everything up, the audience will have a good impression of you as a speaker. On the other hand, if your conclusion abruptly ends or trails off, the audience may have a poor last impression of you as a speaker.

Know Your Audience

Knowing with whom you are speaking is important. The more you know about your *audience* in terms of their attitudes, demographics, and the speaking situation (Audience Analysis Chapter Three), the more you can anticipate their reaction to your speech. It is important to know who your audience is when it comes to selecting a topic, supporting materials, organizational patterns, and visual aids.

Know Audience
Assists a speaker in selecting: a topic, supporting materials, organizational patterns, and visual aids

Select an Appropriate Topic

You will feel less nervous if you choose a topic that may be familiar to you. You should have a basic understanding or "working knowledge" of a potential topic. This is especially true for persons who are not experienced in public speaking. This does not mean it is necessary for you to know everything about your topic. This would be unrealistic. However, having a basic understanding of the *speech topic* facilitates research, organization, and ultimately, delivery of the presentation.

Consider the following example. You are interested in astrology. Although you are not an astrologist and have never taken a course on astrology, you do know a little about astrology. You know there are twelve

Speech Topic
Assists a speaker in: research, organizing information, and delivery

astrological signs and you know the astrological signs are associated with horoscopes. This is probably enough information to consider this a potential speech subject. You should be able to locate and understand the supporting material and effectively organize and deliver your presentation.

In addition to knowing who your audience is, you need to select a topic that is important to you. This enthusiasm will come across in your delivery. If you are not comfortable discussing the subject at hand or if you are not interested in it, it will be very difficult to get your audience involved in your speech. Keep one simple rule in mind: the **Rule of Self-Interest.** Never select a subject you would not want to listen to if you were in the audience. If you find the topic boring, dull, mundane, or outdated, there is a very strong chance your audience will feel the same way.

If you choose a topic which is uninteresting you will have difficulties generating sufficient enthusiasm in your delivery of the speech. Your lack of enthusiasm will be evident in both your **verbal** and **nonverbal** communication, and as a result of your lack of genuine enthusiasm in your delivery, your audience will be able to recognize your lack of interest in the topic. There is an old saying that states, "You cannot fake sincerity." Your audience will be able to tell if you like your own topic. If you are not interested in the topic, your disinterest is contagious. Your audience will probably find your speech just as uninteresting as you do.

Delivery Methods

There are four methods for *delivering* a speech. They are reading from a manuscript, speaking from memory, impromptu speaking, and extemporaneous (conversational) speaking. Each type of delivery is explained in this text; however, the emphasis is on extemporaneous speaking.

Reading Your Speech from a Manuscript

The *manuscript* delivery involves reading a speech that has been written out word for word in essay style. There are occasions where this delivery style is effective. These occasions are usually very formal such as when giving a commencement address, a tribute, a eulogy, or an inaugural address. Because the **contexts** for these speeches are more formal so is the **word choice.** Most of the speeches that are delivered from manuscript are "special occasion speeches" (discussed in Chapter Seven). An advantage of this delivery style is that you can carefully select your words in advance; however, most of us do not speak in these settings on a daily basis. If you are asked to give such a speech, you should practice the speech until you can read it in a natural, conversational manner while maintaining strong eye contact with the audience.

Rule of Self Interest
Choose a topic that is of interest to you

Verbal Communication
Is oral or written

Nonverbal Communication
Consists of: eye contact, fidgeting, tone, volume, gestures, and posture

Delivery
The way an individual presents their speech

Manuscript
Delivering a speech from an essay

Context
Location in which communication is taking place

Word Choice
Important for "connecting" with the audience

Speaking from Memory

This is an ineffective method of delivery for public speakers. *Memorizing* a presentation word for word can result in many problems for both the speaker and the audience. Speakers who memorize speeches take the risk that they may forget portions of the speech or become confused. You may have seen a person who went blank during a speech and was unable to continue. This is because the person memorized the speech.

Impromptu Speaking

An *impromptu* speech is delivered with little or no preparation. This type of delivery is commonly referred to as "off the cuff" speaking. Politicians and community leaders are often asked to speak at functions where they may not have anticipated speaking. You may have been asked to speak at your fraternity or sorority meeting, in a business meeting, or to give a toast at a friend's wedding without any advance notice. In each instance, you had to quickly formulate a presentation in a matter of seconds.

This is not an effective method of delivery for a speech that you are going to have to present. Most inexperienced speakers who deliver an impromptu speech have trouble organizing the ideas of the presentation and may ramble. Do not employ an impromptu delivery style for any of your assigned speeches!

Extemporaneous Delivery

This is the most effective delivery for a public presentation. Using an outline and **speaker cards,** you present your speech in a conversational manner. You have rehearsed the speech several times, but you have not memorized it word for word. You are familiar enough with the information to discuss it with your audience. You may have cue cards in front of you, but they only contain key words on them. You are not reading from your note cards (manuscript style), you have not memorized your speech word for word, and you are not speaking "off the cuff" (impromptu). You have researched your topic, organized your ideas, and familiarized yourself with the information. Now you are sharing that information with your audience in a conversational tone. This is what an *extemporaneous* delivery style is and it is the type of delivery that is the easiest to listen to for most audiences.

Practicing for an Extemporaneous Speech

Before you can begin *practicing* your delivery, you need to complete an outline of the speech. From this outline you will make cue cards to help you recall key points and information while you are delivering your

---

Memorized
Not an effective delivery method

Impromptu
Delivering a speech with little or no preparation

Speaker Cards
Index cards with limited key words— enough to prompt a speaker's memory

Extemporaneous
Speaking from note cards with key terms on them

Practice
This is a key component of speech-making

Speaker Cards
Index cards with
limited key words—
enough to prompt a
speaker's memory

speech. These cue cards, which are usually 3×5 or 4×6 index cards, are called **speaker cards.**

When creating your speaker cards do not write complete sentences on them. Use only key words or phrases that will help you recall information. If you write a complete sentence on a speaker card, you will probably read the complete sentence to the audience, destroying your extemporaneous delivery. Of course, if you are using a direct quote you should write the quote word for word on the speaker card.

Limit the number of speaker cards you use during the presentation. You may begin practicing with several cards, but by the date of the speech, you should have significantly reduced the number of speaker cards. Your instructor may have a maximum number of speaker cards he/she will permit you to use during your speech. Each speaker card should contain a maximum of three points. Each main point (key word or phrase) should be written legibly and large enough for you to see. Speaker cards may look like:

---

150 million years = earth continents formed

80% was ocean

Pangea = Gondwanaland and Laurasia

Practice your delivery using your speaker cards. Hold the speaker cards in your non-dominant hand. If you are right-handed, you would hold your speaker cards in your left hand. If you are left handed, you would hold your speaker cards in your right hand. This enables you to make natural gestures with your dominant hand and solves the problem of not knowing what to do with your other hand. Quite often our non-dominant hand ends up in our pocket or tapping on the lectern.

Place your thumb next to the point you are currently discussing in the presentation. As you progress to the next point, slide your thumb down the index card. Now, when you look down at the index card you only need to look at your thumb to know where you are in the speech.

After completing all the points on a speaker card you need to know what to do with the index card. If you are speaking at a lectern, you should slide the card face up to the immediate right or left with your dominant hand. If you need to look back at the last point you covered, you can easily glance down and locate the previous speaker card. Placing the card face up also reduces the tendency to force a speaker card under the existing pile, which could be disastrous if your speaker cards become mixed up. If you are not using a lectern, then you should place the speaker card at the back of the remaining speaker cards in your non-dominant hand.

Your speaker cards are there to help you recall information and the organization of your presentation. Do not be embarrassed to use a few speaker cards. However, do not use them as a crutch and write every point in the presentation on them. When a speaker uses too many speaker cards the flow of the speaker's delivery is interrupted and the audience can lose interest.

There are several ways to **practice** for a presentation using speaker cards. You may find one method to be more effective for you than another. Briefly, here is a description of the most common ways of practicing for a speech.

- ■ *In front of a mirror*
  By practicing in front of a full-length mirror you can observe your nonverbal communication tendencies. You can see what you look like while you are speaking. What am I doing with my feet? Am I standing still? Do I have proper facial expressions? Do I look tense? Am I using my speaker cards properly?
- ■ *Tape recorder*
  By delivering your speech into a tape recorder you can play the speech back several times and analyze any problem areas. You may notice you spoke too quickly or too slowly, or perhaps you have several "you knows," or "ums" in your delivery. By tape recording your delivery you will be aware of these types of problems and be able to correct them before giving the speech.
- ■ *Video recorder*
  Taping your speech on a video recorder enables you to hear and see your delivery. Not only will you be able to correct any verbal mistakes you may have a tendency to commit, but you can also observe your nonverbal communication.
- ■ *In front of a live audience*
  Before you finally give the speech try to gather a few friends or relatives together and ask them to listen to it. While your friends and relatives may not be overly critical of your delivery, you will have the experience of speaking before a live audience. You can practice recognizing and reacting to feedback.

We cannot stress enough the importance of being properly prepared for a public presentation. This is the most effective method of reducing speech anxiety. The following is a pre-speech checklist:

Practice
This is a key component of speech-making. Speakers must feel comfortable with presentation

In Front of a Mirror
Allows a speaker to see their nonverbal tendencies

Tape Recorder
Allows a speaker to hear their verbal tendencies

Video Recorder
Allows a speaker to see and hear their communication tendencies

In Front of Live Audience
Allows sa peaker to gain some experience speaking to a group of individuals

---

Organizing and Practicing Your Speech

- ◼ I have analyzed my intended audience, including their needs and expectations.
- ◼ I have considered the environment in which I will be speaking.
- ◼ I have selected an appropriate speech topic.
- ◼ I have properly narrowed my speech topic.
- ◼ I have sufficiently researched my topic.
- ◼ I have properly organized the introduction, body, and conclusion of the speech.
- ◼ I have properly outlined my speech using footnotes and a source bibliography.
- ◼ I have practiced my delivery several times out loud until I am comfortable with the information.
- ◼ I have made appropriate speaker cards with keywords on each.
- ◼ I have selected proper visual aids.

Before we discuss the various elements you should consider when practicing the delivery of your speech, we want you to consider a few speakers you found interesting. What characteristics did the speakers share? It is probably safe to assume the speakers you found most interesting had effective delivery skills. They used a conversational delivery. They used appropriate gestures. They spoke with confidence and enthusiasm. They were genuinely interested in the speech subject. They avoided unnecessary terms such as "you know" and "um." They maintained effective eye contact. They kept your attention at all times.

When you are preparing your delivery, you should keep these speakers in mind. This is not to say you should imitate their style of speaking. Each of us has our own unique style. However, you should consider all the elements that made each one successful.

Eye Contact

Eye contact
Important because it supports a speaker's credibility with the audience

Maintain *eye contact* with your audience at all times. In American culture a speaker who does not maintain eye contact is perceived as being less credible, less friendly, and less competent than a speaker who does maintain eye contact. For instance, you may have characterized people as dishonest because they had "shifty eyes" or they never looked you in the eye. The same is true for public speaking.

Approach the front of the audience confidently. Before you begin speaking look directly at the audience for a moment. This will help reduce your pre-speech anxiety. It will provide you with an opportunity to become acquainted with the audience and for your audience to become acquainted with you. As you deliver the speech make direct eye contact with several members of the audience in all portions of the room—left, right, and center. To the extent possible, look members of the audience directly in the eyes but do not stare at people. Of course, it is not necessary to look at every single individual in the audience. However, you should make it evident through your eye contact that you are concerned about the audience's reaction to your words.

You may be asking yourself, "How can I maintain eye contact and also look at my speaker cards?" This is a good question. When you are speaking it is perfectly natural for you to look at your notes from time to time. However, your primary focus must be on the audience. You should avoid nervous tendencies to look out the window, at the ceiling, at the floor, or down at the lectern. This indicates to your audience you are probably uneasy about speaking and it creates many **barriers to listening** for the audience.

You may have heard anecdotal stories of how speakers have faked eye contact. They may have looked over the heads of the members of the audience or looked "through" the audience. This simply does not work. The audience is aware you are not looking at them. When you have a conversation with a person are you able to tell when he/she is looking over your head? Of course you are. Your audience can as well.

Barriers to Listening
Obstacles that prevent a person from listening to a message even though they hear the message

Eye Contact and Culture

The amount and duration of eye contact a speaker has with his or her audience is culturally specific. In the United States, looking directly at your audience members is an important aspect of establishing credibility; it communicates trustworthiness and believability. In the United States, there is even a phrase that supports this notion: "Look me in the eye and say that." The premise is that the speaker will not lie to you if he or she is looking directly at you. However, in Japan, communicators do not use prolonged direct eye contact to establish credibility and audience members may display their attentiveness and agreement by looking down and away from the speaker. The frequency and duration of eye contact while giving a presentation varies across cultures. In general, Arabs, Europeans, Americans, and Latins tend to look directly at their audience while speaking, but the Chinese, Indian, Japanese, and Pakistanis tend to avoid prolonged direct eye contact. Knowing how your audience views eye contact will allow you to adjust to feedback. In the United States, speakers adjust their message based upon the amount of eye contact they receive back from the audience. If your audience is comprised of individuals from cultures, which do not value prolonged direct eye contact, and you are from a culture that does, you may alter your speech, thinking that you are boring the audience. In reality, the audience is showing their respect for you and your speech.

Rate, Tone, Pitch, Volume

Rate
How fast and/or slow an individual speaks

Your **rate** of speech—how fast or slowly you speak—should vary within your presentation. Some of us may naturally speak faster or slower than others. In addition, pre-speech anxiety may increase or decrease your natural rate of speech. Some speakers sound as if they are race cars speeding down the highway—all their words and sentences meld together into one great big long sentence that never seems to end. For others, it seems to take them 30 seconds to get through one simple sentence. As you might have guessed, both of these rates of delivery are ineffective.

Consider your normal speaking voice. When you have a conversation you alter your rate of speech. When you are excited about something you may speak faster. When you want to stress an important point you may speaker slower or even pause after saying it. You should attempt to deliver your speech in the same manner. You should alter your rate of speech, just as you do in your normal everyday conversations.

Avoid running your sentences together and rushing through the presentation. Give your audience an opportunity to absorb and process the information. Keep in mind that your goal at all times is to facilitate the audience's listening, understanding and comprehension of your message. Deliberate pauses in your delivery, perhaps after a rhetorical question or after an important point, gives the audience a chance to absorb or reflect on the information.

Silence and Culture

"Speech is not equally valued in all societies, or even consistently throughout the United States. The qualities of cogency (the ability to be convincing), precision and delivery which may be encouraged in speech communication classes in the United States may, in some cultures, be regarded negatively."[1] The importance given to words varies from culture to culture. To Americans, words are considered very important. We often want to fill what we consider to be awkward pauses of silence with words. We even "give our word' to assure our truthfulness. Other cultures such as Japan, China, Thailand, Swaziland, Ethiopia, and Kenya value silence. Asian cultures associate silence with wisdom and it is used to express power. "The desire not to speak is the most significant aspect or feature of Japanese language life. The Japanese hate to hear someone make excuses for his or her mistakes or failures. They do not like long and complicated explanations. If one has to say something, it is said in as few words as possible."[2] What does this mean for a public speaker? It is important to know which cultures emphasize public speaking, and which do not reward the speech-making process. In some instances, it may be in your best interest to submit a report than to give a speech. It is important to know when which style is preferred. In Korea, oral communication is not valued and written communication is dominant. "To read is the profession of scholars, to speak the act of menials."[3]

1. Candon, J.C., Jr. (1978). Intercultural communication from a speed communication perspective. In F.C. Casmit (Ed.), Intercultural and international communication. Washington, DC: University Press of America.
2. Klopf, D.W. (1991). Intercultural encounters: The fundamentals of intercultural communication. Englewood Cliffs, NJ: Morgan.
3. Yum, J.O. (1987). Korean philosophy and communication. In D.D. Kincaid (Ed.), Communication theory: Eastern and western perspectives. San Diego: Academic Press.

Speaking too quickly or too slowly can lead to numerous problems for the listeners. Your audience may find it very difficult to understand a presentation that is delivered too quickly. On the other hand, a speech that is delivered too slowly may become difficult to follow. The audience may become bored with the information.

Your **tone** of voice is the manner in which you speak. Your mother or father may have said to you at one time, "Don't take that tone of voice with me!" In that particular instance your tone of voice may have been disrespectful or sarcastic.

Tone
The manner in which an individual speaks

When you deliver your presentation you will want to be aware of your tone of voice. Am I being argumentative? Am I condescending? Is my tone formal? Informal? Defensive? Angry? Anxious? Frightened?

You should take into account your speech topic, your speech purpose, your audience, and your own natural style of speaking when determining an appropriate tone of voice. The best advice anyone can give you is to speak in your natural tone of voice. Do not try to imitate your favorite speaker. We cannot all speak like the Reverend Jesse Jackson or former President William Jefferson Clinton.

Pitch
How high or low a speaker's voice sounds

Volume
How loudly or softly an individual speaks

Body Language
A speaker's posture, gestures, facial expressions, and movement

Natural Gestures
Are much better than rehearsed gestures

By altering your **pitch,** how high or low your voice sounds, you can alter your tone of speech. You have probably heard speakers who did not alter their pitch and had a very monotone delivery. This type of delivery is very difficult to listen to and tends to permit the audience to daydream during the speech. I am sure you can think of a speaker who spoke in a monotone voice. It was probably difficult for you to pay attention to the speaker.

Finally, you need to be aware of how loudly or softly you are speaking. Just as you will want to alter your rate and pitch, you will want to alter the **volume** of your delivery. For the audience to listen to your presentation, they first must be able to hear it. People who are not accustomed to speaking before a group have the tendency to speak much too softly or to over compensate and yell at their audiences. Both are equally ineffective. Adapt your volume to the size of room. In most instances this simply means speaking slightly louder than your normal speaking voice. If using a microphones, speak in your normal speaking voice. There is no need to speak louder or softer because of the microphone.

Body Language

Your *body language* says as much or more than your spoken words. Your posture, hand gestures, facial expressions, and physical movement are all examples of nonverbal communication or body language. Consider this description of former President Franklin D. Roosevelt, who was paralyzed from the waist down:

> "His broad friendly smile and highly expressive countenance were important assets to Franklin Roosevelt as a speaker. His mobile face could reflect a wide variety of reactions. It changed expressions with the quickness and sureness of a finished actor's. It was amused, solemn, sarcastic, interested, indignant. It was always strong and confident and it was never dull."[2]

This textbook is not going to prescribe how you should stand, how to make effective hand gestures, or how to make appropriate facial expressions. This would not be effective because each one of us is different. What is appropriate for me may not be completely effective or natural for you. However, there are three guidelines you should be aware of with respect to body language.

■ *Your gestures should be natural.*
We strongly recommend you do not rehearse a series of gestures and attempt to incorporate them into your presentation. Far too

often a rehearsed gesture, such as pounding a fist on the table or
pointing, appears unnatural and out of character for the speaker.
This is not to say you should not pound your fist or point, but
these gestures should be a natural part of the delivery of the presentation. Remember to always be yourself!

■ *You should avoid repetitive gestures.*

By practicing in front of a full-length mirror, using a video
recorder, or practicing before a live audience, you are more likely
to recognize if you have tendencies to make certain gestures more
often than others. For example, you may make most of your gestures with your left hand or you may have a tendency to sway back
and forth when you are speaking.

■ *Your nonverbal communication should be consistent with your*
spoken message.

A speaker who is trying to elicit anger from the audience because
the federal government refuses to address the growing homeless
population should not be smiling throughout the presentation.

Word Choice

Choose your words very carefully. As you recall from Chapter One, The
Communication Process, you, the sender, are ultimately responsible for
the message being sent. We discussed the role of language in the communication process with respect to each participant's **frames of reference**
and in the **context** of the communication process.

If this were not enough, in a public speaking situation you are given
only one chance to state your information clearly. Unlike written communication, where if you make a mistake you can erase it, pause a few
minutes, and re-write it, public speaking does not permit you such luxury. When you are speaking to a friend and you do not understand something, you simply ask a question. Once again, the audience will not be
giving you verbal **feedback** throughout the presentation. You need to be
able to recognize and react to primarily nonverbal feedback. As discussed
in Chapter One, this is much more difficult and ambiguous when delivering a public speech.

In order to overcome some of the natural obstacles to public speaking
you have to select your words and phrases much more carefully than you
would in other forms of communication. When determining appropriate
word choice you must consider the following: (1) your natural vocabulary
and tendencies, (2) the speaking situation, and (3) the expectations of
the audience. All of these are of equal importance.

Each person has different natural speaking tendencies. Some of us have
a greater vocabulary than others. This may be the result of our number of

**Avoid Repetitive
Gestures**
Vary the type of
gestures used

Consistency
Speaker's verbal and
nonverbal messages
should be in agree-
ment

**Frame of
Reference**
An individual's per-
ceptions and/or
interpretations

Context
Location in which
communication is
taking place

Feedback
A response to a
message that is
decoded by the
source

Word choice
Important for
"connecting" with
the audience

years of education, past experiences, personal interests, family upbringing, or many other factors. For some speakers, English may not be their first language.

Despite these possibilities, all speakers should avoid unnecessary **nondescript** terminology. Nondescript terms are terms that we use habitually in our normal speaking voice. These terms have little or no meaning in themselves and are used primarily as "fillers" in our speech patterns. The following is a list of the most common habit phrases or nondescript terms that you should avoid in your delivery:

Nondescriptive
Words or phrases a speaker uses when he/she is not sure what to say next

---

Fillers to Avoid

Um	Etcetera	Ok
Really	Whatever	Uh
Like	Kind of	Yeah
I mean	Mmmmm	You know

In our normal everyday conversations we may find ourselves using profanity, derogatory characterizations, or slang terms. While different situations may govern our use of such words, a public presentation is not a situation where profanity, derogatory characterizations, and slang terms are considered appropriate by most audiences.

Lastly, remember with whom you are speaking. Take into account who your audience is (Audience Analysis Chapter Three). You do not want to talk over your audience's head or, for that matter, below them. You can give a speech on *How Computers Work* to any audience. But depending on the **demographics** of the audience your speech may be substantially altered. For example, the words you choose when speaking to laypersons is going to be different from those you would choose when speaking to computer programmers.

Demographic Analysis
Who the audience members are, in terms of: age, gender, level of education, etc.

Articulation and Pronunciation

Having a pleasant and clear sounding voice is an asset for any speaker. The audience will not only form a first impression based on your physical appearance, they will also form perceptions on the basis of how you sound.

The mechanical process of forming words is called **articulation.** How clearly do you produce sounds when you are speaking? Perhaps you have had the unfortunate experience of listening to speakers who mumbled.

Articulation
The mechanical process of forming words

These speakers were not properly articulating their words. This is the result of poor enunciation of words and sloppy speaking habits. Slurring the sounds of words together and dropping syllables in words are but two examples of poor articulation.

To improve your articulation, try speaking slower and louder. You may also need to open your mouth wider than you normally do when engaged in everyday conversation. If you have poor articulation and you are unable to correct it on your own, you should consider taking a course in voice and diction. Most colleges and universities offer this course in the Speech or Theatre Departments.

Pronouncing words correctly is very important for all speakers. **Pronunciation** is the act of speaking with the proper sound and accent. You should never use words in a presentation that you do not know how to pronounce or that you are intentionally mispronouncing. If you are not sure how to pronounce a word, you should consult a dictionary or eliminate the word from the speech.

Pronunciation
The act of speaking with the proper sound and accent

Both native English speakers and non-native English speakers frequently mispronounce words. If you speak with an accent, whether regional or foreign, it is not necessarily a problem. Your accent is part of your cultural identity and often adds to the presentation. However, if your accent prohibits your listeners from understanding words clearly, this could be a problem. There are times when audiences have little patience for speakers who frequently mispronounce words that are not difficult to pronounce.

If you feel you need help pronouncing words you should consider enrolling in an accent reduction course. Most colleges and universities offer these types of courses through English Language Institutes, or the English, Speech, or Communication Departments.

A Delivery Checklist

On the Day of Your Speech, It Is Important That You Remember

- Relax and be yourself!
- Have confidence in yourself that you have taken the necessary steps in preparing this presentation. You have information the audience *needs* to know!
- Step up to the lectern with confidence and poise.
- Establish eye contact with the audience before you begin speaking.
- Begin speaking without referring to your notes. This is very important in the introduction. You should know your topic and how you want to introduce it to this audience.

- Appropriately thank the person who introduced you.
- Remember to speak conversationally at all times!
- Avoid memorizing or reading material to the audience. If you prepared properly you won't read or memorize information to the audience!
- Avoid *verbal fillers* such as ah, um, ok, like, you know, mmmm. . . .
- Maintain good posture at all times.
- Remember, you establish your credibility with your nonverbal communication.
- Avoid playing with your hair, jewelry, clothing, pencil, note cards, etc. . . .
- Don't chew gum.
- Speak loudly so everyone can hear you, but don't shout at the audience.
- Articulate your words clearly and properly pronounce all your words.
- Don't speak too quickly or too slowly.
- Establish *vocal variety.* Effectively alter your rate, tone, and volume of speech.
- Don't call attention to your mistakes or offer any apologies.
- Don't rush through your concluding remarks.
- Avoid concluding your speech with *"That's it"* or *"I'm done."*
- Don't run off the stage.
- Don't applaud yourself.
- Say *"Thank you"* and exit the stage professionally.

Endnotes

1. McCroskey, J. (1977). Oral communication apprehension: A review of recent theory and research." *Human Communication Research*, 78.
2. Logue, C. (1992). *Briefly Speaking*, (4th ed., p. 198) Boston: Allyn and Bacon.

Chapter Two
KEY TERMS

Articulation: _____
_____

Body Language: _____
_____

Communication
Apprehension: _____
_____

Delivery Methods: _____
_____

Eye Contact: _____
_____

Impromptu: _____
_____

Manuscript: _____
_____

Memorized: _____
_____

Pitch: _____
_____

Pronunciation: _____
_____

Rate: _____
_____

Speaker Cards: _____

_____

Tone: _____

_____

Volume: _____

_____

Ways to Prevent
Anxiety: _____

_____

Ways to Practice: _____

_____

Chapter Two
EXERCISES

Based on your experiences, briefly describe the trait of a speaker you enjoyed. What did he/she do well? What made you want to listen?

_____

_____

_____

_____

_____

_____

_____

_____

_____

Based on your experiences, briefly describe the trait of a speaker you did not enjoy. What did he/she not do well? What made it difficult for you to listen?

_____

_____

_____

_____

_____

_____

_____

_____

_____

_____

Chapter Two
REVIEW QUESTIONS

1. List and briefly define the four methods for delivering a speech.

    a. _____ : _____

    b. _____ : _____

    c. _____ : _____

    d. _____ : _____

2. When would it be appropriate for a speaker to read his/her speech from a manuscript?

    _____

    _____

    _____

3. What problems may result from a memorized delivery?

    _____

    _____

    _____

4. Why is an extemporaneous delivery the most effective delivery for a public presentation?

    _____

    _____

    _____

5. List the four most common methods of practicing the delivery of your speech.

    a. _____

    b. _____

    c. _____

    d. _____

6. Define the following delivery variables:

    a. rate: _____

    b. tone: _____

    c. pitch: _____

    d. volume: _____

Chapter Two
POWERPOINT SLIDES

- Ways to prevent anxiety
- Delivery methods
- Effective ways to practice
- Maintaining eye contact
- Nonverbal guidelines

WAYS TO PREVENT ANXIETY

- Be prepared

- Know audience

- Know intro/con

- Select appropriate topic

54

DELIVERY METHODS

- Impromptu

- Manuscript

- Memorized

- Extemporaneous

EFFECTIVE WAYS TO PRACTICE

- In front of a mirror

- Tape recorder

- Video recorder

- In front of a live audience

56

MAINTAINING EYE CONTACT

- Focus on your audience at all times.

- Make direct eye contact with several members of the audience.

- Scan the entire room.

NONVERBAL GUIDELINES

- Your gestures should be natural.

- You should avoid repetitive gestures.

- Your nonverbals should be consistent with spoke message.

CHAPTER 3
Audience Analysis and Topic Selection

"In all matters, before beginning, a diligent preparation should be made."
Cicero

One of your goals as a speaker is to keep the audience interested in your presentation at all times. The most important method of gaining and maintaining the attention of the audience is to select a topic your audience finds interesting. You may be wondering, "How will I know what interests this particular audience?" Since this is a very difficult question to answer with specifics, it is better answered with generalities about all potential audiences. When an audience perceives that a speaker has genuine enthusiasm for a topic the audience is more likely to be interested in the topic. This is generally true for all audiences regardless of the topic. There are exceptions. Surely you have had experiences where the speaker was genuinely enthusiastic about a topic but you did not share the same enthusiasm. This is why it is essential to consider the general interests of your audience. This is called conducting an **audience analysis.**

Two students were giving speeches on the same topic—skin cancer. They met the night before the speech was due to compare their presentations. The first students said:

> I never knew so much information existed on this subject. I am going to inform the class about the different types of skin cancer with quotes from doctors and statistics from the American Medical Association. I have so much technical information, I hope I can get it all in during the allotted time.

Audience Analysis
Knowing what the interests/needs of the audience are

The second student said:

> I tried something different, I think is important that the audience know all the statistics and research studies related to skin cancer, but they also need to know how and/or why this is important to them.

In this example, the first student was only concerned about the speaker's perspective. This student was concerned with including all the information that was researched, even though most of it was very technical. The second student was looking at the situation from the audience's perspective. He/she wanted to make the message interesting to his/her classmates and was careful to view the information from the viewpoint of someone hearing it in a short speech for possibly the first time.

An audience analysis starts by asking a series of questions about the intended audience.

Audience Analysis

Audience Demographics

You may be asking, "How will I know what my audience is like when I have never met them?" Surprisingly, you do not have to know your audience personally to hypothesize about them. The first portion of an audience analysis is the *demographic analysis*. Questions regarding the audience's average age and income are some of the most basic demographic questions a speaker might need to know when selecting a speech topic. Consider the following demographic questions:

Demographic Analysis
Who the audience members are, in terms of: age, gender, level of education, etc.

- What is the average age of the audience?
- What is the predominant gender of the audience?
- What is the average level of education of the audience?
- What ethnicities will be represented in the audience?
- What is the average level of income of the audience (high, middle, low)?
- What religions will be represented in the audience?
- Does the audience belong to any common clubs or organizations?

You may not be able to hypothesize about all of the demographic questions listed above. That is fine. However, for many of the questions you will be able to make a reasonable guess at the answer. From your answers to the demographic questions you will be able to hypothesize about the next portion of the audience analysis: the psychological analysis of the audience.

Psychological Analysis

Hypothesizing about an audience's *psychological* profile is not difficult, but there are certain dangers of stereotyping people. Beware of jumping to unfounded conclusions based on the answers to a few demographic questions. Having said that, one needs only to look at the advertisements to realize the importance of analyzing an intended audience. Since most of us are not advertisers, consider a more practical example. The last time you selected a gift for a friend or relative did you consider the person's demographics? You probably did not consciously ask yourself each demographic question, but subconsciously they influenced your decisions when selecting the appropriate gift. You did not just buy any gift. You considered what would be appropriate based on the person's age, your relationship to the person, and the person's perceived needs.

Psychological Analysis
What the audience members think

Changing Population and Your Audience

One hundred years ago, the dominant culture in the United States felt threatened by the arrival of the Irish, Italians, Germans, Eastern Europeans, Catholics, and Jews. Now the individuals who are considered racial minorities are individuals from Hispanic, African, Asian, and Native American descent. In fact, the United States Census Bureau believes our country is undergoing significant demographic changes. As many as 1 million immigrants enter the United States each year legally and these immigrants are holding onto their cultural traditions much more than the immigrants of 100 years ago. Whether it is "Little Havana" in Miami or "Chinatown" in San Francisco, the new wave of immigrants is changing the diversity of the United States.

It is not only immigrants that are changing the make-up of audiences throughout the United States. With the Civil Rights Movement of the sixties, the Womens Rights Movement of the seventies, the Gay Rights Movement of the nineties, and the aging of the baby boomers over the next 20 years, which will lead to the largest elderly population in United States history, the demographics of the United States is, without doubt, changing.

What implications does this have for public speakers? For audiences? Audience analysis, an important step that should never be overlooked by good speakers, will become even more rigorous. The less homogeneous your audience is, the greater your chances of both failing to communicate effectively and also failing to understand why you were unable to communicate. Our speeches reveal our worldview and demonstrate, by their content, structure, language, introductions, and conclusions, whether or not we accept culturally diverse audiences.

Topic Analysis

Your perceptions of the audience's needs were based on the hypothesized answers to the demographic questions. This same process should be applied when selecting an appropriate speech topic. Hypothesize about what your audience will find interesting based on the demographics analysis.

Useful

Select a topic your audience will find *useful*. An audience is more likely to find a topic interesting if a speaker can successfully indicate to the audience the usefulness of the information. The audience members will be asking themselves, "How can I use this information in my life?" or "Why do I need to know this?" For example, a presentation to a group of high school students on *How to Select a College* may prove quite useful to them. In this instance, based on the audience's age and level of education, the audience will probably find this information interesting because it is useful. A presentation on *Retirement Benefits,* to the same group of high school students would probably not be considered useful information.

Relevant

An audience will find a subject interesting if a speaker can indicate to the audience how the speech topic is *relevant* to their daily lives. The audience will ask themselves, "How does this information relate to me?" and "How does the information affect me at this time?"

To make a topic relevant a speaker should either attempt to bring the topic to the audience or bring the audience to the topic. The relevance of South Africa could be demonstrated in two ways. If a speaker wanted to bring the topic to the audience, he/she would indicate how the events in South Africa directly affect the United States, or perhaps, their very own city. On the other hand, if the speaker wanted to bring the audience to the topic, he/she may describe the daily life and recent effects of the new policies.

In both instances the speaker is attempting to indicate the relevance of the topic. If you are not certain what topics are currently being discussed, take a few minutes to review a newspaper, a news magazine, or the local or national news. These are excellent sources for generating topic ideas.

Needs

Consider the audience's perceived needs as well. Does the audience have a *need* to know the information? In most cases the audience has voluntarily chosen to listen to you speak. They will expect the information to be of some importance. For example, the importance of a speech on the *Symptoms of AIDS* is not necessarily dictated by the audience's age. This information meets a perceived need of most audiences. On the other hand, it is unlikely the audience will need to know or care to know about your trip to your grandmother's house. Your trip may have been very interesting to you, but when you consider your audience's needs the topic becomes trivial.

A speech on *AIDS Prevention* to a group of college students meets a perceived need. A speech to senior citizens on *Healthcare* meets a perceived need. A speech to kindergarten children on *Fire Safety* meets a perceived need. What do all of these topics have in common? They were all selected based on the speaker's **psychological analysis** of the **audience demographics.**

Significance

When people do not find information *significant*, they do not listen very closely. If your instructor announces before class, "You will not be tested on the following information," do you listen intently? Hopefully you do listen as closely, but you probably do not. If you do not listen as closely it is because you feel the information is not important to you at the time.

Novelty

A successful speaker also attempts to arouse the curiosity of the audience. The audience will often find a topic interesting if they have not heard the subject before or if the speaker sheds some new light on a topic. In these instances, the audience considers the *novelty* of the information. A speaker may choose to inform an audience on the *Theories Related to Marilyn Monroe's Death*. If the audience is of the age to be acquainted with Marilyn Monroe and the situation is conducive to such a topic, the audience may find the topic interesting because it is novel. The death of Marilyn Monroe was a significant event in American culture, and has continued to be discussed and written about to this day; however, the discussion of the *Theories Related to Marilyn Monroe's Death*, is not necessarily based on significance, relevance, or perceived need of the audience. It appeals to listeners because it peaks their curiosity.

Situation Analysis

After determining the interests of the audience, you need to consider the *speaking situation*. Consider the following questions about the speaking situation:

- Why have I been asked to speak?
- How much time am I allotted for the presentation?
- Where will I be speaking?
- When will I be speaking?

Psychological Analysis
What the audience members think

Demographic Analysis
Who the audience members are, in terms of: age, gender, level of education, etc.

Significant
Speech topic is meaningful to the audience

Novelty
Speech topic is new and/or unusual to the audience

Situation Analysis
Under what conditions will an individual be speaking

When selecting a speech topic, consider the reasons you have been asked to speak. Have you been asked to speak for your expertise on the subject? Is the audience attending voluntarily?

Another important factor in selecting a speech subject is the amount of time you have been allotted to speak. Whether your boss has given you ten minutes to speak during a business meeting, or the Kiwanis Club has asked you to speak for an hour at their next meeting, the audience is expecting you to cover your entire stated speech topic within the specified time limits.

Perhaps you can recall listening to a speaker who had not considered the scope of his/her presentation. The speaker either spoke far too long or finished before satisfactorily explaining the subject. In either case, you probably became annoyed at the speaker's lack of consideration to the allotted time limit for the speech. It is a very rare case that a speaker will be given an unlimited amount of time to complete a presentation. As such, you must be aware of your speech goals and narrow your speech topic accordingly. Time limits will probably be provided for each of your presentations. Therefore, you must be aware of your speech purpose and narrow your speech accordingly.

Narrowing your speech topic for your intended audience is not as difficult as it may appear. Let us suppose you have a general idea of what you intend to speak about in your presentation. You have chosen the subject *Business*. You are a business major and the subject interests you. Can you speak about business in ten minutes? Can you speak about business in one hour? As you can see, this is a tremendously broad topic. To narrow your speech topic examine the time you have been allotted to speak and the perceived interests of your audience.

Assume you were given fifteen minutes to complete your speech on the topic of business. If you wish to inform the audience on this topic, you will need to narrow it down considerably. Below is an example of a **spider diagram** used to narrow down a speech topic. It is a method of **brainstorming** for ideas from a main topic with the intention of arriving at a more interesting and relevant topic. In this way a speaker can discuss a topic in more detail in the time allotted for the presentation. A general rule of thumb to follow when narrowing a speech topic, "It is better to know a lot about a little, than a little about a lot."

Spider Diagram
An effective way to narrow down a speech topic

Brainstorming
A method of generating ideas

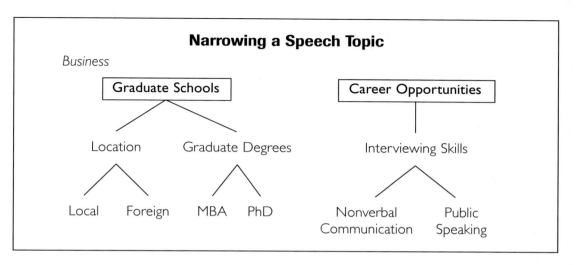

Narrowing a Speech Topic

Business

Graduate Schools

Location   Graduate Degrees

Local   Foreign   MBA   PhD

Career Opportunities

Interviewing Skills

Nonverbal   Public
Communication   Speaking

Potential Broad Speech Topics

abortion	ERA	nuclear power
AIDS	espionage	opera
Amistad, the	euthanasia	Panama Canal
artists	film	philosophy
assassinations	foreign countries	prisons
astrology	forensics	propaganda
Berlin Wall	government	Pyramids
business	Great Wall, the	racism
censorship	history	religion
cloning	homeless	royalty
Constitution, the	inflation	school
crime	insurance	science
criminals	language	solar energy
culture	law	space
currency	leadership	subliminal advertising
Depression, the	literature	taxes
discrimination	management	technology
disease	marriage	television
divorce	mass media	traditions
domestic policies	medicine	treaties
drugs	military	UFOs
education	music	war
Eifel Tower, the	NASA	women's rights

Chapter Three
KEY TERMS

Audience Analysis: _____

_____

Demographics
Analysis: _____

_____

Spider Diagram: _____

_____

Psychological
Analysis: _____

_____

Things to Consider   _____
in Selecting a Topic: _____

_____

Chapter Three

EXERCISES

After selecting a speech topic, conduct a demographic and psychological analysis for the following potential audiences.

AUDIENCE #1: ELEMENTARY SCHOOL CHILDREN

Topic: _____

Situational Analysis:

What is my speech purpose? _____   How long do I have to speak? _____
_____   Will others be speaking? _____
Why have I been asked to speak? _____   Physical environment? _____
_____   _____

Demographic Analysis:

Average Age _____   Average Income _____

Predominant Gender _____   Predominant Religion _____

Average Education _____   Common Groups/Clubs _____

Predominant Ethnicity _____   Other _____

Psychological Analysis:

Why will the audience find the information useful? _____
_____

How is this topic relevant?
_____

Why does the audience need to know this information?
_____

Why will the audience find this topic interesting?
_____

Other Important Information:

Attire _____   Visual Aids _____

Vocabulary/Word Selection _____   _____
_____   Other _____

After selecting a speech topic, conduct a demographic and psychological analysis for the following potential audiences.

AUDIENCE #2: A WOMEN'S ORGANIZATION

Topic: _____

Situational Analysis:

What is my speech purpose? _____ How long do I have to speak? _____
_____ Will others be speaking? _____
Why have I been asked to speak? _____ Physical environment? _____
_____ _____

Demographic Analysis:

Average Age _____ Average Income _____

Predominant Gender _____ Predominant Religion _____

Average Education _____ Common Groups/Clubs _____

Predominant Ethnicity _____ Other _____

Psychological Analysis:

Why will the audience find the information useful? _____
_____

How is this topic relevant?
_____

Why does the audience need to know this information?
_____

Why will the audience find this topic interesting?
_____

Other Important Information:

Attire _____ Visual Aids _____
Vocabulary/Word Selection _____ _____
_____ Other _____

After selecting a speech topic, conduct a demographic and psychological analysis for the following potential audiences.

AUDIENCE #3: A GROUP OF RETIRED PROFESSIONALS

Topic: _____

Situational Analysis:

What is my speech purpose? _____   How long do I have to speak? _____
_____   Will others be speaking? _____

Why have I been asked to speak? _____   Physical environment? _____
_____   _____

Demographic Analysis:

Average Age _____   Average Income _____

Predominant Gender _____   Predominant Religion _____

Average Education _____   Common Groups/Clubs _____

Predominant Ethnicity _____   Other _____

Psychological Analysis:

Why will the audience find the information useful? _____
_____

How is this topic relevant?
_____

Why does the audience need to know this information?
_____

Why will the audience find this topic interesting?
_____

Other Important Information:

Attire _____   Visual Aids _____

Vocabulary/Word Selection _____   _____
_____   Other _____

After selecting a speech topic, conduct a demographic and psychological analysis for the following potential audiences.

AUDIENCE #4: YOUR PUBLIC SPEAKING CLASS

Topic: _____

Situational Analysis:

What is my speech purpose? _____   How long do I have to speak? _____
_____   Will others be speaking? _____
Why have I been asked to speak? _____   Physical environment? _____
_____   _____

Demographic Analysis:

Average Age _____   Average Income _____
Predominant Gender _____   Predominant Religion _____
Average Education _____   Common Groups/Clubs _____
Predominant Ethnicity _____   Other _____

Psychological Analysis:

Why will the audience find the information useful? _____
_____

How is this topic relevant?
_____

Why does the audience need to know this information?
_____

Why will the audience find this topic interesting?
_____

Other Important Information:

Attire _____   Visual Aids _____
Vocabulary/Word Selection _____   _____
_____   Other _____

Upon completing each of the pervious analyses of the speech situation and the potential audiences, answer the following questions.

How would your presentation change if you replaced the first audience of a group of elementary school children with high school students?

_____

_____

_____

_____

If you were speaking to a men's group rather than a women's group?

_____

_____

_____

_____

If you were speaking to a religious organization rather than a group of retired professionals?

_____

_____

_____

_____

If you were speaking to a group of students in one of your other classes rather than to your public speaking class?

_____

_____

_____

Before giving your presentation review the following checklist:

_____ I have analyzed my intended audience.

_____ I have selected an appropriate speech topic.

_____ I have properly narrowed my speech topic.

_____ I have sufficiently researched my topic.

_____ I have properly outlined my speech using footnotes and a source bibliography.

_____ I have practiced my delivery and made appropriate speaker cards.

_____ I have selected proper visual aids.

Chapter Three
EXERCISES

Prepare a *Spider Diagram* for two different topics.

Topic #1: _____

Final Topic: _____

Topic #1: _____

Final Topic: _____

Chapter Three
REVIEW QUESTIONS

1. To what extent is the speaker responsible for the audience's physical and/or mental actions?

   _____

   _____

   _____

2. Define the "Rule of Self-Interest."

   _____

   _____

   _____

3. How does the statement, "You cannot fake sincerity" relate to public speaking?

   _____

   _____

   _____

   _____

4. Why should a speaker conduct a situational, demographic, and psychological analysis prior to speaking?

   _____

   _____

   _____

   _____

5. Explain how a speaker can analyze an audience if he/she has never seen the audience before.

   _____

   _____

   _____

Chapter Three
POWERPOINT SLIDES

- Demographics analysis
- Psychological analysis
- Choosing a topic
- Speaking situation

DEMOGRAPHICS ANALYSIS

What is the audience's:

- Average age?

- Predominant gender?

- Average level of education?

- Average level of income?

- Predominant ethnicity?

PSYCHOLOGICAL ANALYSIS

Is the topic:

- Useful to the audience?

- Relevant to the audience?

- Likely to meet a need?

- Significant to the audience?

- Novelty to the audience?

TIPS FOR
CHOOSING A SPEECH TOPIC

- Usefulness of information

- Relevance to audience's life

- Need for audience to know info

- Significance of information

- Novelty of information

THE SPEAKING SITUATION

- Why have I been asked to speak?

- How much time do I have to speak?

- Where will I be speaking?

- When will I be speaking?

- What is the appropriate dress?

- What equipment is available to display visuals?

- Who else is speaking?

CHAPTER 4
Visual Supporting Material

"A picture is worth a thousand words."

Chinese Proverb

Speakers who are able to effectively integrate visual supporting material into a presentation are generally more successful than speakers who rely solely on the spoken word. When used appropriately, **visual supporting materials** facilitate the audience's understanding and retention of the spoken information in the speech. When used correctly, visual supporting materials make a presentation more polished and professional.

The Value of Visual Supporting Material

Creates Understanding
Appropriate visuals can enhance the audience's understanding of information. There is a scientific reason why visual supporting materials are effective. Think about your five senses—touch, smell, hearing, taste, and sight. You learn more from your sense of sight than the other four senses combined. In fact, it has been estimated that over 80 percent of all information comes to you through sight.

Increases the Audience's Retention of Information
Appropriate visual supporting materials also enhance retention of information. It has been estimated that you remember 10 percent of what you read, 20 percent of what you hear, 30 percent of what you see, and 50 percent of what you see and hear simultaneously.

You may recall a recent lecture when an instructor used visual materials. Did you find it easier to understand and retain the information? If the instructor used the correct types of visual supporting materials and

> **Visual Supporting Material**
> Used to help an audience understand and remember a speaker's message

used them appropriately, your understanding and retention of the information increased.

When to Use Visual Aids

Determining if and when it would be beneficial for you to use visual supporting materials can be difficult. When deciding this consider the following questions: (1) Is the information abstract? (2) Are you using statistics? (3) Are you speaking about a geographical location?

Abstract Information

Abstract Information
Information not easily understood

Often information may be difficult for the audience to visualize mentally. If the audience has the opportunity to see the information they are more likely to understand and retain the information. The basic model of communication presented in Chapter One, The Communication Process, is an example of how abstract information can be effectively visualized by listeners.

Statistical Information

Statistical Information
Numerical information

Statistical information when presented orally can be quite confusing. If the goal is for the audience to understand and retain the statistical information, visual supporting material should be used. Consider this, from *The Car Book* by Jack Gillis:

Your target price should be $100–$200 over the dealer cost on a car costing $10,000–$15,000 . . . $200–$400 extra for a car $15,000–$18,000 . . . and no more than $400–$600 more for a car $18,000–$25,000.

In this instance, visual supporting material could help a listener understand and retain the information. The speaker could have presented the information as follows:

Dealer Cost	$ Over Dealer Cost
$10,000–$15,000	$100–$200
$15,000–$18,000	$200–$400
$18,000–$25,000	$400–$600

It is not necessary to visually depict all statistical information. There are times when a speaker does not necessarily want the audience to remember the specific statistical data. In these instances the statistical information is used to make a general point. Consider this example from Sharon Camp, senior vice-president of Population Action International:

"In sub-Sahara Africa, with food production growing at 2 percent and population growing at 3 percent, per capita food production has already dropped 15–20 percent since 1970".[1]

The purpose of stating the statistical information is simply to indicate the seriousness of the problem. It is not necessary for the listener to remember the exact numbers. Ms. Camp's primary purpose is to show the impact of overpopulation in sub-Sahara Africa with respect to per capita food production and to make the audience aware of the seriousness of overpopulation.

Geography

One of your goals as a speaker is to either bring the topic to the audience or bring the audience to the topic. When you are discussing a geographical location (region, country, state, county, area of a city, etc.), it is often beneficial to visually represent this particular information. It is not wise to assume that your audience is familiar with the exact location or specifics of a geographical area. A presentation on Central America should include a map and/or pictures of the area, as should presentations on the former Soviet Republics, or the projected movement of a hurricane.

Geography
Features (pictures and/or maps) of a specific region

Criteria for All Types of Visual Supporting Materials

Regardless of the types of visual supporting materials you use, all visuals should meet the same criteria to be effective:

- Each must be clearly visible to all.
- Each must be relevant to the spoken material.
- Each must be integrated properly.
- Each must be clear, understandable, and labeled.
- Each must have a professional appearance.

Each Must Be Clearly Visible to All

All visual supporting materials must be *clearly visible* to all listeners. The person in the first row and the person in the last row must both be able to clearly see the visual.

Visibility
Capable of being seen by entire audience

When using a **PowerPoint** slide or a simple transparency, the visual should have bright contrasting colors. Colors such as yellow, beige, light blue, and pink are not easily distinguishable from a distance. When projecting information on a large screen or using a television or computer monitor, be certain the visual can be clearly seen by everyone in the audience. There are times when the lights need to be dimmed to facilitate viewing. When using a visual aid, there are certain rules that should be followed to ensure that the visual is visible to your audience.

PowerPoint
Computer program that integrates text, video, and audio

- You want to use a 30–36 point font.
- Use no more than six lines of information.

- Use no more than 40 characters per line.
- Use phrases not full sentences.
- Use upper and lower case lettering.
- Use a simple typeface.

Each Must Be Relevant to the Spoken Material

Relevant
Directly related to audience

All visual supporting material must be *relevant* to your subject. Visual supporting materials are not to be used as props or background scenery. You are giving a formal public presentation; you are not acting in a short play. If you are informing your audience on the *Life of Elvis Presley,* there is no need to dress the part or place poster boards with screaming adoring fans behind you as a backdrop. Keep this statement in mind when determining the appropriateness of your visual: "My visual aids should help my audience understand and remember some aspect of my speech."

You Must Know How to Integrate Each Visual

Integration
Display visual only when referring to the visual

You should only display visual supporting material when you are discussing the contents of the visual. This is known as *integration.* Consider a presentation on *How to Make a Television Commercial,* you would not want a visual of the first step to remain in view while explaining the second step. Once you have completed discussing the contents of a visual, it should no longer be displayed or it will create a distraction and interfere with the listening process. You will defeat the purpose of having a visual aid in the first place.

Each Must Be Clear, Understandable, and Labeled

Clear, Understandable, and Labeled
Information on visual should be obvious to audience

Visual supporting materials must virtually speak for themselves. The audience should not have to guess at the meaning and its relationship to the subject being discussed. When using PowerPoint or a transparency, always keep the information on the visual simple. Be certain all portions of each visual are clearly labeled. Each visual must have a clear title and, if appropriate, should be properly footnoted.

Guidelines to consider would be:

- Only one picture or graph per visual.
- Never pass anything out.
- You must discuss all information on the visual.
- Maintain eye contact with your audience while discussing your visual.

Each Must Have a Professional Appearance

All visual supporting materials should look *professional* and be of high quality. Only in very rare instances should the speaker write on a visual or produce the visual while speaking.

The text of a visual should always run straight across the page. Even a slight variation, either uphill or downhill, will be greatly magnified when projected. Visuals should never be sloppy, dirty, crumpled, or frayed. Of course, you should check for any misspelled words and be certain your text is grammatically correct.

If you are using a video or an audio recording as your supporting material, be certain that the videocassette, or compact disc, is properly cued before the presentation begins and the volume is properly adjusted. If you are using different portions of one video, or using several videos, edit the information onto one tape.

Always take the time to properly prepare visual supporting materials. The extra effort to prepare properly and become accustomed with the equipment will save you from potentially embarrassing situations. Your **credibility** and professionalism may be questioned if your visual supporting material is not properly prepared and/or not properly used in a presentation.

Types of Visual Support Aids

There are six categories of visual aids that help the audience understand your message. Visual aids can be items you create yourself, or borrow from other sources.

Real Objects

For example, an informative speech on *Getting Started in Scuba Diving* will be more easily understood if you incorporate visuals. Include a wet suit, fins, tank, regulator, and other diving equipment to illustrate each of the required items. This will help the audience to visualize what you are talking about.

Using *real objects*, however, is not appropriate in all speeches. An informative speech on *Choices in Birth Control* will probably not benefit from the display of condoms or other devices. These items add little relevance to the presentation. They may cause some degree of distracting embarrassment among members in the audience. Additionally, these are too small to be seen by everyone in the audience. A much better choice

Professional
Visual must meet high standards

Credibility
A speaker's qualifications in terms of physical appearance, composure, and stated qualifications

Real Objects
Not suitable for all speeches

for a supporting aid would be a graph showing the relative effectiveness of each method of birth control.

Ask two simple questions about real objects: Will the audience better understand my speech if they can see the actual object(s)? Do the real objects meet the criteria of visibility, clarity, relevance, and integration? If your answers are "yes," using real objects is probably appropriate!

Models

Model
Representation of a real object

When you can not use an actual object as a visual aid, consider using a *model*. Models are representations of actual objects. They may be scale models—smaller versions of larger objects, or larger versions of small objects—or actual size substitutes. Models must meet the criteria of visibility, clarity, relevance, integration, and professionalism.

You can improve a speech about *The Architecture of the Roman Coliseum* by using a reduced size scale model of the Coliseum. A speech on *Nuclear Energy* may benefit from an enlarged model of a uranium atom. In a speech about *The Nature of Chiropractic Medicine*, the audience will better understand the process of spinal adjustment if you present a life size model of a skeleton.

Models are easy to obtain. Talk to people who are knowledgeable about your subject. They may have exactly what you need or know where you can get it. An advantage of studying at a college or university is having experts in many fields available right on campus. Most of these experts are delighted to help a determined student.

Pictures

Picture
When a model or real object is not appropriate, a photograph may suffice

When you cannot get the real object or model, a *picture* may be an important and essential substitute. What would a speech on *The Artistry of Michelangelo* be without representations of his paintings? However, you probably do not have an original Michelangelo in your private collection. Although you may be able to get a model of *David* to show the class, it would be impossible to bring the ceiling of the Sistine Chapel to the speech except by pictures. In this case, a picture is an adequate substitute.

Graphics

Graphics
Include diagrams, charts, and graphs

Graphics help the audience understand concepts visually through diagrams, charts, and graphs. Prepare these materials so the content is clear and understandable. Graphics should require only minimum explanation. Limit graphics to a single concept or idea.

Notice that David Letterman reveals his "TOP TEN" lists one at a time. He has no more than five items (usually fewer) on the screen at any one time. Prepare your graphics with a maximum of six lines of information. Use a type style large enough to be clearly seen, and simple enough to be immediately understood.

Diagrams

- Show the parts of an object, an organization, or the steps in a process.

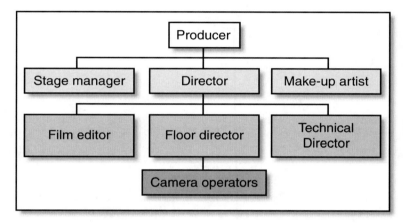

Charts

- Present a list of key words related to your topic.
- Give a definition.

Graphs

- Visually relate similar concepts.
- Show changes over time.

The type of graph you use will depend on the information you need to display. Different graphs include:

- A **pie graph** is particularly effective to show percentages in relation to the whole. For example, your speech on *Curbing the Federal Deficit* can include a pie graph showing the percentages of the pie the government spends on defense, deficit reduction, and other expenses.

Pie Graph
Depicts percentages in relation to the whole

Sample Pie Graph

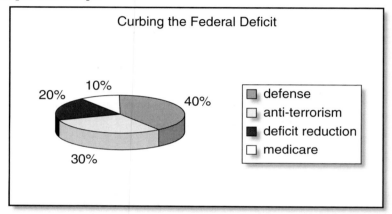

- The **line graph** is useful for depicting relationships that change over time. The audience will understand the growth of the national debt better if you include a line graph showing the increase in the federal deficit during each of the past four decades.

Line Graph
Depicts change over time

Sample Line Graph

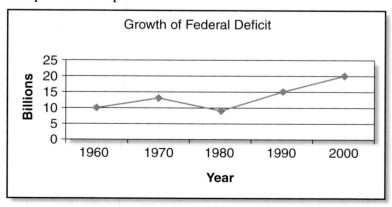

- The **bar graph** is well suited to show relationships between two or more factors. The audience can understand the magnitude of the national debt and recognize their personal involvement if you personalize the graph. Compare the amount the government spends on the military versus education, medicaid, and welfare.

Bar Graph
Depicts a general relationship between two or more factors

Sample Bar Graph

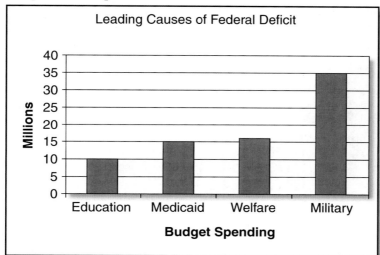

Videos

Videos, with or without sound, offer advantages over other forms of visual aids.

Videos
Show action/motion

- To be understood, does your topic require the audience to see something in motion? (e.g., *Fundamentals of Synchronized Swimming*).
- Time is important in topics with historical elements or in topics that take place too fast or too slow for us to see. You can use documentary video, time-lapse, or time-condensed video to show events beyond the audience's normal perception.

Audio

What we hear is seldom used in presentations because most speakers don't think of *audio* as a "visual aid." However, sound can be very useful. Sound is effective in situations when the audience must hear something to understand your message, but when seeing what creates the sound is distracting or inappropriate. A speech on the *Symphonies of Tchaikovsky* will benefit from a short passage from the *Nutcracker Suite*; however, the audience may become distracted from your main point if you include the video of the ballet.

Audio
Allows the audience hear a message

Computer Generated Visuals

With advancements in computer technology, it is easy to produce sophisticated visuals with color, animation, and sound.

PowerPoint
Computer program that integrates text, video, and audio

Microsoft's **PowerPoint** has templates and instructions to assist you in the creation of your visual. Slides may contain diagrams, charts, graphs, pictures, clip art, video, and sound bites. Because PowerPoint is the first choice, amongst professionals, when it comes to choosing visual support aids; we have included a step-by-step explanation of how to create a PowerPoint presentation.

See the following websites:

http://www.fgcu.edu/support/office2000/ppt/ (PowerPoint 2000)

http://www.ltd.ocps.net (PowerPoint XP)

http://www.library.georgetown.edu (Adding Audio Narration)

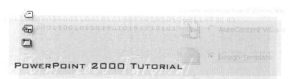

Getting Started
- AutoContent Wizard
- Create a presentation from a template
- Create a blank presentation
- AutoLayout

PowerPoint Screen
- Screen layout
- Views

Working with Slides
- Insert a new slide
- Applying a design template
- Changing slide layuts
- Recording slides
- Hide slides
- Create a custom slide show
- Edit a custom slide show

Adding Content
- Resizing a text box
- Text box properties
- Delete a text box
- Bulleted lists
- Numbered lists
- Adding notes
- Video and Audio

Working with Text
- Adding text
- Editing options
- Formatting text
- Replace fonts
- Line spacing
- Change case
- Spelling check

Color Schemes
- Color schemes
- Backgrounds

Graphics
- Adding clip art
- Adding an image from a file
- Editing a graphic
- AutoShapes
- WordArt

Slide Effects
- Action buttons
- Slide animation
- Animation preview
- Slide transitions
- Slide show options

Master Slides
- Slide master
- Header and footer
- Slide numbers
- Date and time

Saving and Printing
- Save as a web page
- Page setup
- Print

Keyboard shortcuts

Tips
- Design tips
- Presentation basics

Getting Started

Open PowerPoint and you will be prompted by a dialog box with four choices. Each of these options are explained on this page. If PowerPoint is already open or this box does not appear, select **File | New** from the menu bar.

AutoContent Wizard

The AutoContent Wizard provides templates and ideas for a variety of presentation types. Page through the wizard by clicking the **Next** button on the bottom of each page after making necessary choices.

Design Template

PowerPoint provides many templates with different backgrounds and text formatting to begin your presentation. Preview each design by highlighting the template name on the list. Press **OK** after you have chosen the design.

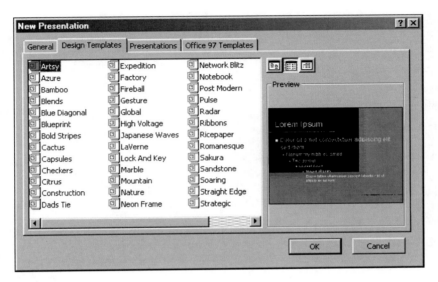

Blank Presentation

Select Blank Presentation to build the presentation from scratch with no preset graphics or formatting.

Open an Existing Presentation

Select this option to open a PowerPoint presentation that already exists. Select the folder the file is located in from the **Look in:** drop-down menu and highlight the file on the list. Click **Open** to open the presentation.

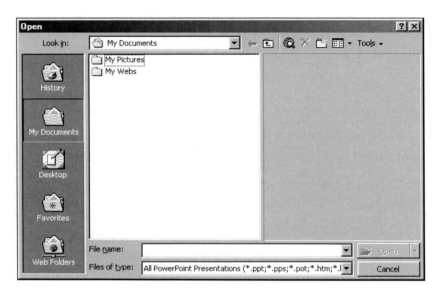

AutoLayout

After selecting the presentation type, you will be prompted to choose the layout of the new slide. These layouts include bulleted lists, graphs, and/or images. Click on each thumbnail image and a description will be printed in the message box. Highlight the layout you want and click. **OK.**

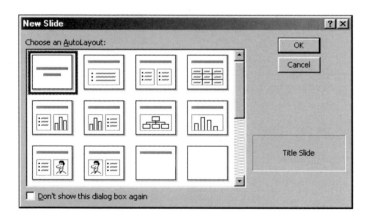

PowerPoint Screen

Screen Layout

The PowerPoint screen layout in **Normal View:**

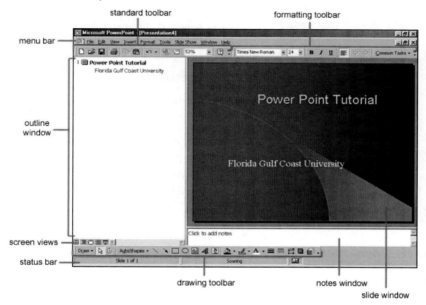

Views

PowerPoint gives you four screen layouts for constructing your presentation in addition to the Slide Show. You can select the page view by clicking the buttons just above the formatting toolbar and the bottom of the page.

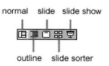

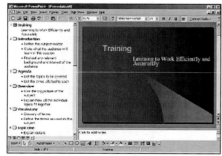

Normal View
This screen is split into three sections showing the presentation outline on the left, the slide in the main window, and notes at the bottom.

Slide View
The slide view displays each slide on the screen and is helpful for adding images, formatting text, and adding background styles.

 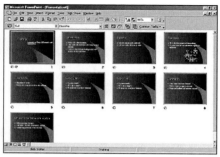

Outline View
The presentation outline is displayed on the majority of the screen with small windows for the slide and notes. This view is recommended for editing text.

Slide Sorter View
A small image of each slide is displayed in Slide Sorter view. Slides can easily be ordered and sorted from this screen.

Click the **Slide Show** button to view the full-screen slide show.

Working with Slides

Insert a New Slide
Follow these steps to insert a new slide into the presentation:
- In the Outline window, select the slide you want the new slide to appear after by clicking the slide's number.
- Select **Insert | New Slide** from the menu bar or click the new slide button on the standard toolbar.
- Choose the page layout from the window and press. **OK**

Applying a Design Template
To add a design template or changing the existing one, selection **Format | Design Template** from the menu bar. Select the template and click **Apply**.

Changing Slide Layouts
To change the layout template of the slide select **Format | Slide Layout** from the menu bar. Select one of the layout thumbnail images and click **Apply**.

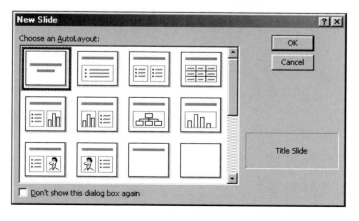

Reordering Slides

To reorder a slide in **Slide Sorter View**, simply click on the slide you wish to move and drag it to the new location. In **Normal** or **Outline View**, click the slide icon ⁵⌷ beside the number of the slide you want to move and drag the icon to a new location.

Hide Slides

If you do not want a slide to appear during the slide show, but do not want to delete the slide as it may be used later, the slide can be hidden by selecting **Slide Show | Hide Slide** from the menu bar. To add the slide back to the slide show, select **Slide Show | Hide Slide** again.

Create a Custom Slide Show

The Custom Slide Show feature allows you to select the slides you want to display in the slide show if not all the slides should be used.

- Select **Slide Show | Custom Slide Show** from the menu bar.

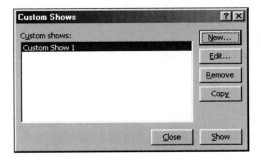

- Click the **New...** button in the **Custom Shows** window.
- In the **Define Custom Show** window, type a name for the slide in the **Slide show name** field.

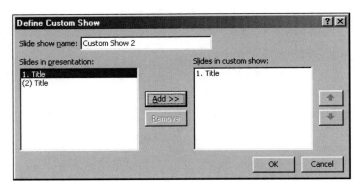

- Add slides to the custom show by highlighting them in the **Slides in presentation** window and clicking the **Add >>** button. Those slides will then appear in the **Slides in custom show** window.
- To remove slides from the custom show, highlight their names in the **Slides in custom show** window and click the **Remove** button.
- To reorder slides in the custom show, highlight the slide that should be moved and click the up and down arrows to change its order in the show.
- Click **OK** when finished.
- Click the **Show** button on the Custom Shows window to preview the custom slide show and click **Close** to exit.

Edit a Custom Slide Show

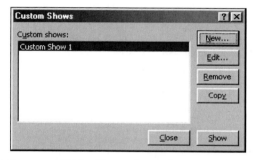

- Select **Slide Show | Custom Slide Show** from the menu bar.
- Edit the show by highlighting the name in the **Custom shows** box and clicking the **Edit...** button.
- To delete a show, highlight the name and click **Remove**.
- Create a copy of a show by clicking the **Copy** button. The copy can then be renamed by clicking the **Edit...** button.
- Click the **Show** button to preview the custom slide show and click **Close** to exit.

Bulleted Lists on Design Templates

Bulleted lists allow you to clearly display the main points of your presentation on slides. The text boxes on design templates already include bulleted lists. Click the place holder on the slide to begin adding text and press the **ENTER** key to return to the next line and add a new bulleted item. To go to the next line without adding another bullet, hold down the **SHIFT** key while pressing **ENTER**.

Adding Content

Bulleted List from a Text Box

If you are not creating a bulleted list from an existing placeholder on a design template, or if you would like to add an additional bulleted list, follow these steps to create a new list:

- In slide view, create a text box by selecting **Insert | Text Box** from the menu bar.
- "Draw" the text box on the slide by holding down the left mouse button while you move the mouse until the box is the size you want it.
- Choose **Format | Bullets and Numbering** from the menu bar.

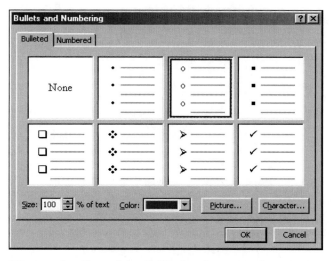

- Change the **Size** of the bullet by changing the percentage in relation to the text.
- Choose a color for the bullet from the **Color** menu. Click **More Colors** for a larger selection.
- Select one of the seven bullet types shown and click **OK**.
  -OR -
  Click the **Picture** button to view the **Picture Bullet** window. Select one of the bullets and click **OK**.
  -OR -

Click the **Character** button to select any character from the fonts on the computer. Select a symbol font such as Wingdings or Webdings from the **Bullets from** drop-down menu for the best selection of icons. Click on the characters in the grid to see them larger. Click **OK** when you have chosen the bullet you want to use.

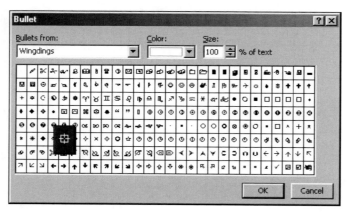

- Click **OK** on the **Bullets and Numbering** window and use the same methods described in the "Bulleted Lists on Design Templates" to enter text into the bulleted list.

Bulleted Lists and New Slides from an Outline

In **Normal** or **Outline** view, text can easily be entered in the outline window and new slides are automatically added. Follow the steps below to become familiar with adding slide content in outline view:

- Next to **Slide 1** the icon, type the title of the slide. The text you type beside the slide icons will be the large-type titles on each slide.
- Press **ENTER** to type the next line. This will automatically create a new slide. To create a bulleted list for the first slide, press the **TAB** key or click the **demote** button on ⊞ the **More Buttons** menu accessible by clicking the "triple arrow" button at the end of the formatting toolbar ⊞.
  -OR -
  Press **ALT+SHIFT+Right Arrow** to demote the selection to a bulleted list item.
- Continue entering text for the bulleted list, pressing **ENTER** at the end of each line to create a new bullet.
- Create a multilevel list by executing the demote action again to create a bulleted sublist. Press the **promote** ⊞ button on the **More Buttons** menu or press **ALT+SHIFT+Left Arrow** to return to the original list.
- Create a new slide by executing the **promote** action until a new slide icon appears.
- Continue creating new slides and bulleted lists by using the demote and promote actions until the presentation is completed. Use the formatting instructions below to format the lists.

If there is more than one bulleted list on the slide, the lists will be designated by numbers enclosed in black boxes. The example below shows the slide created from the outline on the left. The bulleted list on the left side of the slide is labeled list "1"on the outline and the list on the right is labeled list "2". When typing the outline, begin typing in the new list by pressing **CTRL+ENTER**. In this example, **CTRL+ENTER** was pressed after typing "Access".

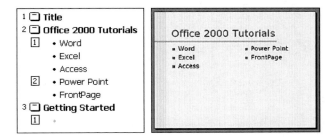

Numbered List

Follow these steps to create a numbered list:

* Create a text box.
* With the text box selected, choose **Format | Bullets and Numbering** from the menu bar.
* Click the **Numbered** tab at the top of the Bullets and Numbering window.

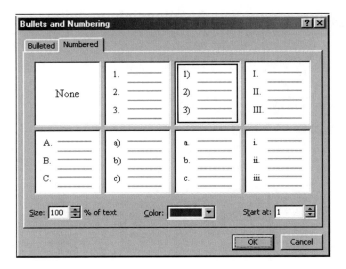

* Change the size of the numbers by changing the percentage in relation to the text.
* Choose a color for the numbers from the **Color** menu. Click **More Colors** for a larger selection.
* Change the **Start at** value if the numbers should not begin with 1.
* Select one of the the seven list types shown and click **OK.**

Resizing a Text Box

Select a text box by clicking on it with the mouse. A border with nine handles will appear around the text box. The four handles on the corners will resize the length and the width of the box at once while the handles on the sides will resize only in one direction. Click one of the handles and drag it with the mouse. Release the mouse button when it is the size you want it to be. Move the text box by clicking and dragging the thick, dotted border with the mouse.

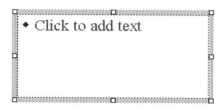

Text Box Properties

Change the colors, borders, and backgrounds of a text box from the **Format AutoShape** dialog box.

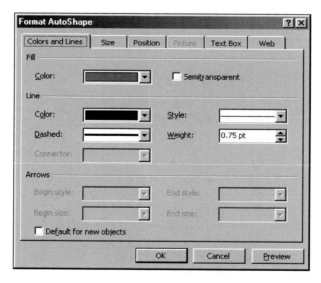

- Activate the textbox by clicking on it and select **Format | Colors and Lines** from the menu bar.
- Under the **Colors and Lines tab,** select a **Fill** color that will fill the background of the text box. Check the **Semitransparent** box if you want the slide background to show through the color.
- Select a **Line** color that will surround the box as well as a **Style** or **Weight** for the thickness of the line and a **Dashed** property if the line should not be solid.

- Click the **Text Box tab.**

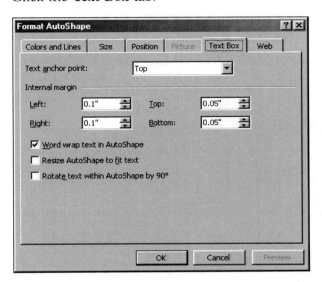

- Change the **Text anchor point** to reposition the text within the text box.
- Set **Internal margins** to the distance the text should be to the text box edges.
- Click **OK** to add the changes to the text box.

Delete a Text Box

To delete a text box from a template, simply click the border of the text box and press the **DELETE** key on the keyboard.

Adding Notes

From **Normal View**, notes can be added to the slide. These notes will not be seen on your presentation, but they can be printed out on paper along with the slide the notes refer to by selecting **Print What: Notes Pages** on the Print menu.

Video

To add a video to our presentation select **Insert | Movies and Sounds | Movie from File** or to insert an animation from Microsoft's gallery choose **Insert | Movies and Sounds | Movie from Gallery**. Select the video file and click **OK**.

Audio

To add sound to your presentation select **Insert | Movies and Sounds | Sound from Gallery** or **Sound from File**. Select a sound file and click **OK**.

Working with Text

Adding Text

If the slide layout includes text boxes, simply click on the text box to add text. To add a text box to the slide, select **Insert | Text Box** from the menu bar and draw the text box with the mouse. Set text editing options by selecting **Tools | Options** from the menu bar and clicking the **Edit** tab.

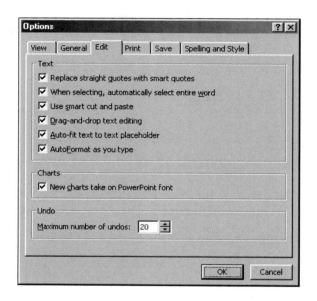

Formatting Text

Select the text that will be formatted by highlighting the text either on the outline or on the slide. Choose **Format | Font** from the menu bar or right-click on the highlighted selection and select **Font** from the popup shortcut menu. Select a font face, size, style, effect, and color from the **Font** dialog box. Click the **Preview** button to see how the changes will appear on the slide before making a decision.

Replace Fonts

Design templates have a preset font that you may want to change or you may want to change the font used on for the entire presentation for a number of reasons. This can be accomplished quickly using the Replace Fonts feature. Select **Format | Replace Font Replace** from the menu bar. Choose the font you want to **Replace** from the first drop-down menu and the font it should be replaced **With** from the second menu, and click the **Replace** button.

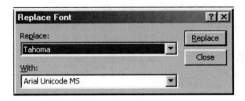

Line Spacing

Change the amount of space between lines in a text box by selecting **Format | Line Spacing** from the menu bar.

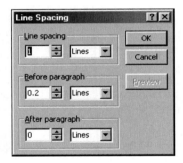

- **Line spacing** - Select the amount of vertical space between lines. A value of "1" is equal to single spacing and "2" is double spacing. Values between and above these numbers are valid as well.
- **Before paragraph and After paragraph** - This value will determine the amount of vertical space before and after each paragraph in a text box.

Change Case

Change the case of the characters in a paragraph by selecting **Format | Change Case** from the menu bar without having to retype the text.

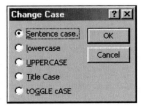

Spelling Options
Select **Tools | Options** from the menu bar and click the **Spelling and Style** tab.

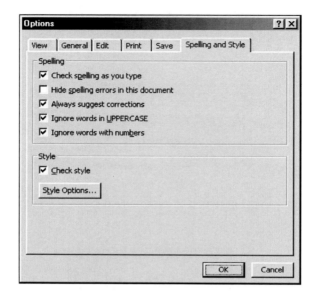

- **Check spelling as you type** - If this box is checked, PowerPoint will check the spelling of every word as you type. Misspelled words will be underlined with wavy red lines.
- **Hide spelling errors in this document** - Check this box to remove the wavy red lines from words that are spelled wrong.
- **Always suggest corrections** - If this box is checked, suggestions for misspelled words will appear when you activate the spell checker.
- **Ignore words in UPPERCASE** - PowerPoint recommends that you don't type slide titles in all uppercase letters so it will treat words like this and other all-uppercase acronyms as misspelled. Check this box to ignore this suggestion and acronyms that are typically typed in all caps.
- **Ignore words with numbers** - Check to ignore words that are combinations of letters and numbers.

Spelling Options

Select **Tools | Options** from the menu bar and click the **Spelling and Style** tab.

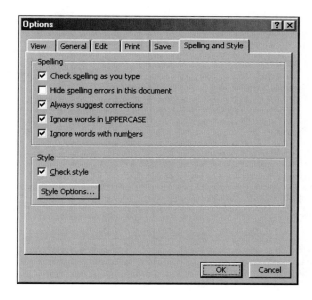

- **Check spelling as you type** - If this box is checked, PowerPoint will check the spelling of every word as you type. Misspelled words will be underlined with wavy red lines.
- **Hide spelling errors in this document** - Check this box to remove the wavy red lines from words that are spelled wrong.
- **Always suggest corrections** - If this box is checked, suggestions for misspelled words will appear when you activate the spell checker.
- **Ignore words in UPPERCASE** - PowerPoint recommends that you don't type slide titles in all uppercase letters so it will treat words like this and other all-uppercase acronyms as misspelled. Check this box to ignore this suggestion and acronyms that are typically typed in all caps.
- **Ignore words with numbers** - Check to ignore words that are combinations of letters and numbers.

Color Schemes

The colors of predesigned slide templates can be changed and a color scheme can be added
to blank presentations. This page explains how to add color schemes and background images
to slides.

• Select **Format | Slide Color Scheme** from the menu bar.
• Click one of the preset color scheme thumbnail images in the **Color schemes** box.

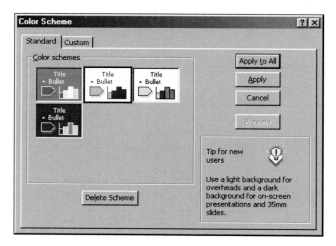

• Click the **Preview** button to see how the scheme will appear on the slide.
• To make changes to the color scheme, click the **Custom** tab on the dialog box.

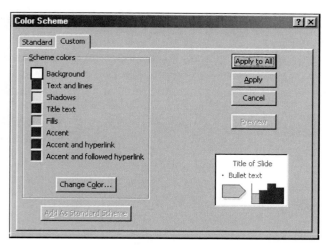

• Change the colors of the slide elements by selecting the color swatch beside the name of
the element and clicking the **Change color** button.

- Highlight one of the colors from the **Text and Line Color** window or select the **Custom** tab to view more color choices and click **OK** when finished.

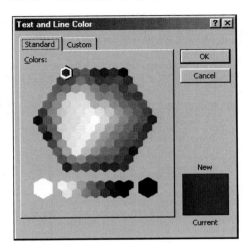

- When you have finished all color formatting, click **Apply to All** to apply the color scheme to all the slides in the presentation or **Apply** to add the scheme only to the current slide.

Backgrounds

Follow these steps to add background colors and patterns to a slide:

- Select **Format | Background** from the menu bar.

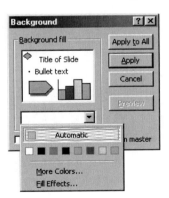

- Select a color from the drop-down menu below the **Background fill** preview or choose **More Colors...** for a larger selection.

- Select **Fill Effects** from the drop-down menu to add gradients, texture, patterns, or a picture to the background.

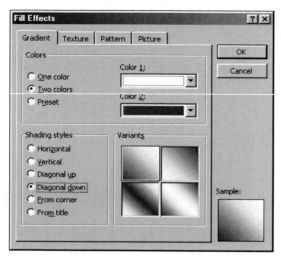

- **Gradient tab**
  - Select **One color** if the color chosen will fade into the background and select the color from the **Color 1** drop-down menu. Choose **Two colors** if the gradient will use two colors and select those colors from the **Color 1** and **Color 2** drop-down menus. **Preset** provides a selection of color combinations. Select one from the **Preset colors** drop-down menu.
  - Select the type of gradient from **Shading styles.**
  - Click one of the four **Variants** of the styles chosen.

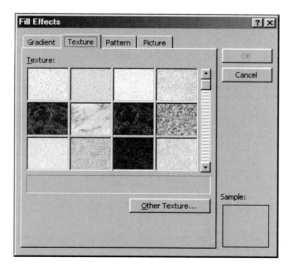

- **Texture tab**

  From the Texture window, select a repeating background by scrolling through the thumbnail images or click **Other Texture...** to select an image from a file.

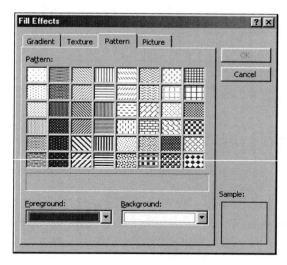

- **Pattern tab**

  Select a two-tone pattern by clicking one of the pattern swatches and selecting the **Foreground** and **Background** colors.

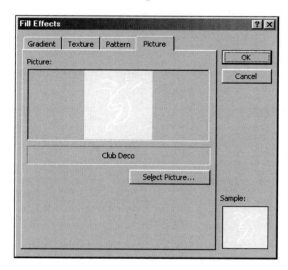

- **Picture tab**

  Click the **Select Picture** button to choose a picture from a file. After the picture is selected, a preview and description will be shown in this window.
- Click **OK** to apply the changes made from the **Fill Effects** windows.
- Click **Apply to All** to add the changes to every slide or **Apply** to make changes only to the current slide.

Graphics

The Drawing Toolbar provides many commands for creating and editing graphics. The toolbar is located at the bottom of the PowerPoint screen or it can be activated by selecting **View | Toolbars | Drawing** from the menu bar.

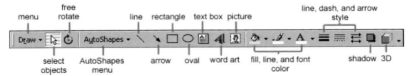

- **Menu** -
  - **Grouping** - Images can be grouped together so they become one image and can be moved together or the same formatting changes can be applied to both at once. Select all the images that will be grouped by holding down the **SHIFT** key and clicking once on each image. Then select **Group** from the **Draw** menu. The images can be ungrouped by selecting **Ungroup** from the same menu. The rectangles in the image to the left are separate images with their own sets of handles and they are grouped together in the image to the right:

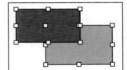 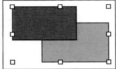

  - **Order** - The order of overlapping images can be changed using this feature. In the example of two rectangles below, the green rectangle is selected and the **Send Backward** command was used to move the image below the blue rectangle. Send Backward and Bring Forward will move elements by one layer. Send to Back and Bring to Front move the elements to the back or top of a series of several overlapping graphics.

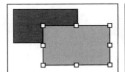 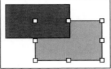

  - **Nudge** - Use the nudge actions to move an object slightly in one direction.
  - **Align or Distribute** - Select a group of objects and choose one of the the commands from the Align or Distribute menu to change the position of the objects in relation to one another.
  - **Rotate or Flip** - Rotate an object 90 degrees or flip the object over its x- or y-axis.

- **Select objects** - Deactivate all drawing functions.
- **Free rotate** - This button will place green handles on certain objects so they can be arbitrarily rotated. Click and drag the handles to rotate the objects.

- **AutoShapes menu** - Click the small down arrow to the right of the "AutoShapes" text to select a shape. [more...]
- **Line** and **Arrow** - Click and drag the mouse on the slide to add lines. Hold down the **SHIFT** key to draw a straight line. Use the end points of the completed line to stretch and reposition the line.
- **Rectangle** and **Oval** - Click and drag the mouse on the slide to add rectangles and ovals. Hold down the **SHIFT** key to add squares and circles.
- **Text box** - Click to draw a text box on the slide.
- **Word art** - Click to add WordArt. [More]
- **Picture** - Click to add a clip art image to the slide.
- **Fill color** - Choose a fill color for rectangles, ovals, and clip art.
- **Line color** - Select a border color for shapes and pictures.
- **Font color** - Highlight text on the slide and click the small down arrow next to the Font color icon to select a color.
- **Line style** - Highlight a line or arrow that has been drawn and click this button to select a thickness or style for the line.
- **Dash style** - Highlight a line or arrow and select a dash style.
- **Arrow style** - Change the arrow head style for an existing arrow or change a line to an arrow.
- **Shadow** - Select a text box to add shadow to text or choose any other object on the slide to add a drop shadow.
- **3D** - Add a three-dimensional effect to text and other objects.

Keyword Outline: _____
_____

Internal Summaries: _____
_____

Magnitude Patterning:_____
_____

Main Points: _____
_____

Outline: _____
_____

Preview Statements: _____
_____

Primary Sources: _____
_____

Pro and Con
  Patterning: _____
Relevance of
  the Topic: _____
Secondary Sources: _____
_____

Significance of
  the Topic: _____
Spatial Patterning: _____
_____

Specific Purpose: _____
_____

- **Insert Clip** to add the image to the slide.
- **Preview Clip** to view the image full-size before adding it to the slide. Drag the bottom, right corner of the preview window to resize the image and click the "**x**" close button to end the preview.

- **Add Clip to Favorites** will add the selected image to your favorites directory that can be chosen from the **Insert ClipArt** dialog box.
- **Find Similar Clips** will retrieve images similar to the one you have chosen.
- Click the **Close** button in the top, right corner of the **Insert Clip** window to stop adding clip art to the slide.

Add An Image from a File

To add a photo or graphic from a file:

- Select **Insert | Picture | From File** from the menu bar.
- Click the down arrow button on the right side of the **Look in:** window to find the image on your computer.
- Highlight the file name from the list and click the **Insert** button.

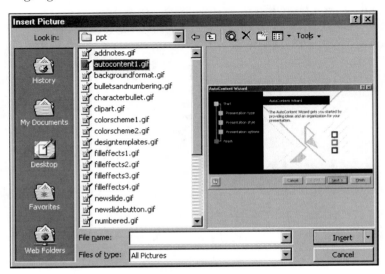

Editing A Graphic

Activate the image you wish to edit by clicking on it once with the mouse. Several handles will appear around the graphic. Click and drag these handles to resize the image. The handles on the corners will resize proportionally while the handles on the straight lines will stretch the image. More picture effects can be changed using the **Picture** toolbar.

Auto Shapes

The AutoShapes toolbar allows you to draw a number of geometrical shapes, arrows, flow chart elements, stars, and other graphics on a slide. Activate the AutoShapes toolbar by selecting **Insert | Picture | AutoShapes** or **View | Toolbars | AutoShapes** from the menu bar. Click the buttons on the toolbar to view the options for drawing each shape.

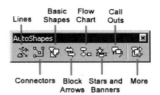

- **Lines** - After clicking the Lines button on the AutoShapes toolbar, draw a *straight line, arrow,* or *double-ended arrow* from the first row of options by clicking the respective button. Click in the slide where you would like the line to begin and click again where it should end. To draw a *curved line* or *freeform shape,* select curved lines from the menu (first and second buttons of second row), click in the slide where the line should appear, and click the mouse every time a curve should begin. End creating the graphic by clicking on the starting end or pressing the **ESC** key. To *scribble,* click the last button in the second row, click the mouse in the slide and hold down the left button while you draw the design. Let go of the mouse button to stop drawing.
- **Connectors** - Draw these lines to connect flow chart elements.
- **Basic Shapes** - Click the Basic Shapes button on the AutoShapes toolbar to select from many *two- and three-dimensional shapes, icons, braces,* and *brackets.* Use the drag-and-drop method to draw the shape in the slide. When the shape has been made, it can be resized using the open box handles and other adjustments specific to each shape can be modified using the yellow diamond handles.

- **Block Arrows** - Select Block Arrows to choose from many types of ***two- and three-dimensional arrows.*** Drag-and-drop the arrow in the slide and use the open box and yellow diamond handles to adjust the arrowheads. Each AutoShape can also be rotated by first clicking the **Free Rotate** button on the drawing toolbar ⟳. Click and drag the green handles around the image to rotate it. The tree image below was created from an arrow rotated 90 degrees.

- **Flow Chart** - Choose from the flow chart menu to add ***flow chart elements*** to the slide and use the line menu to draw connections between the elements.
- **Stars and Banners** - Click the button to select ***stars, bursts, banners,*** and ***scrolls.***
- **Call Outs** - Select from the ***speech and thought bubbles,*** and ***line call outs.*** Enter the call out text in the text box that is made.
- **More AutoShapes** - Click the More button to choose from a list of clip art categories.

Each of the submenus on the AutoShapes toolbar can become a separate toolbar. Just click and drag the gray bar across the top of the submenus off of the toolbar and it will become a separate floating toolbar.

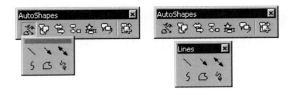

WordArt

Add headlines in striking colors and shapes to your presentation using Word Art.

- Select **Insert | Picture | WordArt** from the menu bar or click the **Word Art** button on the Drawing toolbar.
- Choose a Word Art style from the listing and click **OK**.

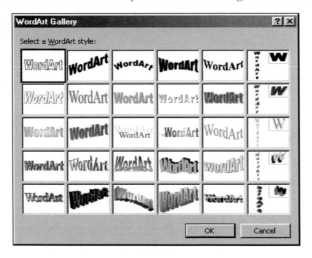

- Enter the text in the **Edit WordArt Text** box and choose the font, size, and style for the text. Click **OK**.

- Use the white box handles around the word art to resize it on the slide.
- Drag the yellow diamond handle to change the shape of the text. To revert back to no shape, double-click the diamond.

Slide Effects

Action Buttons

Use the action button toolbar to add functioning buttons to slides in a presentation.

- Select **Slide Show** | **Action Buttons** from the menu bar. Click the bar across the top of the button menu and drag it off the menu so it becomes a floating toolbar.

- Click one of the button faces and draw the button on the slide using the mouse. The **Action Settings** menu will then appear.

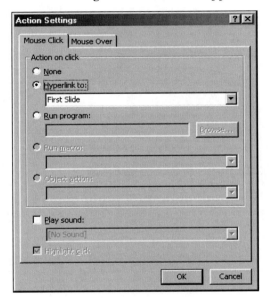

- Set the actions under either the **Mouse Click** or **Mouse Over** tabs. Actions specified for Mouse Click will execute when the button is clicked on the slide while actions for Mouse Over will occur when the mouse pointer hovers over the button.
- Select an action for the button by choosing a **Hyperlink to** destination.
- If you want a sound to be played when the button is clicked, check the **Play sound** box and choose a sound from the drop-down menu.

- Click **OK** when finished.

- The button on the slide can be resized using the white box handles and the depth of the button can be changed by dragging the yellow diamond.

Slide Animation

Several animations for slide objects are available through the drop-down menus on the menu bar. First, select the text box or graphic that will be animated. **Select Slide Show | Preset Animation** and choose from one of the options. To select a different animation or turn the animation off, select the appropriate choice from the same menu. For more options, follow the procedure below:

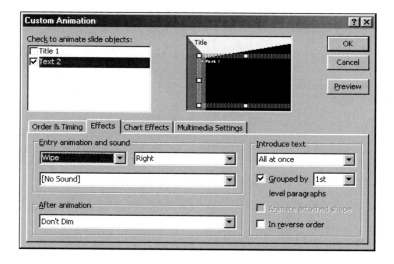

- Select **Slide Show | Custom Animation** from the menu bar.
- Select the object on the slide that will be animated from the **Check to animate slide objects** list.
- Under the **Effects tab,** select the animation type (or select "No Effect" to turn an animation off) and direction from the drop-down menus and select a sound if you wish.
- Select an **After animation** effect if the text should change colors after the animation executes.
  - **Color palette** - Select one of the color swatches or click **More Colors** for a larger selection. The text will change to the selected color when the mouse is clicked during the slide show.
  - **Don't Dim** - This option erases all After Animation effects.

- • **Hide After Animation** - Text will be immediately erased after the animation is completed.
  - • **Hide on Next Mouse click** - The text will be erased when the mouse is clicked.
- • Choose the style of displaying the text under the **Introduce text** section. The drop-down menu provides options for displaying the characters for each bulleted item. Select "All at once" for the text to appear immediately, "by Word" for the text to appear one word at a time, or "by Letter" for a typewriter effect that displays one letter at a time.
- • Click the **Order & Timing tab** to alter the order that the objects appear on the slide. Highlight the object in the **Animation order** box and click the **Move** arrows to move the object's position within the animation sequence. Under **Start animation,** choose "On mouse click" to activate the animation by clicking the mouse or "Automatically" for the animation to execute after a set number of seconds.

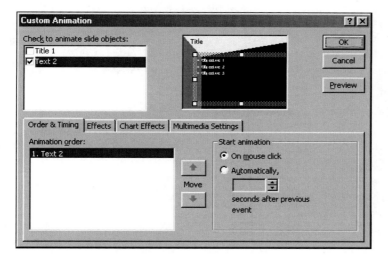

- • Click the **Preview** button at any time to preview the animation on the slide and click **OK** when finished.

Animation Preview

Select **Slide Show | Animation Preview** from the menu bar to view the Animation Preview window. Click anywhere within this window with the mouse to preview the animations that have been set. To hide the window, click the **x** close button in the top, right corner.

Slide Transitions

Add transition effects when changing slides by following these steps:

- Select **Slide Show | Slide Transition** from the menu bar.
- From the **Effect** section, choose a transition from the drop-down menu and notice the preview after the transition is selected. Select a speed for the transition as well.
- Under **Advance,** check "On mouse click" for the slide transition to occur by clicking the mouse or using keystrokes or check "Automatically after" and a number of seconds if the transition should occur automatically.
- Select a **Sound** if necessary and check the **Loop until next sound** if it should keep repeating until the next sound is played.
- Click **Apply to All** if the transition effects should be added to every slide or **Apply** if the effects should be added only to the current slide.

Slide Show Options

Select **Tools│Options** and click the **View** tab to choose from several more slide show options.

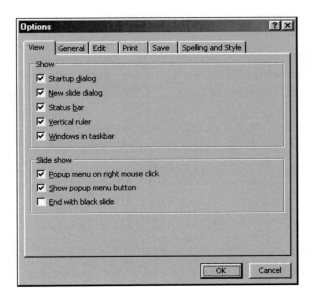

- **Popup menu on right mouse click** - Check this box if you want to be able to access the shortcut menu during a presentation.
- **Show popup menu button** - Check this box to activate the menu button that appears in the bottom, left corner of the screen during a presentation.
- **End with black slide** - Insert a blank, black slide to the end of the presentation.

Slide Master

Change the style of all slides in the presentation by changing the properties on the **Slide Master.** Each Design Template has its own Slide Master that can be altered. If you create slides from scratch, a consistent style can be added to the presentation by formatting the Slide Master.

- Select **View | Master | Slide Master** from the menu bar.

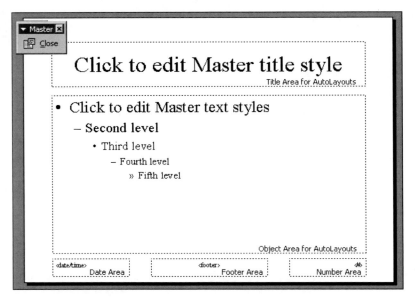

- Format the master slide just as you would format a regular slide by formatting text, formatting lists, adding background patterns and effects, and setting footers.
- Click the **Close** button on the **Master toolbar** to quit editing the master slide and return to the presentation.

Headers and Footers

Add the date and time, slide numbers, and other footer text to the master slide from the Header and Footer window.

- Select **View | Header and Footer...** from the menu bar.

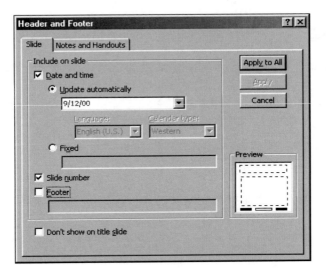

- Check the **Date and time** box to add this feature to the slide. Select **Update automatically** to always display the current date and time or click **Fixed** and enter a date that will not change in the text field provided.
- Check the **Slide number** box to add this feature to the slides.
- Click the **Footer** box and add other text to the footer area of the slide.
- Check the **Don't show on title slide** box to hide these features on the title slide of the presentation.
- Click the **Notes and Handouts** tab to make the same changes to notes and handouts pages.
- Click **Apply to All** to add the changes to every slide or **Apply** to add only to the current slide.

Slide Numbers

To add the slide numbers in a fixed position on the slide, use the **Header and Footer** window detailed above. The slide number can otherwise be added anywhere on the slide by placing the cursor where the slide number should appear and selecting **Insert | Slide Number** from the menu bar. The text of the slide number can be formated just as regular text style is changed.

Date and Time

A date and/or time can also be added using the **Header and Footer** window or anywhere else on the slide. Place the cursor where the date and time should appear on the slide and select **Insert I Date and Time** from the menu bar. Select a format from the **Available formats** box and click **Update automatically** if this feature should always be updated to reflect the current date and time. Click **OK** to finish.

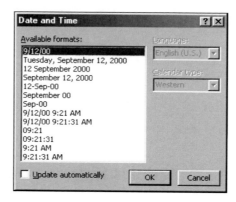

Saving and Printing

Save as Web Page

Presentations can be saved by selecting **File I Save** from the menu bar. However, if you want to post PowerPoint presentations on the Internet, you may want to save them as web pages so students and other visitors to your web site can view the presentation even if they do not have PowerPoint installed on their computers. Select **File I Save As Web Page** from the menu bar. Choose your web page directory on the network from the **Look in:** drop-down menu and name the file in the **File name:** box. Click **Save** to save the presentation in web format.

Page Setup

Select **File I Page Setup** from the menu bar to access options for printing the presentation slides. Select the format the printed slides will be used for from the **Slides sized for** drop-down menu or enter a specific print size using the **Width** and **Height** boxes. Select the page orientation for the slides and for other print material from the presentation in the **Orientation** section.

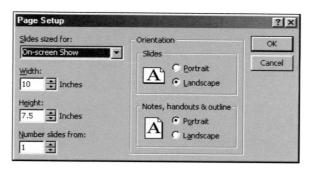

Print

Select **File | Print** from the menu bar to print the presentation.

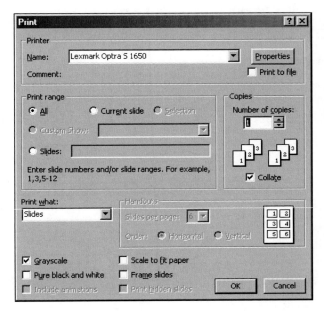

Print range - Select **All** to print all the slides in the presentation, **Current slide** to print only the current slide, or enter slide numbers in the **Slides** field to print only certain slides.

Copies - Enter the number of copies of each slide specified in Print range and check the **Collate** box if necessary.

Print What -
- **Slides** prints a full-page slide on each page.
- **Handouts** prints as many slides as you designate on each page.
- **Notes Page** prints one slide with that slide's notes on each page
- **Outline view** prints the outline of the presentation

Click **OK** to print.

Keyboard Shortcuts

Keyboard shortcuts can save time and the effort of switching from the keyboard to the mouse to execute simple commands. Print this list of PowerPoint keyboard shortcuts and keep it by your computer for a quick reference.

Note: A plus sign indicates that the keys need to be pressed at the same time.

Action	Keystroke	Action	Keystroke
Document actions		**Formatting**	
Open a presentation	CTRL+O	Select all	CTRL+A
New presentation	CTRL+N	Copy	CTRL+C
Save As	F12	Cut	CTRL+X
Save	CTRL+S	Paste	CTRL+V
Print	CTRL+P	Undo	CTRL+Z
Help	F1	Redo	CTRL+Y
		Bold	CTRL+B
Presentation actions		Italics	CTRL+I
Begin slide show	F5	Underline	CTRL+U
Next slide	ENTER or Down arrow key	Left justified	CTRL+L
Previous slide	BACKSPACE or Up arrow key	Center justified	CTRL+E
		Right justified	CTRL+R
Activate pen tool	CTRL+P	Promote list item	ALT+SHIFT+Left arrow
Erase pen strokes	E	Demote list item	ALT+SHIFT+Right arrow or TAB
Deactivate pen tool	CTRL+A		
Show/Hide black screen	B	**Editing**	
Show/Hide white screen	W	Find	CTRL+F
Show/Hide pointer & button	A	Replace	CTRL+H
End slide show	ESC	Insert hyperlink	CTRL+K
		New slide	CTRL+M
		Spell checker	F7
		Macros	ALT+F8

Run the slide show and press the F1 key to view all keyboard shortcuts applicable when running a slide show.

Tips

Design Tips

- Use contrasting colors for the text and the background so the text will be easy to read.
- Use font size large enough to be seen from the back of the room where the presentation will be held. A font size of 24-point or larger is recommended.
- Use short phrases and sentences to convey your message.
- Use simple slide transitions. Too many different transitions will distract your audience from the subject of the presentation.
- Avoid cluttering the slides with too much text or graphics. Your audience should hear what you have to say and not be distracted by a busy screen.
- Keep text simple and easy to read by not using many different text effects such as **bold,** *italics*, underlining, larger font size for emphasis within a sentence, or a different font all on the same slide.

Presentation Basics

- Begin the slide show by clicking the Slide Show button on the bottom of the screen.
- Move to the next slide by pressing the **SPACE BAR, ENTER, PAGE DOWN,** or right arrow keys or by clicking the left mouse button.
- Go back to the previous slide by pressing **BACKSPACE, PAGE UP,** or the left arrow key.
- To end the slideshow before it is complete press **ESC** on the keyboard.
- A pen tool is available for drawing on the screen with the mouse. Press **CTRL+P** or click the right mouse button at any time and a popup window will appear. Choose **Pen** and the pointer will change to a pen that allows you to draw freehand on the screen using the mouse. Press the **E** key to erase all pen strokes. Press **CTRL+A** to disable the pen feature and revert the pen back to a pointer arrow.
- If you would like to use the pen to draw on a blank screen during a presentation, press the **B** or **W** keys, or select **Screen/Black Screen** from the popup menu and the screen will turn black. Press **B** or **W** again or choose **Next** from the popup menu to return to the presentation when you are finished drawing.
- To hide the pointer and button from the screen press the **A** key.
- Be sure to preview the slide show using a projector if one will be used during the presentation. Words or graphics that are close to the edge of the screen may be cut off by the projector.

Endnotes

1. Camp, S. (1993). Population: The critical decade. *Foreign Policy*. 90. 129.

Chapter Four
KEY TERMS

Audio: _____

_____

Bar Graph: _____

_____

Criteria for Visuals: _____

_____

Line Graph: _____

_____

Models: _____

_____

Pictures: _____

_____

Pie Graph: _____

_____

Real Objects: _____

_____

Types of Visuals: _____

_____

Value of Visuals: _____

_____

Video: _____

_____

When to Use Visuals: _____

_____

Chapter Four
EXACTLY EXERCISES

_____ Which type of visual aid would you use in each instance below?

_____ The budget was approved as follows: 25 percent for maintenance, 60 percent for salaries, 15 percent for supplies.

_____ The birthrate is expected to double in the next 10 years.

_____ Former President Nixon's face was pale and withdrawn in his 1960 debate with Senator John F. Kennedy.

_____ There are four steps in preparing a professional resume.

_____ The nucleus has both protons and neutrons.

_____ The Everglades is found in Florida.

_____ The artwork of Michelangelo reflects . . .

_____ Reggae music has a distinct beat.

_____ This presentation will focus on the following three points.

_____ As you can see, the four vice-presidents in this company report directly to the president.

_____ The decline in test scores is directly correlated to class absences.

_____ First you need to mix the sugar, eggs, and flour in the mixing bowl.

Chapter Four
REVIEW QUESTIONS

1. What three questions should you ask yourself when determining if it would be beneficial
    to use a visual aid?

    a. _____

    b. _____

    c. _____

2. What five criteria must all visual supporting material meet in order to be effective?

    a. _____

    b. _____

    c. _____

    d. _____

    e. _____

3. What types of information should be placed on a visual?

    _____

    _____

    _____

    _____

    _____

    _____

    _____

    _____

    _____

    _____

Chapter Four
POWERPOINT SLIDES

- Value of visual aids

- When to use visuals

- Criteria for visuals

- Rules for visibility

- Rules for clarity

- Types of visual aids

VALUE OF VISUAL AIDS

• Creates understanding

• Increases retention of information

WHEN TO USE VISUALS

- Abstract information

- Statistical information

- Geography

143

CRITERIA FOR VISUALS

- Visibility

- Clarity

- Relevance

- Integration

- Professionalism

VISIBILITY

- Maximum 6 lines of text

- Maximum 40 characters per line

- Phrases not full sentences

- Use upper and lower case lettering

- Simple typeface

CLARITY

- Never pass anything out

- Must discuss all information

- One graph/photo per slide

- Maintain eye contact

- Red/green & blue/yellow

SPEECH

TYPES OF VISUAL AIDES

- Real Objects

- Models

- Pictures

- Graphics

- Audio

- Video

PART TWO

INFORMATIVE SPEECHES

CHAPTER 5
Speaking to Inform

"The average man thinks about what he has said; the above average man about what he is going to say."

Anonymous

The most common form of speaking is **informative speaking.** Whether disseminating information on the news, in a business setting, a military briefing, or in a classroom, your primary purpose is to share knowledge with others. However, just presenting information does not necessarily mean that communication has taken place. For example, there is an old saying, "A lecture is a process in which information travels from the mouth of a professor to the notes of the students without passing through their minds." Communication is said to happen when the receivers internalize the information that is presented (the difference between **hearing** and **listening,** Chapter One), but all too often that does not happen. You can speak all you want, but if the audience is not listening, what did you accomplish? It is of the utmost importance that you speak in a clear logical manner about a topic that is important to the needs of your audience. The best speakers **analyze their audience** (Chapter Three), pick an **appropriate topic** (Chapter Three), organize the information they are presenting (this chapter), and practice their **delivery** (Chapter Two).

Although this may seem like a daunting task, it is one of the most skillful techniques you can learn. The great orator Daniel Webster supports this concept:

> If all my talents and powers were to be taken from me by some inscrutable Providence, and I had my choice of keeping but one, I would unhesitatingly ask to be allowed to keep the Power of Speaking, for through it, I would quickly recover the rest.

Informative Speaking
Most common form of speaking

Hearing
A physical process

Listening
A cognitive process

Audience Analysis
Knowing what the interests/needs of the audience are

Topic Selection
A speaker should choose a topic tht is useful, relevant, and significant to an audience

Delivery
The way an individual presents their speech

Informative Speech Types

There are four different types of informative speeches. Although each type of informative speech may use a different organizational pattern (p 168–174), they are all prepared in the same manner. The nine-step procedure is discussed in this chapter.

Demonstrative Speech
The speaker describes a process of how to complete something; also known as a "how to speech"

- ■ *Demonstrative*
  The *demonstrative informative speech* is a "how to" speech. This type of informative presentation demonstrates how to do something or how to complete a process. A presentation on *How to Recognize Child Abuse* or *How to Write a Resume* are examples of speeches of demonstration.

Speech of Definition
The speaker defines a topic for the audience

- ■ *Definition*
  Defining terminology or concepts is another type of informative presentation. In a *speech of definition* your goal is to define a topic for the audience. A presentation defining *The Various Types of Automobile Insurance* or defining *Current Drugs Being Used in AIDS Research* are both examples of speeches of definition.

Descriptive Speech
The speaker describes a person, policy, or event

- ■ *Descriptive*
  Describing a person, policy, or event is the third type of informational speech. Your goal in a *descriptive speech* is to describe your topic to the audience. A biographical presentation on *Winston Churchill*, describing *The Entrance Requirements at Your School*, or describing *The Assassination of John F. Kennedy* are all examples of speeches of description.

Narrative
The speaker tells a story

- ■ *Narrative*
  A *narrative* is a fully developed story with one or more characters, a scene, physical action, and a plot. This type of speech tells the story of how something/someone has developed, changed, or originated. It is told as a story from beginning to end and always uses the chronological organizational pattern.

Informative Speech Types

Demonstrative	Definition	Description	Narrative
"How to" do something "How to" complete a process	Defining terms or concepts or events	Describing a person or policy or event	Tells a story

Putting the Informative Speech Together Is a Nine-Step Process

Step One: The General Purpose

Consider the purpose of your speech. Do you want to teach the audience something? Do you want to inform them on a subject? Do you want the audience to change a previously held opinion or belief? Do you want your audience to physically do something? Do you want to entertain the audience? Perhaps your goal includes some or all of these examples. Your first decision will be to determine the general purpose of your speech. This is what you ultimately want to accomplish in your presentation. A speaker may inform, persuade, or entertain an audience.

Your *general purpose* will never be spoken by you. Its purpose is to help you determine what type of research information you need to locate. If delivering an informative speech you need to find a variety of information that informs your audience about your subject. If you are persuading an audience you will need to build an argument (Chapter Six), and if entertaining your audience with a special occasion speech (Chapter Seven) you will need a different type of **supporting material** all together.

Your general purpose is either:

- To inform
- To persuade
- To entertain

Step Two: The Specific Purpose

Just like the general purpose, your *specific purpose* will never be spoken by you. Its purpose is to help you narrow down your topic sufficiently. After completing your **spider diagram** (Chapter Three), you need to write a specific purpose statement.

By definition, your specific purpose statement is what you want the audience to be able to do at the end of your speech.

- Do you want them to be able to list the different types of abortion?
- Do you want them to be able to explain the different ways to prepare for retirement?
- Do you want them to be able to define the different types of learning styles?

There are five rules for writing a specific purpose statement.

1. Every specific purpose statement should start off with "At the end of my speech, the audience will be able to . . . "

General Purpose
Never spoken by the speaker; helps determine the type of research material required

Supporting Material
The subpoints such as quotes, statistics, definitions, etc. that help build a point

Specific Purpose
Never spoken by the speaker; helps the speaker to stay on point and avoid tangents

Spider Diagram
An effective way to narrow down a speech topic

2. It should contain a number. This number is going to correspond with the number of main points in the body of your speech. For short speeches, up to twenty minutes long, this number should be between two and five.
3. It should be a full sentence not a phrase.
4. It should be a statement not a question.
5. It should have a measurable verb, such as: to list, to explain, to define, to describe.

Examples of specifics purpose statements are as follows:

■ At the end of my speech, the audience will be able to list the four types of abortions.
■ At the end of my speech, the audience will be able to explain the two ways to prepare for retirement.
■ At the end of my speech, the audience will be able to define the three types of learning styles.

Step Three: Thesis Statement

Thesis Statement
A sentence that clearly tells the audience what the speaker will be discussing

Central Idea
A type of thesis statement used with informative speeches; it is a one sentence summary of entire presentation

Unlike the general purpose and specific purpose statements, the *thesis statement* is actually spoken in the introduction. Therefore, it is essential to make certain that the audience is able to identify this statement.

A thesis statement for an informative speech is called a **central idea.** A central idea, while summarizing the speech, does not make conclusions about the subject. Its purpose is to share information and create a general understanding of the topic. The central idea is the most important statement in the introduction. It is the one statement that indicates to the audience your main purpose. You must always keep this statement clear and concise. When writing your thesis statement, there are three rules you should follow: (1) do not propose a particular point of view, (2) do not urge or suggest any physical action by the audience, (3) do not list the main points of your speech. A good thesis statement for an informative speech is a one-sentence summary of your entire speech.

The following examples of central idea statements summarize the informative speech without drawing any conclusions. They do not urge any physical or mental action on the part of the listener. Lastly, they do not mention the specific main points in your speech.

■ The Dragon Boat Festival pays tribute to Qu Yuan.
■ Martin Luther King protested for civil rights in the 1960s.
■ The Bay of Pigs invasion occurred while John F. Kennedy was President of the United States.

Step Four: Conducting Research

After deciding upon a **speech topic** that meets the criteria discussed in Chapter Three, it is necessary to begin planning your research strategy. You should begin by listing a series of pertinent questions pertaining to your speech subject that you feel will need to be addressed in your research and preparation. We will call these questions your **research questions.**

You may be thinking to yourself, "What type of questions should I ask? What questions should my research answer?"

Research Questions

- Who?
- What?
- Where?
- Why?
- How?
- When?

Upon deciding which questions are relevant for your potential speech topic, you can then form a series of relevant research questions. For instance, if you decide to present an informative **demonstrative** presentation on *How to Care for Roses* the following research questions may result:

Topic Selection
A speaker should choose a topic that is useful, relevant, and significant to an audience

Research Questions
Questions your research should answer

Demonstrative Speech
The speaker describes a process of how to complete something; also known as a "how to speech"

Sample Research Questions

- *Who* in the audience will be interested in roses?
- *Why* would the audience need to know this information?
- *Why* would the audience want to know this information?
- *Where* are these particular types of roses grown?
- *What* is the expertise of the audience on this topic?
- *What* is my own level of expertise on this topic?
- *What* types of roses will I be discussing?
- *What* type of visual supporting materials will I be using?
- *What* tools or equipment will be needed?
- *When* should roses be planted? pruned? fertilized?
- *How* much time do I have to research this presentation?
- *How* much background information on roses is necessary for this particular audience?
- *How* are these roses grown?

Supporting Material
The subpoints such as quotes, statistics, definitions, etc. that help build a point

Ethos
Aristotle's term for credibility

Primary Sources
Research materials that are created by individuals directly involved in the event as it was happening

Secondary Sources
Research materials that are created by individuals not directly involved in the event as it was happening

You can probably think of several other pertinent questions on this topic. By writing as many pertinent questions as you can think of before actually beginning to research your speech topic, you will maximize the available time to look for **supporting material.** You will have provided yourself with a good starting point for researching your speech topic. All you need to do now to start your research is begin trying to find the answers to your relevant research questions.

Before you actually begin gathering information you should consider the quality of the information you may find. Keep in mind that not all information is of equal value. The audience must see a speaker as having good sense, good will, and a good moral character. This is what Aristotle called **ethos.** A speaker builds his/her ethos, or what we refer to today as credibility, through good research material.

Research materials are generally divided into two broad categories: primary sources and secondary sources. **Primary sources** are materials created by individuals or groups that were directly involved in the events as they were happening. The three types of primary resources are:

- *Original documents*
  Such as letters, statements, and news footage created by people who were personally involved in the event.
- *Creative works*
  Such as books, poems, paintings, and dances.
- *Relics*
  Cultural artifacts such as jewelry, tools, buildings, and clothes.

Secondary sources are created by persons who were not actual participants in an event. A secondary source is a source that summarizes or interprets the event. Most textbooks, history books, critical reviews, and scholarly articles are considered secondary sources.

There are instances where one source will contain both primary and secondary sources. Consider a newspaper's account of a recent earthquake. If the reporter who wrote the article arrived after the earthquake he/she would be a secondary source. However, if the writer interviewed people who experienced the earthquake, these people would be primary sources.

As you might have guessed, while primary and secondary sources are both useful, in most instances if a primary source is available it is preferable to a secondary source. For example, it is safe to assume that any person who spoke directly to Aristotle is now dead. It would therefore be impossible to find a primary source who spoke to Aristotle. However, there are many people still alive who fought in Vietnam and may be able to give you a first hand account of their experiences in the war. The accounts of these primary sources would be found in diaries, letters, auto-biographies, or through personal interviews.

Armed with a narrowed speech topic and your research questions, you are now ready to begin collecting both primary and secondary sources.

The best place to begin your research is in the library. Many people are tentative about using the library because they are not familiar with how a library is organized and/or they were never instructed on how to use the library effectively. For these reasons many libraries offer short seminars on how to use the various services they offer. Libraries will also familiarize students with current research methods. This is especially important with the recent changes in technology.

Someone who is not familiar with the library may state, "I can't find any information on my topic!" This is probably true. Even you might dis-cover you cannot find any information. This does not mean though that there is no information on your speech subject in the library. Most libraries have more information than you could possibly read on your topic. This is especially true for university, college, and large public libraries. In most instances, if you cannot find enough **supporting mate-rials** for your speech topic, it is probably because you are not looking in the right places.

Think of researching your topic as a mystery that needs to be solved. Consider yourself a detective trying to uncover clues that will help you solve the mystery. Except that instead of looking for "clues" you are try-ing to uncover "facts." Your mystery is the "mystery" of your speech topic.

For beginning library detectives, as well as for super-sleuths, the most logical place to begin gathering "facts" is to ask the reference librarians for assistance. The reference librarians undoubtedly hold most of the keys to solve your mystery. All you need to do is ask for help from these trained professionals and listen intently as they point you in the right direction. Reference librarians may recommend current periodicals or newspapers as the first place to look for information. They may also point you in the direction of a computerized database.

Do not be afraid to ask very specific questions about your speech sub-ject. For example, if you are looking for information on teenage suicides from 2000 to 2004, ask specifically for references and sources of informa-tion on this subject. Do not ask only about teenage suicides or suicide in general.

This may be a little intimidating for most of you. You may be "new" to researching or accustomed to using only a few sources that you are already familiar with from the past. However, do not let your initial reser-vations hold you back. Do not be afraid to ask for assistance. Introduce yourself to the reference librarians and allow them to help you.

Supporting Material
The subpoints such as quotes, statistics, definitions, etc. that help build a point

For most of you the library may be a place to find a quiet study spot, read a book, or meet friends. You may not be aware of all the services the library has to offer. Most libraries are organized very similarly and once you are acquainted with the various resource types a library has to offer, you may actually enjoy uncovering and discovering information.

The following is a brief description of the various forms of resources available to you in most, if not all, libraries.

Computer Databases

Many libraries are now computerized. In most cases the library will have its own databases stored on the library's mainframe computer. You can gain access to most of these databases by using the designed computer terminals in the library.

The most common computerized database in a library is the card catalog or online catalog. It may include a brief description of the book and may indicate if the book is still on the library's shelf or when it is expected to be returned. Most libraries will also have the capability of requesting a book for you from another library through inter-library loan.

In addition to the online card catalog, your library may have other databases stored on the mainframe computer or on CD. Most libraries have computerized indexes on various subjects in journals and magazines. However, you should ask the reference librarians what databases are available in your particular library. In most instances, all you need to do to properly use the computerized databases is follow the instructions provided for you on the screen. Simply read the prompts on the screen and push the appropriate keys.

Microsoft's Encarta is an example of a popular computer CD. It is a multimedia encyclopedia stored on a computer CD that contains 50,000 articles, as well as speeches, sound clips, animations, and even movie segments. Your library may have encyclopedias, newspapers, journals, and/or specialized databases on CD.

Do not be afraid to ask the reference librarians which databases are available on CD and for assistance in using the software. Once again, in most cases all you need to do is place the CD in the computer and follow the instructions on the screen.

Many libraries also provide access to online databases. These online data systems may be expensive to use and you may have limited access to them at some libraries. Most university libraries permit students to use the online databases for no charge but they do require you to make an appointment to use the computer.

One of the most popular online databases is LEXIS/NEXIS. LEXIS/NEXIS provides full text documents, as well as full citations. LEXIS is a database that includes most publications in the field of law, including such items as statutes, cases, reporters, and the administrative codes for statutes at all court levels. NEXIS is an online database that contains hundreds of the nation's leading newspapers and magazines.

Internet

"The Internet, often called the 'information superhighway,' is a world-wide network of computers that links resources and people at colleges and universities, government agencies, libraries, corporations, and homes."[1] This research tool provides access to endless amounts of information that was once limited by inaccessibility.

Even though the Internet contains endless amounts of information, one needs to be able to critically evaluate the information they encounter. Just as with any other research tool, it is imperative to consider the author/source of the information. Just because it is in print, is not necessarily reliable, and since anyone can post information in cyberspace, one needs to be prudent in analyzing from where the information originated.

Books

The library's book collection is indexed in the card catalog or online catalog. The catalog is a listing of the books the library has on its shelves. Additionally, many libraries now offer access to books they do not poses via inter-library loan.

The problem with books, however, is that they do not always contain the most up-to-date information. The time it takes to write, edit, print, and publish a book can sometimes result in the publication of material that is a year or two old.

Periodicals

Periodicals are magazines or journals that are published on a periodic basis. For instance, a magazine or journal may be published weekly, monthly, quarterly, or annually. Because they are published more frequently, periodicals usually provide more current and concise information than books.

To locate the library's periodicals you may consult the card or online catalog. Some libraries, especially smaller ones, publish a list of the periodicals they own. To identify articles in periodicals on a specific subject you may consult an abstract or an index. Traditional paper abstracts and indexes exist for every possible discipline from art to women's studies. Most of these also exist as computerized catalogs on CD or as part of an online catalog or database.

The following is a list of the more common periodical indexes located in most libraries.

- **The Reader' Guide to Periodical Literature: 1915–present**
  This is the most commonly used periodical index. It contains over 200 general-circulation magazines in the United States. It is arranged chronologically and by subject matter. It is published every two weeks. It is available on CD and is updated quarterly. Examples of magazines located in The Reader's Guide are: *Time*, *Newsweek*, *Atlantic Monthly*, and *Sports Illustrated*.

- **ERIC: 1967–present**
  This online database is available in most libraries on CD. It covers all facets of education: elementary, secondary, and higher. It indexes journals as well as technical and unpublished reports on education that are found on microfiche.

- **The Social Sciences Index: June 1974–present**
  Indexed by author and subject, this index of 353 journals focuses on the fields of the social sciences, such as: political science, history, psychology, international relations, and other related areas. It is published quarterly and cumulated annually. It is available on CD and online.

- **The Humanities Index: 1974–present**
  Indexed by author and subject, this index focuses on the humanities: religion, literature, and philosophy. It is available on CD and online.

- **InfoTrac Academic Index: 1985–present**
  A computerized index of popular journals by subject and author. Consult your reference librarians for the InfoTrac link, or similar product, available in your library.

- **Business Index: 1980–present**
  This is an InfoTrac product which lists over 1,000 journals and newspapers which cover all aspects of business. It is available on CD and online.

- **LegalTrac: 1980–present**
  A legal index of more than 800 legal periodical that is updated monthly. It is available on CD.

Newspapers

Another important source of information is newspaper articles. Newspapers offer timely description, interpretations, opinions, and analyses of local, national and international newspapers, will be indexed in the library.

The following is a listing of the more common newspaper indexes:

- **_InfoTrac National Newspaper Index: 1985–present_**
  A computerized index of the nation's most popular newspapers: _New York Times_, _Los Angeles Times_, _Christian Science Monitor_, _Wall Street Journal_, and _Washington Post_. It is available online.

- **_New York Times Index: 1851–present_**
  Indexed chronologically by subject. It contains extensive abstracts of articles appearing in the _New York Times_. It is issued twice a month and is cumulated quarterly and annually.

- **_Official Washington Post Index_**
  This is a very specific index that is issued monthly and cumulated annually.

Several other national and international newspapers are indexed. Check with your library staff to determine which other newspapers they have indexed. _NewsBank_ is a computerized index that references over 450 newspapers. Libraries that have _NewsBank_ will also have the accompanying microfiches of all articles. _Facts On File_ is a weekly publication of US and foreign newspapers and other print publications. One word of caution: If you use _Facts On File_, the articles often do not always contain the original bibliographic sources of information.

Government Documents

The United States government publishes a substantial amount of information on a wide range of topics. In fact, the United States government (the US Government Printing Office) is the largest publisher in the United States.

Various agencies and committees within each of the three branches of the federal government publish information available to the general public. Information such as the census, statistics, reports from congressional committees, and environmental reports are just a few samples of the type of information you can find by using government documents. At various levels, including federal, state, and local, the US government is one of the major collectors and publishers of data and statistics. For example, the _Statistical Abstract of the United States_ is an excellent source of statistical data.

Government documents may appear intimidating, but the information is often quite useful and can be very succinct. Here is a brief listing of the most frequently used government publications.

■ *Monthly Catalog of United States Government Publications*
This index lists documents issued by all three branches of the federal government. The monthly, semiannual, and annual indexes are arranged by author, title, subject, key words, and series/report title. It is available online and updated monthly.

■ *Congressional Record*
The *Record* provides an edited transcript of the activities on the floor of the United States Senate and the House of Representatives. It is published each day that Congress is in session.

■ *CIS Index*
This index is produced by the Congressional Information Service and contains abstracts of all Congressional publications except the *Congressional Record*. It is published monthly and cumulated quarterly and annually.

■ *Congressional Index*
This weekly index is published by the Commerce Clearing House. It provides information on the status of bills and resolutions pending in the United States Congress.

■ *National Journal*
This weekly index contains information about important executive, Congressional, and judicial decisions.

■ *American Statistical Index (ASI)*
This index is produced by the federal government. It is an index to most statistical data, abstracts, and reports compiled by the federal government. There is also microfiche available that contains the full text.

Encyclopedias

There are three types of encyclopedias to choose from when researching a speech topic. You are probably familiar with the traditional multi-volume encyclopedias that offer general information about a variety of subjects. *World Book, Encyclopedia Britannica,* and the *Encyclopedia Americana* are examples of general-information encyclopedias. Often this type of encyclopedia is a good starting point for familiarizing yourself with a certain topic.

Almost every discipline has its own subject encyclopedia and there are several specialized encyclopedias available in the library. Examples include the *Encyclopedia of Black America*, the *Encyclopedia of Medical History*, the *Encyclopedia of Religion*, the *Encyclopedia of Science and Technology*, the *Encyclopedia of the Holocaust*, and the *Encyclopedia of Higher Education*.

As mentioned earlier, there are interactive encyclopedias now available on computer CD, including *New Grollier Encyclopedia*, *Microsoft Encarta*, and *Compton's Multimedia Encyclopedia*.

Personal Interviews

Perhaps the best source of information you will find in your research will be the information you obtain through personal interviews. Conducting a personal interview provides you with the luxury of asking specific questions of an expert on your subject. An expert is someone who has personal experience, either actual physical experience or research experience, with respect to a particular subject.

For example, if you were presenting a speech on the workings of the human heart, you might want to interview a medical professional who has experience in cardiology. By interviewing a person you have the luxury of asking very specific questions. Be sure to ask for clarification if you do not understand the information, especially if it is technical in nature.

Keep in mind that your audience will ultimately determine if your source of information is an expert. If your audience believes your source of information is not credible, knowledgeable, and/or trustworthy, then your source will not be viewed as an expert. For instance, a presentation on abortion that only relied on the Catholic Church or the National Organization of Women for supporting material may not be viewed as credible, knowledgeable, and/or trustworthy by the audience members because each organization has a particular agenda. These may be viewed as biased sources. This does not mean that each source is not credible. This is simply a warning to you to find as much unbiased information as possible for your presentation.

After determining who you want to interview, you need to properly prepare for the interview. By being properly prepared and organized for an interview, you will maximize the potential of obtaining useful and relevant information.

The following guidelines will help you to properly request an interview:

Requesting an Interview

- Contact a potential interviewee and arrange a time that is desirable for him/her.
- Indicate the approximate length of the interview and the specific subject matter you will be discussing during the interview.
- When you make the appointment, request permission to tape record the interview.

After establishing an appointment for the interview, you will need to conduct some preliminary research to prepare for the actual interview. You should know the proper title, qualifications, and relevant experience of the person you are interviewing. If the interviewee has conducted research on a topic, you should locate the documentation and be familiar with it. This preparation will indicate to the person being interviewed that you are serious about your purpose and you will undoubtedly receive better responses to your questions.

Before arriving at the interview you should arrange a series of specific questions to ask. Your previous research on the topic will help you prepare relevant questions. The more pertinent and clear the question, the more likely you will receive a response you can use in your presentation. Keep the questions short and to the point. Do not word the questions so narrowly that the person being interviewed is left with a one-word answer. On the other hand, do not ask broad general questions. This type of question is difficult, and the responses you receive may not be of any use to you in preparing your presentation.

Take the time to write your questions out on a piece of paper. These questions should be arranged in a logical thought pattern. However, you may need to ask additional questions not on your original list based on responses to your original questions. **Listen** intently to each answer and base your next question on the previous response.

When you arrive at the interview you should first thank the person you are about to interview, reconfirm your subject matter, and permission to use a recording device. Conduct yourself in a professional manner. You should dress appropriately and come prepared with a pencil and a notepad. Even if you are recording the interview you should take careful notes of the person's responses.

At the conclusion of the interview you should ask the person if there is anything he/she may want to add and then, once again, thank the per-

Listening
A cognitive process

son for his/her time and knowledge. You may also want to ask if he/she has any recommended written information you could use. When you return home you should take the time to write a brief thank-you note. You may even want to invite the person to your presentation.

Writing or Calling for Information

You may also find it useful to request information via the mail or you may live close enough that you are able to collect the information yourself. For instance, if you were presenting a speech on AIDS you might wish to call the AIDS Hotline at (800) 342-AIDS and request information. Look in the yellow pages of your local phone book for helpful numbers or referral services. Your library may also have the Directory of 800 Numbers. Another important source for telephone numbers, addresses, and general information is the Encyclopedia of Associations. Listed here are only a few of the numbers you may find useful.

Helpful 800 Numbers

Acne Help Line	(800) 222–SKIN
AIDS Hotline	(800) 342–AIDS
Alcohol and Drug Addiction Treatment Center	(800) 382–4357
American Association on Mental Deficiency	(800) 424–3688
American Board of Cosmetic Surgery	(800) 221–9808
American Cancer Society	(800) 227–2345
American Council of the Blind	(800) 424–8666
American Diabetes Association	(800) ADA–DISC
American Infant Sudden Death Syndrome	(800) 232–SIDS
American Kidney Fund	(800) 638–8299
American Liver Foundation	(800) 223–0179
American Parkinson's Disease Association	(800) 223–2732
Arthritis Answer Line	(800) 422–1492
Birth Control Information Line	(800) 468–3637
Bulimia/Anorexia Self-Help	(800) 227–4785
Cancer Information Hotline	(800) 525–3777
Child Abuse Hotline	(800) 4ACHILD
Child Care Information Service	(800) 424–2460
Children's Wish Foundation International	(800) 323–9474

Cocaine Hotline	(800) COCAINE
Consumer Product Safety Commission	(800) 638–CPSC
Cystic Fibrosis Foundation	(800) 344–4823
Domestic Violence Hotline	(800) 333–SAFE
Dyslexia Society	(800) 222–3123
Epilepsy Foundation	(800) EFA–1000
Federal Tax Information	(800) 424–1040
Heartlife	(800) 241–6993
Herpes Hotline	(800) 227–8922
Lupus Foundation	(800) 558–0121
Medicare Information	(800) 332–6146
Missing Children Help Center	(800) USA–KIDS
Missing Children Network	(800) 235–3535
Multiple Sclerosis	(800) 334–7812
National Alliance of Breast Cancer Organization	(800) 221–2141
National Association For Sickle Cell Disease	(800) 421–8453
National Council of Child Abuse/Family Violence	(800) 222–2000
National Down Syndrome Congress	(800) 327–4545
National Highway Traffic Safety Administration	(800) 221–4602
National Parkinson Foundation	(800) 424–9393
National Reye's Syndrome Foundation	(800) 223–7393
Organ Donor Hotline	(800) 24DONOR
Rape Crisis Hotline	(800) 527–1757
Safe Drinking Water Hotline	(800) 426–4791
Shriner's Hospital Referral Line	(800) 237–5055
Spina Bifida Association of America	(800) 621–3141
Spinal Cord Injuries Hotline	(800) 526–3456
Teen Pregnancy Hotline	(800) 522–5006
Veterans of the Viet Nam War	(800) VIETNAM

Step Five: The Body

The body of your presentation is delivered after the introduction and prior to the conclusion. However, in order to effectively organize the introduction and conclusion, you must first organize the main points, subpoints, and connectors in the body of the presentation. This will become more clear when we discuss the proper method of organizing introductions and conclusions, but for the moment let us just focus on the body of the speech—specifically the main points of the presentation. The most effective method of organization for the body of a presentation is to divide the speech into main points.

The **main points** serve as the foundation of the speech and should fully develop the **specific purpose** of the presentation. By understanding the main points of a presentation, the audience should be able to easily understand your specific purpose.

You should limit your presentation to between two and five main points. This enables you to adequately develop each of the main points. It also permits the audience to focus on only a limited number of main points. Each of the main points should be stated through the use of simple and concise language. It is usually unwise to try to use too many words or very complex words when stating your main point. For instance, which of the following main points is easier to understand and remember?

- The continued use of automobiles serves only to increase the amount of carbon monoxide in the air which destroys the ever fragile ozone layer.
- Automobile exhaust destroys the ozone layer.

Clearly the second example is easier to understand, although it basically states the same idea as the first example.

In addition to limiting the number of main points and using clear and concise language, it is also important to keep your main points focused on one idea. A main point expressed as "The University has several majors and offers financial aid" contains more than one idea. These ideas are best expressed in two separate main points:

- The university has several majors.
- The university has financial aid.

Finally, the main points of a presentation must be limited to the specific purpose of the speech. For example, a speech with the specific purpose statement: "At the end of my speech, the audience will be able to describe four basic types of communication styles," would be limited to the four styles of communication as main points.

Rules for Developing Main Points:

- Limit the main points to between two and five if possible.
- Use simple and concise language.
- Use only one idea per main point.
- Be certain the main points are within the realm of the specific purpose statement.

Main Points
Serve as the foundation of the speech and should fully develop the specific purpose of the presentation

Specific Purpose
Never spoken by the speaker; helps the speaker to stay on point and avoid tangents

**Organizational
Patterns**
The order in which
a speaker presents
the main points
and/or subpoints of
the presentation

**Chronological
Patterning**
Main points pro-
ceed from beginning
to end

**Demonstrative
Speech**
The speaker
describes a process
of how to complete
something

**Descriptive
Speech**
The speaker
describes a person,
policy, or event

Narrative
The speaker tells a
story

**Topical
Patterning**
All main points are
of equal relevance

Organizational Patterns

Regardless of whether you are organizing an informative speech or a persuasive speech the following seven *organizational patterns* can be used.
When we discuss persuasive speaking (Chapter Six) we will discuss additional patterns of organization that may be more effective for a persuasive
delivery.

Chronological Patterning

Organizing your presentation based on the order in which the main
points occurred or will occur in time is called *chronological organization*.
Demonstrative or "how to" presentations, **descriptive speeches,** and **narrative speeches** usually follow a chronological form of organization.

Specific purpose: At the end of my speech, the audience will
                      be able to list the three steps in obtaining a
                      driver's license.

A. The written test
B. Restricted license
C. The driving test

Specific purpose: At the end of my speech, the audience will be
                      able to list the three steps in applying for a
                      job.

A. Submit a letter of application
B. Prepare for an interview
C. Send a follow-up letter

Topical Patterning

Topical organization is organizing the main points of a presentation into
categories or topics. Unlike a chronological organizational pattern it is
irrelevant which topic or category you speak about first.

Because each main topic is of equal importance with respect to the
others, the order in which each is discussed is irrelevant. As you can see
from the example below, the third point "liability insurance" could have
been discussed prior to the first point, or the second point could have
been discussed first. These changes would not have prevented the audience from logically following the speech.

Specific Purpose: At the end of my speech, the audience will be able to describe four types of automobile insurance terms.

A. Comprehensive insurance
B. Collision insurance
C. Liability insurance
D. No fault insurance

Specific Purpose: At the end of my speech, the audience will be able to list the three branches of the federal government.

A. The legislative branch
B. The executive branch
C. The judicial branch

Topical Compare and Contrast Patterning

Topical internal organizational patterns may also be used to *compare and contrast* main points. If you wish to inform your audience of the similarities and differences of two local universities, you may want to use a topical-compare-and-contrast pattern. Consider the following two examples of topical-compare-and-contrast organization. Notice how the presentation can be organized two different ways using a compare-and-contrast organizational pattern.

Compare and Contrast Patterning
Used to state the similarities and the differencs in the speakers main points

Specific Purpose: At the end of my speech, the audience will be able to compare and contrast three things about University A and University B.

A. The tuition
    1. University A
    2. University B
B. The academic programs
    1. University A
    2. University B
C. The athletic programs
    1. University A
    2. University B

Specific Purpose: At the end of my speech, the audience will be able to compare and contrast three things about University A and University B.

A. University A
    1. The tuition
    2. The academic programs
    3. The athletic programs
B. University B
    1. The tuition
    2. The academic programs
    3. The athletic programs

Topical Causal Patterning

Causal Patterning
Used to examine the causes and effects

Topical causal organization examines the causes (reasons for) and effects (results of) of a speech subject. There are only two structures for this type of pattern: causes and effects or effects and causes. This organizational pattern is usually too broad for a short speech.

Specific Purpose: At the end of my speech, the audience will be able to list three of the causes and effects of tobacco-related products.

A. Causes
    1. Cigarette smoking
    2. Cigar smoking
    3. Chewing tobacco
B. Effects
    1. Lung cancer
    2. Heart disease
    3. Mouth cancer
    4. Poor personal hygiene

Specific Purpose: At the end of my speech, the audience will be able to explain four effects and causes of child abuse.

A. Effects
    1. Poor self-esteem
    2. Drug addiction
    3. May also abuse children
B. Causes
    1. Prior abuse
    2. Mental illness
    3. Drug abuse

Topical Pros and Cons Patterning

When you wish to present two sides of an issue, reasons for and against, you might use a *topical pros and cons pattern*. If you feel this sounds more appropriate for a persuasive speech you are partially correct. When a speaker presents both sides of an issue equally—that is, the pros and cons are equal in importance and the speaker remains neutral—a topical pros and cons pattern can be used to organize the informative presentation.

If you choose to present an informative presentation using a topical pros and cons pattern, be certain the information is equally balanced in time, content, and delivery. You cannot give greater significance to one side, for instance the pros, by presenting more recent or credible information or by orally delivering the speech in such a manner that your audience gives more credence to one side of the topic. Obviously, if in the conclusion of the presentation you decide to defend one of the positions, then this presentation clearly would become persuasive. Although it is a useful organizational pattern, like the causal pattern, it too is often ineffective for short speeches.

Pros and Cons Patterning
Used to present both sides of an issue equally

Specific Purpose: At the end of my speech, the audience will be able to explain the two pros and cons of socialized medicine in the United States.

A.   Pros of socialized medicine
  1.   Reduced cost of healthcare
  2.   Universal coverage for all citizens
B.   Cons of socialized medicine
  1.   Reduction in medical research
  2.   Less competent healthcare

Specific Purpose: At the end of my speech, the audience will be able to list three of the advantages and disadvantages of legalizing marijuana.

A.   The benefits of legalization
  1.   Reduced crime rate
  2.   Reduced number of addicts
  3.   An increase in prison space for violent offenders
B.   The disadvantages of legalization
  1.   An increase in addiction
  2.   An increase in the crime rate
  3.   Will lead to use of more harmful drugs

Topical Spatial Patterning

Presentations that are organized *spatially* are based on geographic location or physical proximity of the main points. For instance, a presentation that discusses the east, west, north, and south branches of a bank,
the design of the atom from the nucleus outward, or the parts of an air-
plane from the tail forward would be informative presentations organized
spatially.

> **Specific Purpose:**   At the end of my speech the audience will be
> able to describe five parts of an airplane.

    A.   The tail
    B.   The fuselage
    C.   The wings
    D.   The engine
    E.   The propeller

Magnitude Patterning

This organizational pattern assigns importance to the main points. With
the topical patterning, it is irrelevant to the logical organization of the
presentation which main point is discussed first, second, etc. This is not
the case with the *magnitude patterning.*

Let us suppose you have decided to inform the audience about the
President of the United States. This would be a **descriptive** informative
presentation. After considering your audiences needs, you have narrowed
your main points on how the President feels about (A) the national debt,
(B) tax increases, and (C) abortion. If you feel the order of these three
main topics will significantly increase the logical order of your presentation you will be using the topical magnitude pattern.

If you feel your audience is most interested in tax increases you may
want to make this your first topic discussed in the speech. By placing tax
increases as the first topic in the presentation you feel you will increase
your chances for gaining the audience's attention. If your next two main
topics are deemed unimportant by the audience, you now face the risk of
the audience "tuning out" after the first main topic.

You may decide to save your most interesting topic for the last main
point of the speech. This pattern is used to build suspense. However, by
saving your most interesting topic or most relevant topic until the final
main point you may never gain the audience's attention. The best solution to these two examples is to select main points that are all interesting
and relevant, but, inevitably some may be more interesting and/or more
relevant than the others.

This ensures your audience will be interested in the entire presentation and you can still build suspense if you so desire be saving the most important or most relevant main point for the final point in the presentation.

Specific Purpose: At the end of my speech, the audience will be able to discuss three of the President's most important issues in the next election.

A.   Abortion
B.   The national debt
C.   Tax increases

Cultures Influence on Organizational Patterns

Cultures have different preferences for organizing ideas. Which patterns or organization is preferred is taught by one's culture. Cultures, which employ linear organization patterns, present ideas differently than cultures that organize ideas according to the circular pattern, preferred by most Asian cultures.

German and English speaking cultures follow the linear approach. The structure of a good essay or speech is built around a thesis statement found in an introduction. The essay or speech will then support the thesis statement in a straightforward manner, with each paragraph building on the previous one. The main idea of each paragraph is also clearly laid out for the reader or the listener by the use of a topic sentence. Information that is not directly related to the topic sentence does not belong in said paragraph.

The traditional method of organizing ideas in Asia is dramatically different. Organizational patterns "depend on indirection and implication rather than on explicit links to connect ideas and provide a main point. The rules for language use in Japan demand that the speaker does not tell the listener the specific point being conveyed; to do so is considered rude and inappropriate. Rather, the Japanese delicately circle a topic in order to imply its domain. The US concepts of thesis statement and paragraph topic sentences have no real equivalent."

The preferred pattern of organization in Russia is deductive. Russians reason from the general to the specific. This is the opposite of the inductive pattern used in the United States, which is to reason particular facts to a general conclusion. The preferred form of organization in Arab cultures is built primarily on the intuitive-affective pattern. Speakers of Arabic emphasize their history and use emotional appeals as their supporting data.

What this means to a public speaker is that audience members will be drawn to speeches that present ideas in an organizational pattern which is familiar to them. To cultures that employ the linear approach to organization, the circular pattern appears to have no direction; the deductive pattern is considered to be vague; and the use of emotion is thought to be off the point. Structuring a speech that uses an organizational pattern that you are not familiar with is a difficult task. However, if you want to be an effective communicator it may be a necessity.

Lusting, M., & Koester, J. (1996). *Intercultural Competence: Interpersonal Communication Across Cultures.* New York: Harper Collins.

Subpoints
The supporting material such as quotes, statistics, definitions, etc. that help build a point/argument

Supporting Material
Information that defines, supports, explains and/or clarifies a point/argument

Audience Analysis
Knowing what the interests/needs of the audience are

The **subpoints** of a presentation are all the information that support the main points. For the same reasons main points are limited to between two and five, so should the subpoints be limited to between two and five. The subpoints of your speech are comprised of supporting material.

Supporting material is the information in your presentation that defines, supports, explains and/or clarifies what you are saying. When used effectively it:

- Captures and maintains the audience's interest in your presentation.
- Increases your credibility with the audience.
- Helps the audience to remember important points.

A successful speaker knows which type of supporting material to use, where to find it, and based on a thorough **analysis of the audience** (Chapter Three), when each would be most appropriate in the presentation.

Types of Supporting Material
The six most common types of supporting material are:

- Definitions
- Examples
- Narratives
- Analogies
- Testimony
- Statistics

There will be many instances where you will be able to combine two or more forms of supporting material. For example, you may use testimony to support an analogy and statistics within your narration.

Definitions

When the audience is unfamiliar with a word, concept, or phrase you should *define* it within the presentation. If you don't you will lose the attention of the audience. One of the biggest mistakes speakers make is assuming that the audience has the same definition for an idea that they do. For instance, if you were speaking on the relationship of pornography and art, it would be absolutely necessary for you to define what you mean by each term. How do you define pornography? How do you determine if something is pornographic? Who do you feel should determine what is pornographic? What do you consider to be art? Who determines what is art and what is not art? Do you think art can be good or bad? As you can see, if you want to be clear all of these questions will need to be answered.

    You can define words, concepts, or phrases in a variety of ways. One of the easiest is to look in a dictionary. For instance the word "pyrotechnics" according to *Webster's Dictionary* is clearly defined as "the art of making fireworks." You may also provide examples as definitions.

    Art Deco Architecture could be clearly defined by showing the audience a few examples of that particular style of architecture. Similarly, you may find it more effective to play a short recording of a blue jay's call instead of trying to define it by using words (see Chapter Four, Visual Supporing Material).

Definitions
State the percise meaning

Examples

Examples are specific instances that support a general conclusion. Apples, pears, and plums are examples of fruit. Unlike examples used to define words, concepts, or phrases, this type of example simply provides a specific instance of a general idea or conclusion.

    There are times when you will need only a few examples to support your general conclusion as in the example above. At other times, based on your analysis of your audience, you may decide you require several examples to support your general conclusion. Consider this portion of a student speech on why the university registration and student advising process should be changed:

Examples
A representative of a group and/or whole

> Let me give you some examples of why the registration process should be changed. At nine o'clock I went to my academic advisor as scheduled. When I arrived the advisor offered this piece of advice, "You decide what you want to do." With this pearl of wisdom to guide me, I left the office and proceeded to select possible courses for the semester. These would ultimately be courses which did not count towards my major. Next, I went to registration and stood in line for over three hours just to hear the words, "Your advisor needs to sign this!" Despite my explanation that my

advisor doesn't care what I take, I was not allowed to register. I returned to my advisor, who said, "You must have misunderstood me." After changing all my courses I returned to registration to find out two of the courses I had selected were now not available. I had to return to my advisor again! By this time it was almost five o'clock on Friday and registration was closed until Monday!

This speaker provided several examples of why the registration and student advising process should be changed. If these examples were true, they would be called *actual examples*. However, not all examples have to be true. A *hypothetical example* is an example that is not necessarily true but is believable. Quite often hypothetical examples are preceded with the words, "imagine that," "suppose that," or "what if."

Narratives

Narratives are stories that explain a process or describe an event. Narratives, like examples, may be *actual* or *hypothetical*. Most people like to listen to a well-told story. When used appropriately stories add interest, excitement, suspense, clarity, and vividness to presentations.

Consider the following story of a student about to meet his future in-laws:

> As the day approached my general questions such as "Will they like me?" gave way to very specific questions: "What should I wear?" "What should I say?" "What should I call them?" The day finally arrived. I was about to meet my future in-laws. I was very nervous. Not the type of nervousness that makes you feel paralyzed, but the kind that makes you anxious. My heart was pounding. My palms were sweating. My mind was racing. As they walked through the doors of the airport I uttered my first words to them. I said . . .

(Sorry, we are going to leave the rest to your imagination.) See how interesting a story can be when told appropriately?

Analogies

When you compare two people, objects, events, or ideas you are using an *analogy*. Before using an analogy be sure the audience is familiar with the items being compared. If the audience is not familiar with one of the items being compared, then the analogy will not be very effective.

There are two basic types of analogies: literal and figurative. *Literal analogies* are comparisons of like items. For example, comparing the crime in Chicago to the crime in New York is a literal analogy.

Figurative analogies are comparisons of unlike items. Comparing your friend's face to the sun does not mean your friend's face is a big glowing

---

Actual
Based on fact

Hypothetical
Not based on a fact, but is plausible

Narratives
Tell a story

Analogy
Compares things that are similar or assimilar to each other

Literal
Comparisons of similar items

Figurative
Comparisons of dissimilar items

ball of hot gasses. It probably means you see your friend's face as glowing and radiant.

Testimony

When you quote or paraphrase another's words, opinions, or ideas you are using *testimony*. Speakers often rely on expert testimony to increase their credibility. Here is an example of a speaker explaining the influence of Russia's small political parties:

> According to Yekaterina Yegorava, the co-director of a political image-making firm that has advised democratic reformers and centrists, "All of these leaders of parties are trying to find their own places, to show they are the leader and the boss."[2]

You probably noticed in the above example the speaker cited the source's qualifications. This is to add to the credibility of the information. However, what makes someone an expert? Before deciding to use testimony make sure that the quote meets the following criteria:

- Is the quote accurate?
- Is the source unbiased and trustworthy?
- Is the source credible?

Quoting or paraphrasing from a source that does not meet any of the three tests may work against you. To illustrate this point all you need to do is consider the various witnesses used in the O.J. Simpson case. The jury asked themselves, "Do these witnesses have knowledge of what they are speaking about?" "Are the witnesses biased?" "Are they trustworthy?" and "Are these sources believable?" The audience in a public presentation will be asking themselves the same questions about the sources you quote or paraphrase in your presentation.

Statistics

One of the most common types of supporting material used is *statistics*. Statistics are information presented in a numerical fashion. All we need to do to see the influence of statistics is look at the importance television networks place on ratings and politicians place on public opinion polls. Many important decisions are based on the use of statistics.

Let us look at a few of the most popular forms statistics take in a presentation. They are:

- the average or mean
- the median
- percentages
- ratios

Testimony
To quote or paraphrase

Statistics
Numerical information

■ *Averages/Means*

This is probably the most popular form of statistics. The mean or average is obtained by adding all the numbers in a set together and then dividing by the total number of instances.

For example, suppose you were trying to determine the average number of students in each public speaking class at your school. You would total the number of public speaking students and then divide this total by the number of public speaking classes. The result would be the average or mean number of public speaking students in each class.

■ *Median*

This is the number in the middle of a group of numbers that have been rank ordered. That is, the median has an equal number of items above and below it.

Consider the following set of numbers: 76, 88, 91, 94, and 62. The median would be 88. First you need to rank order the numbers. They would look as follows: 94, 91, 88, 76, and 62. Now it is apparent that 88 have an equal number of numbers above and below it.

The median is used in instances where a very high or low number may skew the mean. Your instructor may present the results of your examinations or presentations in the form of the median rather than the mean or average score.

■ *Percentages*

These are also a very popular form of statistic. When you present a statistic as a portion of the whole, represented by 100, you are using percentages. A student presentation on smoking and teenagers explained that in the United States, "approximately 80–90 percent of smokers began before they were 18 years old."[3]

Often percentages are expressed in terms of trends, which are increases or decreases in the percentage across time. The same speaker stated that "between 1991 and 1994 smoking among eighth graders increased by 30 percent."[4]

■ *Ratios*

These are used when percentages are very small. For example, .000001 percent is much easier to understand if stated as the ratio 1 in 100,000. Common percentages such as 10%, 25%, 50%, 75% and 90% are also more commonly expressed as ratios. For instance, "1 in 10," "1 in 4," "1 of every 2," "3 out of 4," or "9 out of 10."

When you use statistics in your presentation you should consider several guidelines.

- Round off your statistics. 48 percent is much easier to understand and remember than 47.578 percent.
- Do not use misleading statistics.
- Do not use statistics you do not understand.
- Do not overwhelm your audience with statistics.
- Use visual aids to clarify statistics when it is necessary.

Connectors

The next part of the body that you need to be concerned with are the different connectors. *Connectors* help a speaker move smoothly from one section of a speech to another. Connectors should not be choppy or obvious; they should flow with the speech. There are three types of connectors.

- *Transitions*
  Transitions are words or phrases such as: therefore, because, likewise, all and all, however, on the other hand, due to the fact, etc. Transitions are found between the **subpoints** in the body of your speech. They are a type of connector because they connect the supporting material together, thereby making the research flow smoothly.

- *Preview Statements*
  The final statement in the introduction should briefly *preview* the **main points** of the presentation. Previewing a presentation's main points has been practiced for 2,500 years. Ancient rhetoricians such as Corax, Aristotle, and Cicero all stressed the importance of briefly forecasting the main points in a presentation in order to facilitate the audience's understanding of the speech. The preview statement briefly and clearly indicates what the main points of the presentation will be. You want to list the main points in the order that they will be presented in the body of your presentation.

  - I will be discussing the three branches of the federal government: the executive, the legislative, and the judicial.
  - In today's speech, I will be explaining to you the symptoms of AIDS, which are high fever, exhaustion, and nausea.

  The preview statement is the connector from the introduction to the body of the speech. After previewing the main points pause for a brief moment to permit the audience to remember what the main points will be and in which order they will be addressed.

Connectors
Help a speaker move from one section of a speech to another smoothly

Transitions
Words or phrases that connect the subpoints

Subpoints
The supporting material such as quotes, statistics, definitions, etc. that help build a point/argument

Preview Statement
Found in the introduction; this is where a speaker lists the main points of the presentation

Main Points
Serve as the foundation of the speech and should fully develop the specific purpose of the presentation

Internal Summaries
Found between the main points in the body of the speech

Noise
Interference with encoding and decoding of a message, there are two types: internal noise and external noise

Final Summary
Found in the conclusion; a speaker restates the thesis and summarizes each main point

■ *Summaries*

Internal summaries are found between the main points in the body of the speech. They are a sentence or two that connect(s) the main points together. Internal summaries are relatively new to the standard American Speech Format. They are used as a means of summarizing and forecasting your main points.

Americans, unfortunately, have poor listening habits. **Internal noise** (Chapter One) affects us all, causing our minds to wander. Internal summaries, therefore, help clarify information for those who are not fully paying attention.

The following are examples of internal summaries:

The main points of the speech are: child models, fashion models, lifestyle models, and runway models.

■ If you think that it is hard to get a job as a child model, agents are even more selective with the category of fashion models.
■ Even though men and women are not equal in the category of fashion models, they are in the next category I wish to discuss, called lifestyle modeling.
■ Jobs for lifestyle models in Miami are abundant, as are jobs in the runway industry.

The main points of the speech are: politics, medical professionals, and gay community.

■ Having discussed all of the shortcomings of the Reaganites and other politicos it is a miracle that any of the early medical professionals pioneered research into this obscure disease.
■ In the discussion about the medical profession, we recognize a willingness to perform their duties to the best of their abilities. However, it was the gay community that provided the leadership and activism that would guide the research and educate their community, and inevitably everyone else.

The *final summary* is found in the conclusion (for exact location see Step Seven of this process entitled Conclusions). In the final summary you need to restate your central idea and summarize each of your main points.

The following is an example of a final summary:

Scientific research is creating many questions in the field of male thinking versus female thinking.

1. The results indicate that there are differences in thinking linked to the functions of the brain but researchers are skeptical about drawing conclusions.
2. Since men and women do think differently they also carry a conversation differently.
3. The results of my survey indicated that most people know about these differences and they do cause problems in the communication process.

Step Six: Introductions

The first few words out of your mouth may be the most difficult and, perhaps, the most important of a presentation. "What do I say first? How do I start this speech?" You may have experienced the same problems when writing a composition or a letter to a friend. You may have spent many long hours trying to write that first line or opening paragraph. Speechmakers often have the same difficulties when trying to formulate an introduction to a speech.

After determining how to begin a presentation many have trouble knowing how to effectively end a presentation. This may seem a bit premature to you now. You may be thinking to yourself, "I am not worried about the ending. I don't even have a beginning."

However, you will shortly realize the introduction and the conclusion are very closely related when organized properly.

There is an old saying that every speechmaker should keep in mind when organizing a presentation. That saying advises:

The Three Parts of a Speech

- In the introduction, "Tell then what you intend to tell them." You accomplish this by previewing your main points.
- In the body, "Tell them." This is where you present your main points.
- And in the conclusion, "Tell them what you just told them." This is done by summarizing your main points.

Of course the introduction, body, and conclusion of a speech are more complex, but put simply those are the main goals of each portion of a presentation.

The Goals of an Introduction

1. Gain the audience's attention.
2. Clearly indicate the significance (importance) of the topic.
3. Clearly indicate the relevance of the topic to this particular audience at this particular time and place.
4. Establish credibility with the audience.
5. Clearly state the presentation's central idea.
6. Clearly, but briefly, preview the presentation's main points.

All these goals are of equal importance and an effective introduction will contain all six elements. The ultimate goal of an introduction is to introduce the speech topic to the audience and facilitate the audience's listening and understanding of the speech's purpose.

The next few pages explain each of the six goals of an introduction in more detail and provide numerous examples of how to achieve each goal. You should keep in mind that there might be instances where you are able to achieve more than one goal at a time. For instance, when attempting to gain the attention of the audience, you may try to do so by stressing the importance and/or relevance of the speech subject.

Cultural Influence on Introductions

In the United States, public speakers are taught to develop attention-getting statements so as to capture the concentration of audience members. Gaining an audience's attention can be accomplished in several ways: an actual or rhetorical question, a startling fact or statistic, an example, a short story, a brief demonstration, a quote or phrase, reference to a specific event, or a joke or humorous story.

Humor is not only considered to be appropriate to the speech-making process in the United States, it is often sought after by audience members. This, however, is not true of all cultures. President Carter would have been wise to look into the use of humor related to public speaking in Japan. While in Japan, delivering a speech to a group of Japanese businessmen, a translator prevented an awkward moment from occurring. You see, President Carter opened his speech with a joke. In Japan, this is not customary. The translator informed the audience that President Carter was telling a joke and when he finishes, laughter would be appropriate.

Other cultural differences related to the structure of the introduction involve the Chinese. The Chinese do not rely on a preview statement to provide the listener with an idea of where the speech is heading. This is because the Chinese culture is a listener-responsible culture. Unlike the United States, which is a speaker-responsible culture, listener-responsible cultures believe it is offensive to tell an audience what they should listen for. In listener-responsible cultures, the listener is responsible for constructing the meaning of the message based on the common beliefs, values, and norms between the sender and the receiver.

1. Gain the Audience's Attention

Your first goal as a speaker is to gain your audience's attention. If you have properly selected your speech topic (Chapter Two), then:

- You have considered your speech purpose.
- You have considered your own interests.
- You have considered the interests of your audience by conducting an audience analysis.
- You have properly narrowed the topic for the occasion and for this particular audience.

If you have met these first four criteria you have won half the battle of gaining your audience's attention.

There are several methods for *gaining the attention* of the audience. What follows are various techniques and examples for breaking the ice with your audience and getting those first few very important words out of your mouth.

Gaining the Attention
This is the first sentence a speaker will say to the audience

Make Reference to the Occasion

Often it is appropriate for you to *make reference to the speaking occasion*. For example, if you were speaking at a graduation ceremony, a memorial service, or an awards banquet, you may consider beginning your presentation by making reference to the occasion.

- It is my pleasure to be here this evening on such a happy occasion. Before I begin I would like to congratulate each and every graduate. Give yourselves a big round of applause.

Reference to the Occasion
A statement indicating why the speaker and audience are present

Begin with a Pertinent Illustration

A *pertinent illustration* is a short story that is representative of your entire speech topic. An illustration may be factual (true) or hypothetical (probable, but not necessarily true). For instance, a presentation designed to

Pertinent Illustation
A story related to the speech topic

Factual
Based on reality/truth

alleviate the fear of donating blood may begin with a *factual illustration* of the time you donated blood.

> ■ I would like to share a story with you. I had never given blood before and had no idea what to expect. I thought for sure it was going to hurt. How could it not? Well, let the world's biggest chicken reassure you. It was painless and very safe. When it was over, I left feeling ten times better because I knew my blood might save another person's life.

Hypothetical
Not based on reality/truth, but is plausible

A presentation on recognizing the signs of child abuse might begin with a *hypothetical illustration* of a child who was abused. This particular child may or may not actually exist, but the illustration of the abuse is unfortunately believable and representative of examples of child abuse.

> ■ He was so cute. And smart. Sure, he had a few bruises on his arms and legs. What seven-year-old didn't? Sure, he cried and told me his Mommy and Daddy spanked him. Don't all parents spank their children sometimes? What I didn't know, because I was unable to recognize it, is that Johnny was being physically and mentally abused at home. To this day I regret not recognizing the signs of abuse and finding him help sooner.

Create Suspense About the Speech Topic

Create Suspense
Increases the audience's curiosity with the speech topic

You may be able to *create suspense* about your speech topic in order to increase the audience's curiosity. See if you can guess the speech topic from the first few sentences.

> ■ I was petrified. I had trouble sleeping the night before. My stomach was churning. My palms were sweaty. I felt feverish. I knew that this was going to be the worst experience of my life. . . .

Do you know what the topic is? Here is the final sentence.

> ■ No, I wasn't about to enter the hospital for major surgery. I was about to take my first trip by plane.

Use Startling Facts or Opinions

Startling Facts or Opinions
Statistical information that shocks the audience

You may decide to begin your presentation with a *startling fact* or a *startling opinion*. Your goal when using this technique is to grab the audience's attention by startling them. Assume you are trying to convince an audience to take safety precautions in order to prevent them from becoming a victim of crime. You may begin the presentation by offering this personal observation.

■ Of the 50 people in this room, it would not surprise me to find out that 25 of you have been victims of some sort of crime.

The previous example was not necessarily a fact but the speaker's opinion. The next example attempts to gain the audience's attention by using a startling fact.

■ The first case of AIDS was reported over two decades ago. However, according to an article in *Medicine and Science in Sports and Exercise* printed in 1994, in 1993 there were 339,250 reported cases of AIDS and over one million people infected with the HIV virus.

If you should decide to begin a presentation by using a startling fact or opinion, you must be careful not to mislead the audience by sensationalizing or trivializing the speech subject. Always be certain your information can be substantiated, is realistic, and is representative of other opinions and facts.

Begin with a Rhetorical Question

A *rhetorical question* is a question you ask the audience but not one that requires a verbal response. The goal of a well-planned rhetorical question is to get the audience thinking about the answer. It is the answer you are most concerned with. For example, a speech on self-defense might begin with this rhetorical question:

Rhetorical Question
A question the speaker does not expect to be answered

■ What would you do if you were walking alone at night and a strange person approached you and tried to mug you?

This rhetorical question could have numerous responses. This is not necessarily an effective rhetorical question because the responses could be so varied. A more effective example might include more than one rhetorical question, each phrased to create a more precise mental answer from each audience member.

■ What would you do if you were walking alone at night and a strange person approached you and tried to mug you? Would you run? Would you scream? Would you panic? Or, would you be able to fight back?

In the first example the audience's mental response may have been vague. "Oh, I am not really sure what I would do in that instance." If that were the case the rhetorical example is of no use to the speaker. In the second example, where you used a series of rhetorical questions, the audience was given four realistic choices. They have the option of choosing one of the examples and are likely to do so if the choices are realistic. "Yeah, that is what I would probably do." In this example, the answer to the rhetorical question has served its purpose by focusing your audience on the speech subject.

If you should decide to use a rhetorical question be certain to allow your audience sufficient time to mentally answer the question or questions. This may mean pausing for a few seconds. However, you should never wait for a verbal response or direct the question to an unsuspecting audience member.

Open with a Pertinent Quotation

A *pertinent quotation* is an effective way to begin a presentation. If you decide to begin a speech with a pertinent quotation be certain you interpret the meaning of the quotation for the audience. Unlike a rhetorical question, which may have more than one answer or interpretation, you will want the audience to understand exactly what the quotation means. Always keep your quotation limited to a few short lines because long quotations are difficult for the audience to follow. Quotes can also be presented in the form of questions.

■ "He says: Why can't a woman think like a man? She says: Why can't a man think more like a woman? I answer: Because men and women have different thinking styles"[5]

Open with a Humorous Remark

We hesitate to mention this introductory technique. Often speakers feel the best way to break the ice is to begin a presentation with a relevant *humorous story, joke,* or *anecdote.* Using humor can be quite effective when used appropriately and in conjunction with other introductory techniques. This is especially true for **after-dinner speeches** and/or speeches to entertain (see Chapter Seven).

Having said this, we urge you to explore the other introductory methods before deciding to use humor. Quite often a speaker's good intentions to create a light hearted moment fall on deaf ears or may insult the sen-

Pertinent Quotation
The speaker uses the words of someone else

Humorous Remark
Used to entertain the audience

After Dinner Speeches
Festive/light hearted speeches to entertain an audience

sitivities of the audience. As a result, instead of relieving speech anxiety the speaker actually creates more for him or herself. For example:

- Insert the last joke you told that someone did not laugh at.

Open with a Brief Demonstration

The Chinese proverb, "A picture is worth a thousand words," is the idea behind this technique. Sometimes the best way to gain your audience's attention is to show them a photograph.

You are presenting a speech on the dangers of drunk driving. It is possible to give the statistic of how many people die in drunk driving accidents, and it is possible to give a quote from someone who has lost a loved one due to drunk driving; however, the photo of a wrecked car might do more to gain your audience's attention than either of these devices.

Brief Demonstration
Instead of stating something, the speaker shows something

2. *Indicating the Significance of the Topic*

Ask yourself why you feel it is important for the audience to understand your presentation. The answer to this question should then be incorporated into the introduction of the speech. When selecting your speech topic you conducted a **demographic** and **psychological** analysis of your intended audience (Chapter Three). One of the variables you considered was the importance or significance of the speech topic.

Do not take for granted that the audience will find your subject important simply because you find it important. You need to verbally indicate the *significance* of the topic to human kind. You need to make it very clear that your speech subject is important and worth listening to.

There are several variables to consider when determining the importance of a speech topic. You should consider the *urgency*, the *propensity*, and/or the *usefulness* of the subject matter. Ask yourself once again, "Why is my topic important?" Is it because the topic you are discussing requires immediate attention or action? Is it because there is a likelihood the problem you are focusing on will become worse without immediate attention or action? Or, perhaps your subject is important because the audience can use the information for personal, educational, and/or potential financial profit?

Demographic Analysis
Who the audience members are, in terms of: age, gender, level of education, etc.

Psychological Analysis
What the audience members think

Significance
Tells the audience why this speech topic is important to humankind in general

Importance of Your Topic

Urgency:
- Firearms rank as the second leading cause of fatal injuries in the United States. (*Adolescent Medicine: State of the Art Reviews*, October 1993)

Urgency
Of pressing importance

■ More than 1,000,000 teenagers in the United States become pregnant each year. Most of these pregnancies are unintentional. (*USA Today, July 1992*)

Propensity
Innate tendency

Propensity:
■ The United States is heading toward a 40-year low in the real value of the current minimum wage. (*Los Angeles Times, February 1995*)
■ Every year more and more manatees die due to human carelessness. (*Florida Department of Natural Resources, 1995*)

Usefulness
Capable of being used

Usefulness:
■ I will provide you with a method for landing the job you have always wanted.
■ There are more than 1,000 drawings and some 800 paintings of Vincent VanGogh on display at our local museum. (*International Dictionary of Art and Artists, 1990*)

You will need to decide how you can best indicate the subject's importance to the audience. While we cannot give you a simple technique for indicating to your audience why your subject is important and, therefore, why they should listen to the presentation, we can give you a bit of advice on a technique that will not work. One method you do *not* want to use is simply stating to your audience, "My topic is important because . . . and therefore you should listen!" This is sure to fall on deaf ears.

3. Indicating the Relevance of the Topic
Indicating the significance of a speech subject is not always sufficient to generate interest in a presentation. Quite often it is necessary to clearly indicate why the subject is important to this specific audience at this particular time and place. Once again ask yourself the same questions you asked yourself when selecting the speech topic.

■ How does this information relate to the audience?
■ How does this information affect them at this particular time and place?

Relevant
Tells the audience why this speech topic is important to them

Once you have identified why the subject is *relevant* to the audience you need to incorporate that information into the presentation's introduction.

For instance, the relevance of the events in the former Yugoslavia could be demonstrated by how the events may affect the United States. You may want to hypothesize how the events may affect the audience's own family if American soldiers are sent into combat or how the Serbian policy of "ethnic cleansing" is relevant to all civilized human beings. Each example serves to indicate to the audience how the subject relates to them at this particular time and place.

4. Enhancing Your Credibility

As part of your introduction you will need to prove to the audience that you are knowledgeable about the speech subject and you are trustworthy.

The audience will expect you to be knowledgeable about the subject. This is one of the primary reasons all presentations must be fully researched and information must be supported with reliable, credible, and knowledgeable sources.

The audience will determine if you, as a speaker, are *credible* by evaluating three criteria:

- your stated qualifications
- your general physical appearance
- your composure

Stating Your Qualifications:

If you have first hand knowledge about the speech subject you should indicate this fact to your audience. By indicating your qualifications you are strengthening your credibility.

For instance, if you are presenting a speech on the famous Italian Renaissance artist and inventor Leonardo DaVinci and you are an art historian, you will want to indicate this to the audience. If you are discussing magic and you are a magician, you will also want to state this to the audience.

What if you do not have any personal experience with the subject or your personal experience is limited? For example, you have decided to speak about the federal deficit and you have just completed an introductory course in economics. Is the fact that you have taken an economics course enough to persuade the audience you are knowledgeable about the federal deficit? What if you did not have any previous experience on the subject but you have researched the topic throughout the past three weeks?

These are difficult questions to answer but very common questions for students in a beginning public speaking class. After **analyzing your intended audience** and their knowledge of the subject, (Chapter Three) you must answer these questions for yourself: "If I were in the audience what would convince me that the speaker is knowledgeable about the topic?" or "What would convince me that the speaker is knowledgeable, trustworthy, and has a similar value system to my own?" In most cases, a

Credibility
States the speaker's qualifications on the subject matter, their physical appearance, and their composure

Stating Qualification
Telling the audience the scope of your knowledge on the topic

Audience Analysis
Knowing what the interests/needs of the audience are

speaker who indicates his/her expertise is based on only three weeks of research is on shaky ground. However, since most of you are students who are choosing topics of interest to you and your audience, this may be the best that you can do.

When stating your qualifications to speak on a subject you need to do so with caution. You must be completely honest about your qualifications on the subject. Overstating or exaggerating your credentials can be disastrous. A "little white lie" can destroy your credibility with the audience and may result in the audience not believing anything you have to say. Always be completely honest with the audience even if this means you do not have a strong credibility statement in the introduction.

Physical Appearance:

In many cases you may find it difficult to verbally enhance your credibility; however, this does not mean that the audience will not perceive you as a credible speaker. When determining your credibility the audience will also be evaluating your overall physical appearance. They will attribute characteristics to you based on your appearance. This is called formulating a first impression and in most cases is based solely on your physical appearance.

You may feel this is quite unfair and very naive. However unfair, this is the case. Once again place yourself in the audience. Have you made first impressions based on physical appearance? Consider your first impression of teachers, co-workers, and even of your friends. While your first impression of any of these individuals may have changed, you still established a first impression of each primarily based on his/her physical appearance.

When you walk to the front of the room the audience will be forming a general first impression of you. They will be attributing characteristics to you such as your overall intelligence, your general trustworthiness, and your personality. They may even be making assumptions about your background. Each of these assumptions will be a factor in the audience's reception and attention to your speech.

While you cannot control your body type or your height, you can control how you dress for the presentation. Put very simply you must dress appropriately for the occasion. This means you should dress in accordance with the audience's expectations and for the purpose of conveying a positive self-image.

In most instances the audience will expect you to be dressed nicely and be neatly groomed. If the occasion is formal, such as a funeral, graduation ceremony, or business meeting, then formal attire will be expected by the audience. Speakers who do not dress appropriately for the occasion

Physical Appearance The audience's first impression of a speaker based on how he/she is dressed

will not be evaluated positively by the audience and probably will not be successful.

Composure

Simply stating your qualifications and dressing appropriately for the occasion may not be enough to ultimately convince the audience you are credible and worth listening to. Consider the example of a teacher who is qualified to teach the class and is dressed appropriately, but appears extremely unsure of him or herself. Perhaps he/she is mumbling, speaking very quickly and/or avoiding making eye contact with people in the audience. In this instance you may have questioned the speaker's ability to teach the course.

This is why it is extremely important to be prepared to speak on a subject. A successful speaker has practiced the delivery of the presentation and is able to discuss the topic conversationally and with very little prompting.

A successful speaker speaks clearly and at an appropriate **rate** and **volume** (Chapter Two). A successful speaker is able to recognize and react to **feedback** (Chapter One). In other words a successful speaker is one who is perceived by the audience as credible, who is prepared, and maintains his/her composure throughout the presentation regardless of the circumstances.

Do not underestimate the importance of being prepared—both physically and mentally. Practicing your delivery, dressing appropriately, and being neatly groomed helps to create a positive self-concept. You will feel better about yourself. You will be more confident. You will convey a self-assured and positive image. The audience will view you as confident and poised and they will be much more likely to listen to and enjoy the presentation.

5. Stating Your Thesis Statement

(Previously discussed in Step Three of this process, p. 154)

A *thesis statement* for an informative speech is called a central idea. A **central idea,** while summarizing the speech, does not make conclusions about the subject. Its purpose is to share information and create a general understanding of the topic. The central idea is the most important statement in the introduction. It is the one statement that indicates your main purpose to the audience.

You must always keep this statement clear and concise. It neither urges or suggests any physical action by the audience, proposes a particular point of view the speaker might believe to be accurate, nor does it list the main points of your speech.

Composure
Having or showing confidence

Rate
How fast and/or slow an individual speaks

Volume
How loudly or softly an individual speaks

Feedback
A response to a message that is decoded by the source

Thesis Statement
A sentence that clearly tells the audience what the speaker will be discussing

Central Idea
A type of thesis statement used with informative speeches; it is a one sentence summary of entire presentation

When you read the following examples, note that they summarize the informative speech without drawing any conclusions. They do not urge any physical or mental action on the part of the listener. Lastly, they do not mention the specific main points of your speech.

- ■ The Dragon Boat Festival pays tribute to Qu Yuan.
- ■ Martin Luther King protested for civil rights in the 1960s.
- ■ The Bay of Pigs invasion occurred while John F. Kennedy was President of the United States.

6. *Briefly Previewing Your Main Points*
(Previously discussed in Step Five (connectors) of this process, p. 179)

The final statement in the introduction should briefly preview the main points of the presentation. The *preview statement* introduces the main points of the presentation in the order that they will be presented in the body of the speech.

- ■ In this presentation, I will tell you about visual learners, auditory learners, and kinetic learners.
- ■ I will be discussing the three branches if the federal government: the executive, the legislative, and the judicial.
- ■ In today's speech, I will be explaining to you the symptoms of AIDS which are: high fever, exhaustion, and nausea.

The preview statement is the connector from the introduction to the body of the speech. After previewing the main points, pause briefly to give the audience time to remember what the main points are and the order in which they will be addressed.

Step Seven: Conclusions

A *conclusion* has three main purposes:

- ■ To cue the audience that you are ending your speech.
- ■ To summarize the main points of the speech.
- ■ To effectively bring closure to the speech.

Just as the introduction is designed to gain the audience's attention and preview the main points, the conclusion is designed to review those main points and effectively end the presentation. Cueing the audience of the end of your speech lets the audience know that you are going to wrap up your speech and allows the audience to focus in on your summary. This is, after all, you parting message to the audience.

In the summary (see final summary in Step Five of this process, p. 180–181), you need to restate your **central idea** and summarize each of

Preview Statements
Found in the introduction; this is where a speaker lists the main points of the presentation for an informative speech

Conclusion
Brings the speech to a close by cueing the ending of a presentation, summarizing the main points and linking the exit line to the attention getting statement

Central Idea
A type of thesis statement used with informative speeches; it is a one sentence summary of entire presentation

your main points. As you can see, this satisfies the earlier recommendation to "tell them what you just told them" from page 180."

The third requirement of a conclusion is to end the presentation effectively. Your goal is for the audience to realize the presentation has ended and to feel satisfied. Therefore, you should never end a presentation by saying, "That's it," "I'm finished," or "The end." These are not effective methods for ending a presentation. An extremely effective way to exit a presentation is to return to the **attention-getting method** you used in the introduction. For example, if you began the speech with a rhetorical question you may choose to answer that question in the conclusion.

■ *Attention Step*
What would you do if you were walking alone at night and a strange person approached you and tried to mug you? Would you run? Would you scream? Would you panic? Or, would you be able to fight back?

■ *Conclusion*
Earlier I asked you, "What would you do if you were walking alone and a stranger approached you?" I hope your answer now to this question, after completing a self-defense course, is "I would be able to fight back."

Another example of how to link the attention getter with the **exit line** would be by using the story format. In the introduction draw your audience into your speech by telling them a story. In the conclusion finish the story and effectively end your speech.

■ *Attention Step*
He was so cute. And smart. Sure, he had a few bruises on his arms and legs. What seven-year-old didn't? Sure, he cried and told me his mommy and daddy spanked him. Don't all parents spank their children sometime? What I didn't know, because I was unable to recognize it, is that Johnny was being physically and mentally abused at home. To this day I regret not recognizing the signs of abuse and finding him help sooner.

■ *Conclusion*
Johnny, the abused child I spoke of earlier is now fourteen years old and I am happy to tell you he is doing fine. He is on the high school basketball team and a constant member of the honor roll.

By returning to the attention-getting device your speech has become circular. You have returned back to the beginning. A presentation without an exit line—a speech that does not return to the introductory remarks—may leave the audience unsatisfied at the completion of the presentation.

Attention-Getting Method
The first sentence a speaker will say to an audience

Exit Line
Last sentence of speech, linked to attention getter

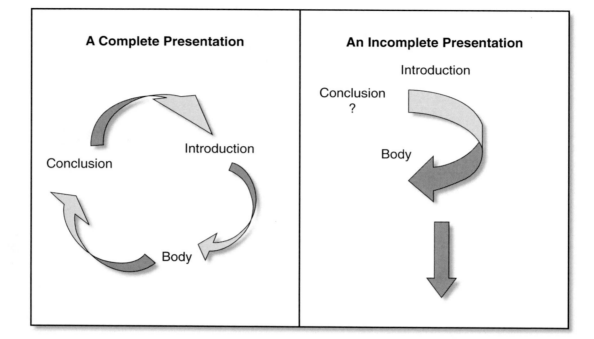

A Complete Presentation	An Incomplete Presentation
Introduction → Body → Conclusion	Introduction → Body → Conclusion ?

Rate
How fast and/or slow an individual speaks

When concluding your presentation always pause before presenting the final exit line. You may find it effective to state your concluding remarks slightly slower than your normal **rate** of speech to indicate to the audience the presentation is concluding. After making your last statement pause and thank the audience for their attention.

Cultural Influence on Conclusions

Americans structure conclusions in a very low context manner by stating "in conclusion" followed by a brief review of the main points. Nothing is left open to chance as far as decoding is concerned; all information is explicitly stated. Low context cultures such as: Americans, British, Swedish, and Germans employ messages that are explicitly coded. These are also cultures that are speaker responsible. This means that the speaker is accountable for providing the structure and the specific meaning of the information provided. Very little information is left open for interpretation in low context cultures.

High context cultures, on the other hand, infer the structure and meaning of their communication based on the shared knowledge of the sender and the receiver. High context cultures such as Asian and Arab cultures close a speech by discussing future relationships without stressing the ideas presented in the body of the speech.

Step Eight: Soliciting and Answering Questions

Depending on the speaking situation, you may find it useful and courteous to invite questions from the audience. Therefore, it is important to anticipate some questions the audience may ask you and prepare answers to these questions in advance. You may even decide to reorganize your presentation to include the answers. Of course not all of the questions the audience will ask you can be anticipated, but with the proper preparation and practice, you will be able to answer any question the audience may have.

You will find the following strategies helpful when answering questions from an audience.

Handling the Q & A Session

- ■ Anticipate as many questions as you can and prepare responses to each question. You may even want to consider preparing speaker notes and including additional supporting material for your responses.
- ■ Keep your answers focused on the questions, avoid rambling from topic to topic, and answer the question as thoroughly and concisely as you feel is appropriate.
- ■ If confronted with negative, attacking questions, or with questions that were obviously answered in the presentation, remain positive at all times. Once again, stay focused on the question and answer it honestly and to the best of your ability. Do not attack the questioner under any circumstances or ask him/her if they were listening to your presentation.
- ■ Never make up an answer to a question. Even the most well prepared and knowledgeable speakers encounter questions they cannot answer. If you do not know the answer to a question, you may want to consider apologizing for not being able to answer the question, offer to find the answer, and get back to the person at a later date.
- ■ If you are asked a vague question, you may ask for clarification before answering.
- ■ Finally, avoid prefacing every answer with, "Good question." This can become very redundant and patronizing to the audience. If every question is a "good question," you probably should have included the information in your presentation.

Step Nine: Outlining

By this time you should have a general idea of how to organize the body, the introduction, and the conclusion of an informative presentation. You are aware of what the goals of an introduction are, how to organize the main points of the body, and what the essential goals of a conclusion are. After successfully researching your speech subject, you need to begin to formally organize your information in the form of an *outline*.

Before discussing how an outline is organized we think it is important for you to understand the benefits of an outline. Quite often students feel they can jump right from researching the presentation to putting notes on a piece of paper, and then delivering the speech. You could do this but there is a high probability your presentation will be disorganized and very difficult for the audience to understand. Therefore, it is necessary to outline the presentation first. Let us further explain the benefits of outlining a speech.

An Outline Enables You To See How the Speech is Organized.

By outlining a presentation you will be able to see if portions of the speech are missing and if each is in the proper sequence. Do I have an attention-getting device? Have I indicated the significance and the relevancy of the subject? If appropriate, have I indicated my expertise on the subject? Do I have a clear thesis statement? Have I briefly forecasted the main points? Have I limited the main points in the body to between two and five? Is each main point adequately supported? Have I cued the audience I was ending my speech? Have I summarized the main points? Finally, have I effectively and appropriately ended the presentation?

An Outline Enables You To See the Amount Of Supporting Material for Each Main Point.

By outlining a presentation you will be able to see if you have too much material for the time allotted for the speech. If this is the case, you may need to use a **spider diagram** to narrow your speech topic (Chapter Three). You will also be able to see if a main point is not sufficiently supported. If a main point is lacking sufficient supporting material, then you will need to research that particular point in more detail.

An Outline Enables You To Revise Your Speech.

Upon completing your speech outline you will be able to begin to make changes in the presentation. By examining the outline you will be able to see if any portion is missing or unclear or if you have too much or too little supporting material. Once you have determined where changes are necessary you can incorporate these changes into the outline.

Outline
A "road map" to follow while delivering a presentation

Spider Diagram
An effective way to narrow down a speech topic

An outline is a working document. It is designed to be changed, changed again, and changed again if necessary. There is no limit to the amount of times you may change the outline and the contents of the speech.

An Outline Enables You to Receive Feedback from the Instructor.

Your instructor will probably require you to submit an outline prior to presenting a speech. The reason your instructor requires the outline is so he/she is able to make constructive criticism on the format and contents of the speech. By reviewing an outline the instructor may reduce the risk of organizational and logical errors in a presentation before they are committed in front of an audience.

If you complete a preliminary outline of a presentation, your instructor will be able to recommend changes to the speech. For example, your instructor may be able to suggest where information is unclear and/or not properly supported. Your instructor may also be able to indicate where **visual supporting material** may be necessary and what form of visual aid would be most effective.

An Outline Enables You to Practice Your Delivery.

While you should not actually speak from your outline, the outline should be used to practice your **delivery.** After completing the outline to your satisfaction you should begin practicing your delivery. While practicing the speech, you will need to make brief notes that you can use during the presentation. The note cards you speak from are called **speaker cards** (see Chapter Two).

The speaker cards should be used to help you remember key information during the presentation. Please notice, we did not say memorize the information. As you recall, in a speech that is memorized you are unable to react to **feedback** and less likely to be successful. Therefore, you should present the speech in a conversational manner.

The speaker cards should ideally be 3x5 or 4x6 index cards. You should avoid writing complete sentences on your speaker cards unless you are using a direct quote in the presentation. If you write a complete sentence on the speaker card you are likely to read this information to the audience and destroy the natural flow of the speech. After practicing your delivery and becoming familiar with the organization, you should write only key words or phrases on the speaker cards. These key words or phrases will help you remember the proper organization and main points of the presentation while you are speaking.

Visual Supporting Material
Used to help an audience understand and remember a speakers message

Delivery
The way a speaker presents their speech

Speaker Cards
The note cards you speak from

Feedback
A response to a message that is decoded by the source

Preparing an Outline

There are three types of outlines: *complete sentence outlines, abbreviated outlines,* and *key word* or *phrase outlines.* A complete sentence outline is an outline that consists of full sentences. It contains the **general** and **specific purpose** at the top of the outline and your **internal summaries** are embedded between the main points. An abbreviated outline is a bulleted outline. A key word or key phrase outline is an outline that consists of only key words and/or key phrases.

The complete sentence outline is a more useful outline for students learning how to give a speech. As you become more accustomed to organizing a presentation and more comfortable delivering a presentation, you may be able to use an abbreviated outline or a key word outline. The major drawback of a key word or phrase outline is that often there is not enough information in the outline. This may result in two problems: (1) you may forget certain points, and (2) your instructor is unable to provide you with feedback because he/she may be unclear as to your intent. Therefore, this text focuses on the complete sentence outline.

There are four general rules for all types of outlining. By following these rules you will be able to more effectively organize your presentation and your instructor will be able to provide you with relevant feedback.

You Should Use a Consistent Form of Notation.

The outline must follow a consistent pattern of letters and numbers. Traditionally, roman numerals are used sequentially prior to each main heading of the speech. For example, your informative presentation has three main headings:

I.   The Introduction
II. The Body
III. The Conclusion

Capital letters are used for each main point within a heading. Remember, the body of an informative speech should be limited to between two and five main points.

    A.   First Main Point
    B.   Second Main Point
    C.   Third Main Point

Under each capital letter Arabic numbers are used to represent subpoints. Subpoints contain information that supports the main point. Subpoints define, explain, describe and/or serve as examples of a main point. Just as main points should be limited to between two and five, so should each series of subpoints.

    A. First Main Point
        1. Subpoint of A
        2. Subpoint of A
    B. Second Main Point
        1. Subpoint of B
        2. Subpoint of B
    C. Third Main Point
        1. Subpoint of C
        2. Subpoint of C

If a subpoint has a subpoint (sub-subpoint), then lowercase letters are used. This is usually as detailed as the outline should be. If your outline requires additional notation, you may want to reconsider how you have organized the presentation. It may be too complicated for the audience to follow clearly.

    A. First Main Point
        1. Subpoint of A
           a. Subpoint of 1
           b. Subpoint of 1
        2. Subpoint of A
           a. Subpoint of 2
           b. Subpoint of 2

You Should Be Consistent in Your Indentation.
To make an outline easier to use, the main points and subpoints should be indented consistently. In the previous examples, note how each subpoint is indented an equal number of spaces. The main points would also be indented equally.

You Should Limit Each Letter or Number in the Outline to One Complete Sentence or Phrase.
Each letter or number in the outline represents one idea. As such, only one complete sentence containing one idea should follow each letter or number. You should never have more than one sentence per letter or number, nor should you try to combine two ideas into one statement. Keep in mind the purpose of the outline is to help you organize information clearly. In order to most effectively organize the information you need to have only one idea next to each letter or number.

You Should Reference All the Information in the Outline.
Any information that is not your own idea should be footnoted in the outline. In addition, a complete bibliography should accompany the outline.

Outline Format for the Informative Speech

I. Introduction
- A. Attention getting device
    1. Significance of topic to humankind
    2. Relevance of topic to audience
    3. Speaker's credibility
- B. Thesis (Central Idea)
- C. Preview Statement

II. Body
- A. First Main Point
    1. Supporting material for A
    2. Supporting material for A
    3. Supporting material for A
    INTERNAL SUMMARY
- B. Second Main Point
    1. Supporting material for B
    2. Supporting material for B
    3. Supporting material for B
    INTERNAL SUMMARY
- C. Third Main Point
    1. Supporting material for C
    2. Supporting material for C
    3. Supporting material for C

III. Conclusion
- A. Cue ending of speech
- B. Restate central idea from introduction
    1. Summarize 1st main point
    2. Summarize 2nd main point
    3. Summarize 3rd main point
- C. Exit line linked to attention getter in introduction

Criteria Used for Evaluating Speeches

The average speech (grade C) should meet the following criteria:

- Conform to the kind of speech assigned (informative, persuasive, special occasion).
- Be ready for presentation on the assigned date.

- Conform to the time limit.
- Fulfill any special requirements of the assignment—such as preparing an outline and using visual aids.
- Have a clear general purpose, specific purpose, and central idea.
- Have an identifiable introduction, body, and conclusion.
- Show reasonable directness and competence in delivery.
- Be free of serious errors in grammar, pronunciation, and word usage.

The *above average speech* (grade B) should meet the preceding criteria and also:

- Fulfill all functions of a speech introduction and conclusion.
- Display clear organization of main points and supporting materials.
- Have a variety of supporting material that is used correctly.
- Exhibit proficient use of connectors—transitions, preview statement, internal summaries, and final summary.
- Be delivered skillfully enough so as not to distract attention form the speaker's message.

The *superior speech* (grade A) should meet all the preceding criteria and also:

- Constitute a genuine contribution by the speaker to the knowledge or beliefs of the audience.
- Sustain positive interest, feeling, and/or commitment among the audience.
- Contain elements of vividness and special interest in the use of language.
- Be delivered in a fluent, polished manner that strengthens the impact of the speaker's message.

The *below average speech* (grade D or F) is deficient in the criteria required for the C speech.

Sample Outlines

The 1930 Hollywood Production Code
Josell Galis-Menendez, Student

General Purpose: To inform

Specific Purpose: At the end of my speech, the audience will be able to explain three aspects of the Hollywood Production Code.

Thesis: From its installment in 1930, the Hollywood Production Code had a monumental influence on film history.

I.   Introduction
    A.   Mobsters, hit men, adulterous affairs hidden in dark motel rooms, passionate lustful embraces, perversion, vulgarity, obscenity, sacrilegious comedies by the dozen, and all the nudity and sex audiences can bare, for many years this has seemed to be the ingredients to making Hollywood hits, however there was a time when every one of these things were forbidden and banished from the coveted silver screen.
        1.   Understanding the hurdles filmmakers overcame in the past to bring their audiences the quality of entertainment they felt was deserved can provide viewers with greater respect for what we can enjoy and appreciate in today's films.
        2.   As young men and women in the twenty-first century, most, if not all of us have at some point watched a great film; it is important to understand the significance of being able to enjoy something as easily overlooked as an on-screen kiss.
        3.   After having researched this topic extensively in the past and over the last few days, I have acquired certain information that you will find interesting and perhaps surprising.
    B.   From its installment in 1930, the Hollywood Production Code had a monumental influence on film history.
    C.   Today, I am going to discuss the formation of the Hollywood Production Code, its strict guidelines, and why it was finally abandoned in 1968.

II.   Body
    A.   The Hollywood Production Code was adopted in March of 1930, fueled by Catholic religious leaders and the censors' panic concerning the overwhelming development of the much racier talking films.
        1.   The major studios hired publicist Will Hays, who convinced studio heads the Production Code would be the most economic option and their best chance at avoiding federal censorship.
        2.   However, between 1932 and 1933, films were still making excellent use of the mass appeal of sex and violence; the "bad girls," such as Jean Harlow and Mae West were still what sold big.

3. To battle this the Hollywood Production Code Administration (PCA) was formed, headed by Joe Breen.
4. Everything put on a reel fell under the iron fist of the PCA; beginning in 1934 the films were radically different.
   a. Film historian Thomas Doherty explains, "It's the difference between Mae West and Shirley Temple."

After seeing that issues of morality and the studio's fear of federal censorship were what drove the Hollywood Production Code into practice, I will now demonstrate to you the severity of the code itself.

B. The Hollywood Production Code was a brutally specific set of guidelines for what was appropriate to be seen in film.
   1. The General Principles of the code were as follows:
      a. No picture shall be produced that will lower the moral standards of those who see it. Hence, the sympathy of the audiences should never be thrown to the side of crime, wrongdoing, evil, or sin.
      b. Correct standards of life, subject only to the requirements of drama and entertainment, shall be presented.
      c. Law, natural, or human, shall not be ridiculed nor shall sympathy be created for its violation.
   2. Subcategories of the code included: crimes against the law, sex, vulgarity, obscenity, and costume.
   3. Examples of certain guidelines for sex in films were:
      a. Excessive and lustful kissing, lustful embraces, and suggestive postures and gestures are not to be shown.
      b. Sex relationships between white and black races are forbidden.
      c. Scenes of actual childbirth, in fact or in silhouette, are never to be presented.
      d. Sex hygiene and venereal diseases are not subjects for motion pictures.
   4. Examples of certain guidelines for costume included:
      a. Indecent or undue exposure is forbidden.
      b. Complete nudity is never permitted. This includes nudity in fact or silhouette, or any lecherous or licentious notice thereof by other characters in the picture.
      c. Dancing or costumes intended to permit undue exposure or indecent movements in the dance are forbidden.

During the code's reign, filmmakers were thrown into a labyrinth of rules and regulations and audiences were given films that lacked all the gritty realism and edge they craved. However, after more than a decade, the code's time was reaching its end.

C. In 1952, the Production Code's days were numbered when movies were finally granted free speech protection from the First Amendment.

    1. In 1968, the code was officially abandoned.

    2. It was replaced by the rating system still in practice to date.

    3. Jack Valenti, President of the Motion Picture Association of America declares, "I have a right to compose a song or write a book or make a movie about anything I choose, but a theater owner has a right to say 'no I don't want to play it.' Or a retail video store says 'no, I don't want to stock it.' That's called freedom. That's called democracy."

III. Conclusion

A. In short, whether someone was in support of or in disagreement with the Hollywood Production Code, it is undeniable that it was a vital part of film history, one that clearly marks how far the industry and its craft have come.

B. From its installment in 1930, The Hollywood Production Code became a monumental time in film history.

    1. The Code was initially created by those who viewed it as the saving grace of morality in films.

    2. Once in place, it set rigid guidelines that dictated everything from the costume choices to the onscreen embraces.

    3. That was, until 1968, when it was finally abandoned due to the protection of films under the First Amendment.

C. The next time any of you sit down to enjoy one of your favorite films, please stop and take a moment to appreciate every wonderfully immoral and indecent scene, storyline, and costume, and your Constitutional right to enjoy or criticize it.

Bibliography

http://www.pbs.org/wgbh/cultureshock/beyond/hollywood.html. Culture Shock; The TV Series & Beyond.

http://www.artsreformation.com/a0001/hays-code.html. Arts Reformation.COM

http://www.pbs.org/wgbh/cultureshock/flashpoints/theater/maewest.html. Culture Shock; Theater, Film and Video.

The Atomic Bomb
Elizabeth Auer, Student

General Purpose: To inform

Specific Purpose: At the end of my speech, the audience will be able to list three main reasons why the atomic bomb was built.

Thesis: The atomic bomb was built for many reasons that to this day do not justify the destruction that it caused.

I.   Introduction
  A.   Fifty-eight years ago over 240,000 Japanese men, women, and children were killed by two of the most destructive weapons ever known to man. We still continue to build these weapons today.
    1.   Understanding the reasons why the atomic bomb was built may prevent the proliferation of these weapons in the future.
    2.   As human beings, we need to have a reason behind the massive loss of life in order to put our minds and hearts at rest.
    3.   After studying this topic for the past week, here is some information I think you would like to know.
  B.   The atomic bomb was built for many reasons that still to this day do not justify the destruction that it caused.
  C.   Today I am going to discuss the three main reasons why the atomic bomb was built, which were: military expansion, the attack on Pearl Harbor, and the Cold War.

II.   Body
  A.   The expansion of the United States military played a vital role in the creation of the atomic bomb.
    1.   At this time the US military was in need of a bigger and better defense weapon.
    2.   The egos that belonged to the leaders of our country were slightly out of hand.
    3.   Albert Einstein wrote a letter to President Franklin D. Roosevelt recommending that atomic bombs be made in the US.
    4.   This launched the American atomic program in 1939, which was called the Manhattan Project.
    5.   The team of people put together by the President began researching and developing atomic energy.
    6.   Henry L. Stimson, Roosevelt's Secretary of War, stated that, "At no time, from 1941 to 1945, did I ever hear it suggested by the President, or any other responsible member of government, that atomic energy should not be used in the war. The entire purpose was the production of a military weapon."

Military expansion was a very important aspect of American strategy. However, the horror and shock of the Japanese attack on Pearl Harbor captured the attention of many Americans.

    B.   The attack on Pearl Harbor was a devastating experience that fueled the American's desire for more military strength.

        1. On December 7, 1941, the Japanese attacked an American fleet of 19 ships and 17 battleships, which were all sunk.

        2. There was estimated to be about 2,400 American soldiers and sailors killed during the surprise attack.

        3. The events of Pearl Harbor eliminated many of the reservations that the Americans had had regarding the use of an atomic bomb in the war.

        4. America wanted revenge and the atomic bomb seemed like the perfect way to achieve it.

        5. The United States' attack on Japan was 100 times more destructive than the Japanese attack on Pearl Harbor.

        6. The launching of the atomic bomb on Japan ultimately brought an end to World War II.

The consequences of Pearl Harbor will forever be in the minds and hearts of everyone involved. However, the Cold War actually brought an end to the madness that had begun with the first atomic bomb.

    C.   The Cold War was a time of heightened nuclear proliferation.

        1. Many countries were in fear of what might happen if one country decided to deploy nuclear radiation into the Earth's atmosphere.

        2. The United States and Russia entered into an arms race to see which country could be the most powerful, militarily.

        3. With the development of nuclear weapons, the arms race became a great fear in everyone's mind.

        4. The countries were developing weapons, which were nicknamed MAD.

           a. Mutual Assured Destruction meant that both countries were so powerful, that if one were to attack the other, both would definitely be annihilated.

        5. This fear is what eventually brought an end to the Cold War.

  III. Conclusion

    A.   And thus, the atomic bomb has still been a very influential and deadly invention throughout history.

    B.   The atomic bomb was built for many reasons that still until this day do not justify the destruction that it caused.

        1. The expansion of the military caused by the egos of America's leaders brought about the beginning of he atomic bomb.

        2. The attack on Pearl Harbor brought about the reality of the existence and power of the atomic bomb.

   3. The events of the arms race during the Cold War have brought about awareness and respect for these weapons.

   C. 240,000 Japanese dead; that is a large number. The road ahead is not paved or straight for us, but if we can keep these destructive monsters under control, then maybe we can hold out hope for the future.

Bibliography

Goodman, P. (2000). *Hiroshima and Nagasaki.* Maryland.

Maddox, R. (1995). *Weapons for Victory.* Missouri University of Missouri Press.

Seddon, T. (1995). *Atom Bomb.* New York: W.H. Freeman and Company.

Sherrow, V. (1994). *Hiroshima.* New York: MacMillan.

The Effects of Cigarette Smoking
Phuoc Nguyen, Student

General Purpose: To inform

Specific Purpose: At the end of my speech, the audience will be able to explain two major effects of cigarette smoking.

Thesis: Studies have indicated that cigarette smoking is a significant risk factor for developing chronic disorders.

I.   Introduction

   A. Each year, an estimate of a half a million Americans die from smoking related diseases. That is more than AIDS, drug abuse, car accidents, and murder combined (Life Extension, 2003)

      1. Understanding the effects of cigarette smoking can influence a person's choice to smoke or not.

      2. As college students, you are usually faced with the pressure of cigarette smoking; therefore, it is important to realize the effects of smoking.

      3. After studying this topic for the past week, I have gathered information that you will find very interesting.

   B. Studies have indicated that cigarette smoking is a significant risk factor for developing chronic disorders.

   C. Today I am going to discuss two major effects of cigarette smoking, which are emphysema and coronary heart disease.

II.   Body

   A. Emphysema is defined as the over-inflated and eventual destruction of the tiny air sacs in the lungs called alveoli (Life Extension, 2003).

      1. During the respiratory process, the alveoli expand and contract in unison as air is inhaled and exhaled. In emphysema patients, these chambers lose their elasticity, becoming more and more like a balloon that is flabby from

overuse. To compensate for their inefficiency, the air sacs overexpand and may rupture and form cysts (Life Extension, 2003).

    a. When the chambers become damaged, the carbon dioxide cannot be expelled completely. It therefore, accumulates as stagnant air, interfering with the ability of the lungs to achieve a full intake of oxygen. Shortness of breath results, and as breathing requires more effort, the muscles of the neck, chest, and abdomen have to work much harder to get enough oxygen into the bloodstream. The over development of these muscles results in the "barrel-chested' look of the emphysema patient (Life Extension, 2003).

    b. Other symptoms include: weight loss, memory loss, insomnia, chronic cough with thick mucus, morning headaches, and cyanosis.

  2. There are about three million emphysema patients in the United States.

  3. It is more common in males than females and is manifested between the ages of 50 and 60.

  4. Emphysema is irreversible, but there are treatments to reduce symptoms.

    a. Antibiotics, bronchodilators, exercise, quitting smoking, eating a balanced and nutritious diet, avoiding areas that are dusty and polluted, flu and pneumonia vaccines, surgery, and lung transplants are some treatments used with emphysema patients.

Emphysema not only damages your lungs, but can also harm your heart, an illness known as coronary heart disease.

  B. Coronary Heart disease is a condition caused by an interrupted or diminished blood flow through the coronary arteries to the heart muscle (American Heart Association, 2002).

    1. The most common way that this flow of oxygen-rich blood becomes reduced is by the build up of fatty deposits or the formation of a blood clot in the arteries. When the blood supply to the heart is interrupted it sometimes causes a severe chest pain known as angina. When the blood supply is cut off completely, a heart attack occurs (American Heart Association, 2002).

    2. The number one risk factor for coronary heart disease is cigarette smoking, which can also lead to other risk factors.

      a. High blood pressure, high cholesterol, physical inactivity, obesity and overweight, diabetes, and alcohol are other risk factors (American Heart Association, 2002).

      b. The nicotine in cigarettes makes your body release adrenaline. Adrenaline causes your blood vessels to constrict and your heart to beat faster, which raises your blood pressure (American Heart Association, 2002).

    c. In addition, carbon monoxide inhaled through smoking robs the body's needed oxygen, since the red blood cells are quicker to attach on the poisonous gas than oxygen (American Heart Association, 2002).

   3. A cigarette smoker has two or three times the risk of having a heart attack than a nonsmoker.

   4. Males who are 65 and older are more susceptible to the disease.

   5. Studies have also shown that women who smoke and use oral contraceptives greatly increase their risk of coronary heart disease compared with nonsmoking women who use oral contraceptives (American Heart Association, 2002).

   6. There are no cures for coronary heart disease, but medications and surgery are available to suppress the symptoms.

III. Conclusion

  A. Finally, I do not completely understand why cigarettes are still on the market, when they are harmful to one's health.

  B. Studies have indicated that cigarette smoking is a significant risk factor for developing chronic disorders.

   1. The results indicated that cigarette smoking can lead to emphysema, which is a case that progresses slowly and persistently, gradually reducing the patients ability to breathe and ultimately leading to death.

   2. The primary factor of coronary heart disease is cigarette smoking, which can lead to other factors, and cause the patients to experience angina and unfortunately a heart attack.

  C. Over 40,000 medical studies detail the evidence that smoking causes diseases and death. Each year, an estimated half million Americans die from smoking-related diseases. That is more than AIDS, drug abuse, car accidents, and murder combined (American Heart Association, 2002).

Bibliography

Emphysema and Chronic Obstructive Pulmonary Disease, Life Extension 1995–2003, Retrieved May 28, 2003, from http://www.lef.org/protocols/prtcl-046.shtml

Risk Factors and Coronary Heart Disease, American Heart Association 2002, Retrieved May 31, 2003, from http://www.americanheart.org/presenter.jhtml?identifier=4726

Melanoma Skin Cancer
Jacqueline L. Ruiz, Student

General Purpose: To inform

Specific Purpose: At the end of my speech, the audience will be able to identify three major factors of melanoma skin cancer.

Thesis: Unprotected exposure to ultraviolet (UV) rays is the most important environmental factor in the development of melanoma skin cancer, which fortunately is often curable if detected and treated early.

I.   Introduction

   A.   Melanoma skin cancer is the most serious and deadly cancer of the skin. Each year in the United States, more than 53,600 people learn they have melanoma, and of those people, about 7,600 will die of the disease. In the US alone, the percentage of people who develop melanoma has more than doubled in the past 30 years causing more than 75 percent of all skin cancer deaths alone (American Cancer Society).

      1.   Understanding melanoma skin cancer will aid men and women of all ages to attain the behavior skills needed to prevent skin cancer.

      2.   As men and women you will unquestionably be exposed to UV radiation and it is necessary to identify melanoma skin cancer in order to begin UV-protection practices as early as possible.

      3.   Nonetheless, raised in a family of doctors and mothered by a dermatologist, I have gathered information throughout the years that I feel is crucial to every individual.

   B.   Unprotected exposure to ultraviolet (UV) rays is the most important environmental factor in developing melanoma skin cancer, which fortunately is often curable if detected and treated early.

   C.   I am going to discuss the risk factors, preventions, and early signs of melanoma skin cancer.

II.   Body

   A.   Studies of skin cancer have found that certain risk factors are involved in developing melanoma.

      1.   Research has shown that people with many ordinary moles, fair skin, a history of melanoma, and a weakened immune system are more likely to develop melanoma.

      2.   Moreover, people who have had at least one severe, blistering sunburn as a child, teenager, or adult, are at increased risk of developing the disease.

      3.   Experts believe that much of the worldwide increased melanoma is related to an increase in the amount of time people spend in the sun and in artificial sources of UV radiation.

Having covered the risk factors of melanoma, I am now going to describe the doctor recommended steps to help prevent and reduce the risk of melanoma caused by UV radiation.

      B.   Doctors recommend that individuals take the proper steps in aiding the prevention and reduction of the risk in developing skin cancer.

          1.   Avoid exposure to the midday sun (from 10 a.m. to 4 p.m.) whenever possible.

          2.   If you must be outside, wear long sleeves, a hat, and wear clothes that can penetrate light.

          3.   In addition, help protect your skin by using a lotion, cream, or gel daily that contains sunscreen with an average sunburn protection factor (SPF) from 15 to 30.

          4.   Finally, wear sunglasses that have UV-absorbing lenses that are at least 99 percent of UVA and UVB radiation protection which protect the eye and the skin around the eyes that are also at risk for skin cancer.

After listing steps to help in the prevention of melanoma, I will describe probable signs and symptoms of skin cancer that are often curable if detected ad treated early by a healthcare provider.

      C.   Thinking the "ABCD" (asymmetry, border, color, and diameter) about skin can help you remember what to watch for on your skin that may lead to melanoma if not treated early (NCI).

          1.   Often, the first sign of melanoma is a change in shape on a mole or freckle that seems abnormal or may appear as a new mole.

          2.   The mole or freckle that is malignant is often ragged, blurred, and the pigment spreads into surrounding skin.

          3.   Moreover, the color of a dangerous mole/freckle is usually uneven, having shades anywhere from black, brown and tan, and areas of white, gray, pink, or blue.

          4.   Most importantly, melanomas often have a change in size larger than the eraser of a pencil (1/4 of an inch).

   III. Conclusion

      A.   In closing, I cannot stress enough the importance of protecting yourself daily from UV-radiation. The number of people afflicted with melanoma skin cancer is increasing daily, which is ironic because it is one of the few cancers that can easily be avoided when taking the appropriate behavioral prevention factors.

      B.   Unprotected exposure to ultraviolet (UV) rays is the most important environmental factor in the development of melanoma skin cancer, which fortunately is often curable if detected and treated early.

          1.   Science has proven that the risk factors involve a family history of melanoma and unprotected exposure to UV radiation from the sun and

artificial sources causes premature aging and skin damage that may cause melanoma.

2. Moreover, taking the proper recommended steps of staying away from UV radiation and wearing sunscreen for protection will aid in preventing and reducing the chances of skin cancer.

3. Also, thinking of the "ABCD" of melanoma symptoms and a routine skin examination is often the best way to check the skin for new growths and other changes that may be dangerous to all individuals of all ages.

C. Nevertheless, it is important to detect melanoma as early as possible. The American Cancer Society recommends that people aged 20–40 have a skin check up every three years and people over the age of 40 have one every year with a professional healthcare provider. You do not want to be one of the 53,600 individuals who are diagnosed with melanoma cancer each year in the US, nor do you want to be one of the 7,600 that are estimated to die.

Bibliography

http://www.americancancersociety.org/melanomainfo—American Cancer Society
http://www.nci.nih.gov/cancerinfo/wyntk/melanoma—National Cancer Institute

Publication Manual of the American Psychological Association (APA)

Books
- Single Author:
  Author's Last name, First Initial. (Year of Publication). *Title Of The Book*. Publishing City, State: Publisher's Name.
- Multiple Authors: ·
  Author's Last Name, First Initial, Author's Last name, First Initial. (Year of Publication). *Title Of The Book*. Publishing City, State: Publisher's Name.

Magazines
- Weekly Magazine:
  Author's Last Name, First Initial. (Year of Publication, Month and Day of Publication). Title of the article. *Title Of The Magazine*, Page(s).
- Monthly Magazine:
  Author's Last Name, First Initial. (Year of Publication, Month). Title of the article. *Title Of The Magazine*, Page(s).
- No Author:
  Title of the article. (Year of Publication, Month and Day of Publication). *Title Of The Magazine*, Page(s).

Journals
Author's Last Name, First Initial. (Year of Publication). Title of the journal article. *Title Of The Journal*, Volume (Number), Page(s).

Newspapers
Author's Last Name, First Initial. (Year of Publication, Month and Day of Publication). Title of the article. *Title Of The Newspaper*, Section, Page(s).

Encyclopedias
Author's Last Name, First Initial. (Year of Publication). *Title Of Encyclopedia*, Edition Number. (Volume Number, Page(s)). Publishing City, State: Publisher's Name.

Interviews
Last Name of the Person Interviewed, First Initial. (Year of the Interview, Month and Day of Interview). Indicate Type of Interview.

Internet
Author's Last Name, First Initial. Title of Document. Retrieved Month Day, Year, from *http://www*.

Modern Language Association (MLA) Handbook for Writers of Research Papers

Books
- Single Author:
  Author's Last Name, Author's First Name. *Title Of The Book*. Publishing City, State: Publisher's Name, Year of Publication.
- Multiple Authors:
  Author's Last Name, Author's First Name, and Author's Last Name, Author's First Name. *Title Of The Book*. Publishing City, State: Publisher's Name, Year of Publication.

Magazines
- Weekly Magazine:
  Author's Last Name, Author's First Name. "Title Of The Article." *Title Of The Magazine* Day Month Year of Publication: Page(s).
- Monthly Magazine:
  Author's Last Name, Author's First Name. "Title Of The Article." *Title Of The Magazine* Month Year of Publication: Page(s).
- No Author:
  "Title Of The Article." *Title Of The Magazine* Day Month Year of Publication: Page(s).

Journals
Author's Last Name, Author' First Name. "Title Of The Journal Article." *Title Of The Journal* Volume Number. Issue Number (Year of Publication): Page(s).

Newspapers
Author's Last Name, Author's First Name. "Title Of The Article." *Title Of The Newspaper* Day Month Year of Publication: Section, Page(s).

Encyclopedias
Author's Last Name, Author's First Name. "Title Of The Article." *Title Of The Encyclopedia*. Year of Publication ed.

Interviews
Last Name of the Person Interviewed, Interviewee's First Name. Indicate Type of Interview. Day Month Year of Interview.

Internet
Title of Site. Ed, First Name of editor Last Name. Date of last update. Retrieved Day Month Year <http://www.>.

Endnotes

1. Quaratiello, A.R. (1997). *The College Student's Research Companion*. New York: Neal Schuman.
2. Hoffman, D. (1995). Political parties multiply-and divide-in Russia. *Miami Herald*, p. 24A.
3. Bartecchi, M.D., C. and et. (1994). The human costs of tobacco use. *The New England Journal of Medicine*, p. 910.
4. *Federal Register*. (1995). V.60, n.155, p. 41313–41375.
5. Gorman, C. (1995). How gender may bend your thinking. *Time*, p. 51.
6. Lusting, M & Koester, J. (1996). *Intercultural Competence: Interpersonal Communication Across Cultures*. New York: Harper Collins.

Chapter Five
KEY TERMS

Abbreviated Outline: _____

_____

Causal Patterning: _____

_____

Chronological
Patterning: _____

_____

Central Idea: _____

_____

Compare and
Contrast Patterning: _____

Complete Sentence
Outline: _____

_____

Connectors: _____

_____

Credibility: _____

_____

Ethos: _____

_____

Final Summary: _____

_____

Gaining
Attention: _____

General Purpose: _____

_____

Keyword Outline: _____

_____

Internal Summaries: _____

_____

Magnitude Patterning:_____

_____

Main Points: _____

_____

Outline: _____

_____

Preview Statements: _____

_____

Primary Sources: _____

_____

Pro and Con
  Patterning: _____

Relevance of
  the Topic: _____

Secondary Sources: _____

_____

Significance of
  the Topic: _____

Spatial Patterning: _____

_____

Specific Purpose: _____

_____

Subpoints: _____

_____

Summaries: _____

_____

Thesis Statement: _____

_____

Topical Patterning: _____

_____

Transitions: _____

_____

Types of Supporting _____

   Material: _____

Chapter Five
EXERCISES

Rearrange the following sentences to form an *introduction* to an informative speech.

- Germany is one of the most significant countries in Western Europe.
- I would like to speak to you this afternoon about why the Berlin Wall was originally built.
- Imagine yourself waking up one morning only to find that your city had been walled in.
- The Berlin Wall fell on November 9, 1989.
- I visited the Berlin Wall before it was knocked down.
- What happens in Europe directly affects the United States.

Attention:_____

_____

Significance:_____

_____

Relevance:_____

_____

Credibility:_____

_____

Thesis:_____

_____

Preview:_____

_____

Rearrange the following sentences to form an *introduction* to an informative speech.

- Although living only 37 years and dying at his own hand, Vincent VanGogh shined brighter than the stars that so fascinated him.
- Everybody interprets art in their own way.
- In the next few minutes I will be discussing Vincent VanGogh's Starry Night through brush stroke and color choice.
- I viewed VanGogh's Starry Night at the Metropolitan Museum in New York City.
- There are more than 1,000 drawings and some 800 paintings still on display today.
- Vincent VanGogh's struggle to find an identity was what led to his experimentation in art.

Attention:_____

_____

Significance:_____

_____

Relevance:_____

_____

Credibility:_____

_____

Thesis:_____

_____

Preview:_____

_____

Chapter Five
EXERCISES

Rearrange the following sentences to form a *conclusion* to an informative speech.

- There are three developmental stages in the first six months after a child is born.
- In summary, I wish all of you the joy and happiness in parenthood that my daughter has brought to my wife and me.
- The cognitive development stage is when babies start to display their personalities.
- The most rapidly changing part of a person's life is the first six months.
- The physical development is associated with the baby's length and weight.
- The sensory-motor development is a baby's ability to move.

Cue Ending:_____

_____

Thesis:_____

_____

    1st main point:_____

_____

    2nd main point:_____

_____

    3rd main point:_____

_____

Exit Line:_____

_____

Rearrange the following sentences to form a *conclusion* to an informative speech.

- The results of my survey indicated that most people know about these differences and they do cause problems in the communication process.
- In conclusion, I am reminded of the scenario where a man gets in trouble with his girlfriend because he forgot their anniversary yet he can remember statistics of most of the players on his favorite sport team.
- Since men and women do think differently, they also carry a conversation differently.
- So if you ever her a man ask why a woman can't think more like him or a woman why a man can't think more like her, just tell them it's not possible because it's biological and environmental.
- The results indicate that there are differences in thinking linked to the functions of the brain but researchers are skeptical about drawing conclusions.
- Scientific research is creating many questions in the field of male versus female thinking.

Cue Ending:_____

_____

Thesis:_____

_____

    1st main point:_____

_____

    2nd main point:_____

_____

    3rd main point:_____

_____

Exit Line:_____

_____

Chapter Five
EXERCISES

This exercise is designed to stress the importance of trying several different methods of gaining attention. In the space provided, briefly indicate how you might try to gain the audience's attention for each given speech topic. While we normally do not recommend speakers write their opening remarks word-for-word, this exercise is an exception.

TOPIC: THE MASS MEDIA

Methods of Gaining Attention:

Joke/Funny Story: _____
_____
_____
_____
_____
_____

Startling Facts/Opinions: _____
_____
_____
_____
_____
_____

Pertinent Quotation: _____
_____
_____
_____
_____

This exercise is designed to stress the importance of trying several different methods of gaining attention. In the space provided, briefly indicate how you might try to gain the audience's attention for each given speech topic. While we normally do not recommend speakers write their opening remarks word-for-word, this exercise is an exception.

TOPIC: **OUTER SPACE**

Methods of Gaining Attention:

Joke/Funny Story:
_____
_____
_____
_____
_____
_____
_____

Startling Facts/Opinions:
_____
_____
_____
_____
_____
_____
_____

Pertinent Quotation:
_____
_____
_____
_____
_____
_____

Chapter Five
EXERCISES

Using your original ideas for gaining attention, prepare an effective method of exiting the speech.

TOPIC: THE MASS MEDIA

Effective Exit Lines:

Joke/Funny Story:

    _____

    _____

    _____

    _____

    _____

    _____

Starting Facts/Opinions:

    _____

    _____

    _____

    _____

    _____

    _____

Pertinent Quotation:

    _____

    _____

    _____

    _____

    _____

Using your original ideas for gaining attention, prepare an effective method of exiting the speech.

TOPIC: **OUTER SPACE**

Effective Exit Lines:

Brief Demonstration: _____
_____
_____
_____
_____
_____
_____
_____

Create Suspense: _____
_____
_____
_____
_____
_____
_____

Rhetorical Question(s):   _____
_____
_____
_____
_____
_____

Chapter Five
EXERCISES

Indicate the *significance* and the *relevance* for the following potential speech topics.

TOPIC: **HOW TO WRITE A RESUME**

Significance:

_____

_____

_____

_____

_____

_____

Relevance:

_____

_____

_____

_____

_____

_____

Write a *central idea* for the following potential speech topics.

Benjamin Franklin:_____

_____

Crime in the US:_____

_____

Heart Disease:_____

_____

Solar Energy:_____

_____

Immigration:_____

_____

Nutrition:_____

_____

Teenage Pregnancy:_____

_____

Chapter Five
EXERCISES

Using the same potential speech topics and your central idea, write a *preview statement*.

Benjamin Franklin:_____

_____

Crime in the US:_____

_____

Heart Disease:_____

_____

Solar Energy:_____

_____

Immigration:_____

_____

Nutrition:_____

_____

Teenage Pregnancy:_____

_____

Chapter Five

EXERCISES

Informative Outline Preparation Sheet

General Purpose: _____

Specific Purpose: _____

Thesis: _____

I. Introduction

Attention: A. _____

_____

_____

_____

Significance: 1. _____

_____

_____

Relevance: 2. _____

_____

_____

Credibility: 3. _____

_____

_____

Thesis: B. _____

_____

_____

_____

Preview: C. _____
                 _____
                 _____
                 _____

                 1. _____
                    _____

                 2. _____
                    _____

                 3. _____
                    _____

II. Body
First Main Point   A. _____
                       _____
                       _____
                       _____

Subpoint of A   1. _____
                       _____

Subpoint of A   2. _____
                       _____

Subpoint of A   3. _____
                       _____

Second main point   B. _____
                       _____
                       _____
                       _____

Subpoint of B   1. _____
                       _____

Subpoint of B   2. _____
                       _____

234

Subpoint of B   3. _____

_____

Third Main Point   C. _____

_____

_____

_____

Subpoint of C   1. _____

_____

Subpoint of C   2. _____

_____

Subpoint of C   3. _____

_____

III. Conclusion
Cue Ending   A. _____

_____

_____

Final Summary   B. _____

_____

_____

1. _____

_____

2. _____

_____

3. _____

_____

Exit Line   C. _____

_____

_____

Chapter Five
REVIEW QUESTIONS

1. What are the benefits of using supporting material in a presentation?

   _____

   _____

   _____

2. What are the differences between primary and secondary sources?

   _____

   _____

   _____

3. Explain the goal of informative speaking.

   _____

   _____

   _____

4. List and define the four types of informative speeches.

   a._____

   b._____

   c._____

   d._____

5. Which part of a presentation should you organize first—the introduction, the body, or the conclusion?

   _____

   Why? _____

   _____

6. Define the following organizational patterns:

   a. Chronological:

   _____

   _____

b. Topical:

_____

_____

c. Topical Compare and Contrast:

_____

_____

d. Topical Causal:

_____

_____

e. Topical Pro-Con:

_____

_____

f. Topical Spatial:

_____

_____

g. Magnitude:

_____

_____

7. List the six primary goals of an introduction.

a. _____

b. _____

c. _____

d. _____

e. _____

f. _____

8. Explain the difference between significance and relevance.

_____

_____

_____

9. When determining the significance of a speech topic, explain how each of the following variables relates to forming an introduction of a presentation:

   a. Urgency: _____

   _____

   b. Propensity: _____

   _____

   c. Usefulness: _____

   _____

10. Explain why simply indicating the significance of a speech topic may not be enough to generate audience interest in the presentation.

    _____

    _____

    _____

11. Why should a speaker preview his/her main points in the introduction of a presentation?

    _____

    _____

    _____

12. What are the three main purposes of a conclusion in an informative speech?

    a. _____

    b. _____

    c. _____

13. Generally, what is the most effective method for exiting an informative presentation?

    _____

    _____

    _____

14. List and provide an example for each of the four types of connectors a speaker may use in a presentation.

    a. _____   :   _____

       _____

       _____

b. _____ : _____
_____
_____

c. _____ : _____
_____
_____

d. _____ : _____
_____
_____

Name: _____   **Date:** _____

Narrative

Speaker's Name: _____

	(needs work)						(excellent)	
Posture	1	2	3	4	5	6	7	8	9
Clear\loud voice	1	2	3	4	5	6	7	8	9
Variation tone\pitch	1	2	3	4	5	6	7	8	9
Uses of um or uh	1	2	3	4	5	6	7	8	9
Organization	1	2	3	4	5	6	7	8	9
Eye contact	1	2	3	4	5	6	7	8	9
Confidence	1	2	3	4	5	6	7	8	9
Overall rating	1	2	3	4	5	6	7	8	9

Comments:_____

_____

_____

_____

_____

_____

_____

_____

_____

_____

_____

Student Critique Sheet— Informative Speech

Speaker's Name: _____

Rate the speaker on each point:

5	4	3	2	1	0
excellent	good	average	fair	poor	not present

_____ Pause

_____ Gained attention of listeners

_____ Significance of topic to humankind

_____ Relevance of topic to our times

_____ Credibility statement

_____ Previewed main points of speech

_____ Main points clear and logical

_____ Variety of supporting material

_____ Main points fully supported

_____ Internal summaries effective

_____ Cue audience of ending

_____ Summarized main points of speech

_____ Effective exit line linked to attention getter

_____ Strong eye contact with entire class

_____ Extemporaneous/conversational delivery

_____ Words articulated clearly

_____ Appropriate nonverbal communication

_____ Problem with um's and uh's

_____ Rate of speaking (too fast or too slow)

_____ Visual aids meet five criteria

_____ Visuals strengthen impact of message

Speech Evaluation Form

5	4	3	2	1	Time: _____
excellent	good	average	fair	poor	

Introduction
_____ gained attention and interest
_____ introduced topic clearly
_____ established credibility
_____ thesis
_____ previewed body of speech

Body
_____ main points clear
_____ main points fully supported
_____ organization well planned
_____ language accurate
_____ language clear, concise
_____ effective internal summaries

Conclusion
_____ prepared audience for ending
_____ final summary
_____ effective exit line

Delivery
_____ maintained eye contact
_____ used voice effectively
_____ used nonverbal communication effectively
_____ presented visual aids well

Overall Evaluation
_____ topic challenging
_____ specific purpose well chosen

Chapter Five
POWERPOINT SLIDES

- Informative speech types
- General purpose
- Specific purpose
- Rules for specific purpose
- Research resources
- Rules for developing main points
- Types of supporting material
- Guidelines for using testimony
- Connectors
- Introduction
- Attention getting devices
- Significance statement
- Relevance statement
- Credibility statement
- Thesis statement
- Preview statement
- Conclusion
- Full circle
- Benefits of an outline
- Tips for preparing an outline
- Different types of outlines
- Q & A

INFORMATIVE SPEECH TYPES

- Demonstration

- Description

- Definition

- Narrative

GENERAL PURPOSE

- To Inform

- To Persuade

- To Entertain

SPECIFIC PURPOSE

- At the end of my speech, the audience will be able to explain 4 treatments for cancer.

- At the end of my speech, the audience will be able to list 2 contributions Hemingway has made to the literary world.

RULES FOR SPECIFIC PURPOSE

- 12 Words

- Contain a number

- Full sentence

- Statement not a question

- Measurable type of verb

RESEARCH RESOURCES

- Internet

- Books

- Periodicals

- Newspapers

- Computer Data Bases

252

RESEARCH RESOURCES

- Government documents

- Encyclopedias

- Personal interviews

- Writing for information

- Calling for information

253

RULES FOR
DEVELOPING THE MAIN POINTS

- Limit the main points

- Use simple and concise language

- Use only one idea for each main point

- Be certain the main points are consistent

254

TYPES OF
SUPPORTING MATERIAL

- Definitions

- Examples

- Narratives

- Analogies

- Testimony

- Statistics

GUIDELINES
FOR USING TESTIMONY

- Make sure quotations are accurate.

- Use testimony from unbiased sources.

- Use testimony that your audience will respect.

- State the credentials of your source.

CONNECTORS

- Transitions

- Preview Statements

- Summary Statements
  1) Internal
  2) Final

INTRODUCTION

- A. Gain Attention

    1. Significance

    2. Relevance

    3. Credibility

- B. Central Idea

- C. Preview Statement

ATTENTION GETTING DEVICES

- Startling facts

- Actual or rhetorical questions

- Joke or humorous story

- Actual or hypothetical illustrations

- Reference to specific occasion

- Quote or phrase

- Brief demonstration

SIGNIFICANCE STATEMENT

- **Urgency**
  - Immediate attention to the topic is required.

- **Propensity**
  - The problem is likely to get worse.

- **Usefulness**
  - The audience can use the information now.

RELEVANCE STATEMENT

- How does this information relate to this audience?

- How does this information affect this audience at this particular time and place?

261

CREDIBILITY STATEMENT

- State your qualifications

- Dress appropriately

- Maintain your composure

262

THESIS STATEMENT

- **Central Idea**
  - **One sentence summary of entire topic.**

- **Claim**
  - **One sentence summary of your position on your subject.**

    Policy

    Fact

    Value

PREVIEWING
YOUR MAIN POINTS

- List all of your main points

- State in chronological

- Be brief and to the point

- Connection to the body of speech

- Pause prior to the body of the speech

SPEECH

CONCLUSION

- A. Cue audience of ending

- B. Final summary

- C. Conclude in memorable way

FULL CIRCLE

Introduction

Body

Conclusion

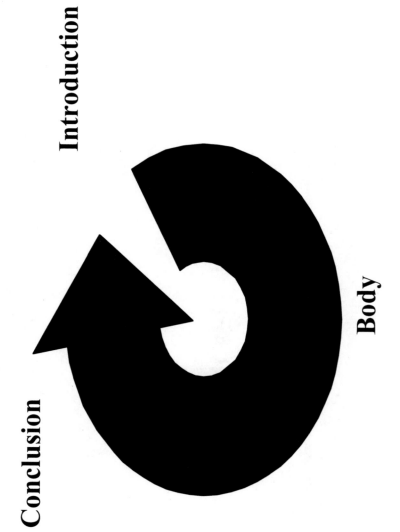

BENEFITS OF OUTLINING

Enables You To:

- See how speech is organized

- See amount of supporting material

- Revise speech

- Receive feedback

- Practice

267

TIPS FOR
PREPARING AN OUTLINE

- Consistent notation

- Consistent indentation

- One phrase/sentence per entry

- Reference material

DIFFERENT TYPES OF OUTLINES

- **Full content**

- **Abbreviated**

- **Key word**

Q & A SESSION

- Anticipate questions

- Keep answers short and focused

- Admit if you do not know answer

- Incorporate question into your answer

- Never point or use arm to call on audience member

PART THREE

PERSUASIVE SPEECHES

CHAPTER 6
Speaking to Persuade

"Speech is power: Speech is to persuade, to convert, to compel."
Ralph Waldo Emerson

The art of persuasion is as old as oral communication itself. From the earliest of times human beings have verbally tried to persuade others to change an existing opinion or to take or avoid a physical action.

History has recorded several speakers who were very persuasive, including: Gorgias, Cicero, Adolph Hitler, and John F. Kennedy. These speakers are well-known for their rhetorical skills. You too face everyday situations that require you to be persuasive. Trying to convince your parents to raise your allowance or to borrow their new car, convincing your friends to see a movie, or speaking before the student council prior to an important school election are all examples of communicating for the purpose of persuasion.

Informative versus Persuasive Speeches

There are three basic types of public presentations—the speech to inform; the speech to persuade; and the speech to entertain. The ancient Greek philosopher Aristotle referred to these presentation types as **docere, movere,** and **placere,** respectively. If your intent is to inform your audience, you are simply trying to raise their level of knowledge about the topic. For an informative speech, you do not have any intentions of promoting a desired course of action nor are you trying to make the audience agree with any of your opinions. Remember, from Chapter Five, an informative presentation may define, clarify, and/or explain a subject.

In contrast to the informative speech, a persuasive presentation has, as its goal, one or more of the following: (1) to change an already existing belief, attitude, or value held by the audience, (2) to reinforce an existing belief, attitude or value, (3) to promote a physical action and/or (4) to discourage a physical action.

Docere
Informative speech

Movere
Persuasive speech

Placere
Special occasion speech

Goals of Persuasion

Goals	Example
■ to change an already existing belief, attitude, or value	You are wrong about nuclear energy.
■ to reinforce an existing belief, attitude, or value	You are wrong about nuclear energy.
■ to promote a physical action	You should protest against nuclear energy.
■ to discourage a physical action	You should not join in the protest against nuclear energy.

Please notice that each example has a different goal. You are either trying to change, reinforce, promote, or discourage the audience.

Claim
A type of thesis statement that states a speaker's position on an issue; it is used with persuasive speeches

Persuasive Speech Types

To clarify the different goals of persuasive speaking and differentiate between persuasive speech types, it is necessary to understand the role of the thesis statement (the claim) in a persuasive speech. A **claim** is the conclusion you want your audience to adopt at the completion of the presentation. It is not necessarily your stated goal, but rather the actual conclusion you want the audience to adopt.

Your claim will assert one of the following three conclusions:

- Something is true or false. (a fact)
- Something or someone is "good" or "bad." (a value)
- Something should or should not be done. (a policy)

Central idea
A type of thesis statement used with informative speeches; it is a one sentence summary of entire presentation

Just as the **central idea** served as the thesis statement in an informative presentation, the claim serves as the thesis statement in a persuasive speech. Your claim should be one concise statement in the introduction of the speech that clearly indicates what you want the audience to believe, feel, and/or do at the completion of the presentation.

While there is only one type of central idea for the informative speech, there are three very distinct types of claims for persuasive presentations. These are claims of fact, value and policy. These claims closely coincide with the stated goals of persuasive speech types. This will become more clear as you understand the different types of persuasive speeches.

Persuasive Speeches of Fact

The first type of persuasive presentation is a speech where you are attempting to convince the audience that your view of reality is accurate. Basically, you are trying to convince the audience that your conclusion on the speech subject is correct or true. In this type of persuasive presentation you would use a claim of fact. A **claim of fact** states the speaker's opinion on the topic as if it were true.

Do not confuse a claim of fact with an actual fact. A claim of fact is simply the speakers assertion that something is a fact (true). For example, claims of fact might be:

- Sexual harassment in the workplace increased during the past five years.
- Global warming is a hoax.
- Permitting homosexuals in the military will hurt morale.

In each example you would be attempting to convince the audience that your view on the subject is correct: sexual harassment actually did increase during the past five years, global warming is really a hoax, or, permitting homosexuals in the military will indeed hurt morale. In each case you are stating your opinion on the subject. You are either attempting to change or reinforce an existing **belief** about the subject. If you look at the three examples more closely, you will notice that each claim of fact is slightly different. The first example, *Sexual harassment in the workplace increased during the past five years*, is a factual claim regarding the past. This claim is concluding that something has occurred. The second example, *Global warming is a hoax*, is a factual claim with respect to the present. This claim is concluding that something is happening now. The third example, *Permitting homosexuals in the military will hurt morale*, is a factual claim about the future. This claim is predicting what will happen in the future.

Persuasive Speeches of Value

When you are trying to convince an audience that a proposition is either good or bad, just or unjust, moral or immoral, right or wrong, and so on, you are asking them to make a value judgment. A speaker who makes an evaluation of a person, object, or situation is asserting a value claim. A **claim of value** states a value judgment the speaker wants the audience to conclude. The following are examples of claims of value.

- The death penalty is just punishment for convicted murderers.
- It is wrong to cheat on examinations.
- The healthcare system in the United States is better than socialized medicine in Canada.

Claim of Fact
States the speaker's opinion as if it were true

Belief
A non-evaluative assertion that individuals believe to be true or false

Claim of Value
States a value judgment the speaker wants the audience to conclude

Just as a factual claim tries to change or reinforce a belief, a value claim attempts to change or reinforce an existing attitude or value.

Absolute Value Claim
Judges an entity according to a fixed standard

There are two different types of value claims. An *absolute value claim* judges an entity according to a fixed standard. For example, the claim *Abortion is morally wrong,* is an absolute value claim. This statement asserts that there is a fixed standard, an absolute moral principle, that abortion always violates. Under no circumstance would abortion be morally acceptable. Other examples include, *Physician-assisted Suicide is Just* and *Exploitation of the Environment is Reprehensible.*

Relative Value Claim
An assertion that one entity is preferred over another

In contrast to absolute value claims, there are claims that are relative. A *relative value claim* is an assertion that one entity is preferred over another. For example, *The Legalization of Narcotics is Preferable to the Overcrowding of the Country's Prison System,* is a relative claim. This claim is not evaluating the legalization of narcotics against an absolute value and concluding that in all instances the legalization of narcotics would be beneficial. Instead, it is asserting that in this particular instance, the legalization of narcotics is preferable to the overcrowding of the country's prisons. The speaker is evaluating one entity versus another entity and concluding that on a hierarchal scale, one is preferable to the other. Other examples include, *City University is Not as Good as State,* or *Ronald Reagan Was a Better President than Lyndon Johnson.*

It is especially important to choose the value term for your claim of value very carefully. Notice the following examples of claims of value and how the intensity of each increases:

- The use of animals for cosmetic testing is wrong.
- The use of animals for cosmetic testing is unjust.
- The use of animals for cosmetic testing in immoral.

In each claim of value the intensity of the value term increases. The original claim asserts that testing is "wrong." The second claim is a bit stronger and uses the word "unjust." The third example and the use of the word "immoral" is worded the strongest.

Persuasive Speeches of Policy

Claim of Policy
States a desired course of action

The final type of persuasive speech promotes or discourages a course of action. A **claim of policy** clearly states a desired course of action and in most instances contains the word "should." There are three basic types of policy claims.

Current Policies Should Change

- The Food and Drug Administration should adopt federal standards for seafood.

■ Congress should pass stricter legislation in support of President Clinton's initiative to restrict the sale of cigarettes to minors.

Current Policies Should Not Change

■ The government should not increase the national minimum wage.
■ The university should not impose a mandatory 15 credit hours per semester.

Current Behaviors Should Change

■ Everyone should become an organ donor.
■ All students should register for a course in public speaking.

A persuasive presentation that has as its intention the adoption of a physical action or the discouragement of a physical action should use a claim of policy as the **thesis statement.**

Once again, there are three basic types of persuasive presentations. Your goal may be to reinforce or change a factual belief, to change or reinforce an existing attitude or value, and/or promote or discourage a course of action or behavior.

Thesis Statement
A sentence that clearly tells the audience what the speaker will be discussing

---

Persuasive Claims

Claim of	Goal
FACT:	Change or reinforce an existing belief.

Past
    Present
    Future	

VALUE:	Change or reinforce an existing attitude or value.
Absolute Relative	
POLICY:	Promote or discourage change, a course of action, or behavior

Keep Existing Policy
    Do Not Change Existing Policy
    Change Behavior	

Selecting a Persuasive Speech Topic

To select a persuasive speech topic, you should follow the same guidelines you used for selecting an informative speech topic (Informative Speeches Chapter Five). Your topic should meet the following criteria:

- The topic should be interesting to you.
- You should have a working knowledge of your topic.
- The topic should be appropriate for the occasion.
- The topic should be appropriate for the audience.
- The topic should be narrow enough to be adequately covered in the specified time limit.

Current
Of present time

Controversial
A subject that sparks different viewpoints

There are two additional guidelines that may be useful when selecting a persuasive speech subject. Your speech topic should be **current** and **controversial.** It is best to speak about a subject that is timely. It does not have to necessarily be on the front page of the newspaper, but your subject should be one that the audience will find relevant and *current.* The second additional criteria for a persuasive presentation is that the subject should be *controversial.* By selecting a subject that is debatable you will increase your chances of selecting a subject that your audience will find interesting.

Brainstorming
A method of generating ideas

When **brainstorming** for potential topics to speak about it is helpful to review popular news magazines such as *Time, Newsweek,* and *US News and World Report.* These magazines are easy to read and they report on national and international news items of interest. You should also review your local newspaper or, if you do not live in a large city, you should read the *New York Times,* the *Washington Post, The Los Angeles Times,* the *Chicago Tribune,* or another national newspaper. For local topics, which may not necessarily be of national interest, you should review your local newspapers, campus newspapers, the local evening news on television, and your local and campus radio stations.

Potential Topics for Persuasive Speeches

- The President should (or should not) be limited to a single six-year term.
- Drug addicts should or (or should not) be put in hospitals for medical treatment instead of in prisons for punishment.
- Solar energy is (or is not) a viable alternate fuel source.
- All owners of firearms should (or should not) be required to register their weapons with the police.
- The Social Security System should (or should not) be voluntary for employees.

- The death penalty for murderers should (or should not) be abolished.
- The death penalty should (or should not) be imposed on juveniles.
- Electroshock treatment is (or is not) a humane form of therapy.
- Every student should (or should not) be required to learn a foreign language.
- American workers should (or should not) be guaranteed a three-day weekend by law.
- Assault weapons should (or should not) be outlawed.
- Immigration into the US should (or should not) be restricted.
- Churches should (or should not) be required to pay taxes.
- The US should (or should not) cut off all foreign aid to dictatorships.

The Persuasion Process

While many people think that a single message has the power to persuade, this is usually not the case. It is best to think of persuasion as a **process** rather than a single event.

Just like the communication process, there are several factors that work together over a period of time to achieve a desired result. In each process the following variables must be accounted for:

- The speakers perception of the audience.
- The audience's perception of the speaker.
- The actual formulation and organization of the message.

The Audience

It is essential that speakers conduct a thorough **situational, demographic, and psychological analysis** of their intended audiences before preparing a speech. You should always consider your speech's purpose and goals, where you will be speaking, the length of time permitted for the speech, and your intended audience. To hypothesize about what your audience believes or may find appealing, you must conduct a demographic and psychological analysis of the audience. You originally considered the audience's demographics and perceived needs when selecting a speech topic (Chapter Three). However, when presenting a persuasive speech it is important that you consider your audience's beliefs, values, and attitudes in more detail.

Advertisers are very aware of the need to take into account the perceived beliefs, values, and attitudes their audiences. When a company markets a product it first considers the attributes of the product and then how best to convince a particular audience to purchase the product.

Process
A series of actions, changes, or functions that bring about an end or a result

Situational Analysis
Under what conditions will an individual be speaking

Demographic Analysis
Who the audience members are in terms of: age, gender, level of education, etc.

Psychological Analysis
What the audience members think

Pepsi's *A New Generation,* and Oldsmobile's *It's Not Your Father's Oldsmobile Anymore,* are both persuasive appeals based on the companies' perception of what a younger audience would like. Ford's *Have You Driven A Ford Lately* campaign was geared towards reclaiming customers who began purchasing other manufacturer's automobiles. Knowing your audiences perceived beliefs, values, and attitudes will help you tailor your speech to fit their needs.

Belief
A non-evaluative assertion that individuals believe to be true or false

A **belief** is a non-evaluative assertion people believe to be true or false. For example, each of the following assertions are classified as beliefs:

- God exists.
- The United Nations has outlived its usefulness.
- Defendant X is guilty.

Attitudes
Govern our predispositions

While beliefs are non-evaluative—they do not assert if something is good or bad—they are the basis for making evaluative assertions which are called **attitudes.** For instance, the assertion that drinking and liver disease are related is a belief. As a result of this belief, you may conclude drinking is bad. The conclusion "drinking is bad" is an attitude you formulated based on your beliefs about drinking.

As you might have imagined, not all people believe the same things to be true or false. Different people/cultures have different sets of beliefs, as do individuals within each culture. For example, people raised in predominately Christian cultures probably believe that Jesus Christ is their means to salvation. Hindus, Jews, Muslims, Buddhists, and many others probably do not agree with this belief. In addition, not all people may believe an assertion equally. You may believe "Defendant X" may be guilty and I may be certain "Defendant X" is guilty. Therefore, beliefs are best thought of on a continuum.

The Belief Continuum

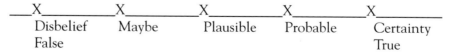

Disbelief	Maybe	Plausible	Probable	Certainty
False				True

Supporting Material
Information that defines, supports, explains and/or clarifies a point/argument

Generally, the more evidence or **supporting material** a person accepts in support of the assertion, the higher the belief will be on the continuum. The less evidence or supporting material a person accepts in support of the assertion, the lower the belief will be placed on the continuum.

In Chapter Five, Informative Speeches, we discussed several types of evidence or supporting material. At this point let us reconsider the role evidence has on beliefs by looking at the first example, *God exists.* If we were to ask you to determine if the statement *God exists* is a fact or an opinion, we are certain that we would have many people claiming it is a fact and many people claiming it is an opinion. For those of you who answered that the assertion *God exists* is a fact, you could probably list several reasons why you believe God exists. You may have listed a few of the following reasons:

- The Bible
- My Religious upbringing
- I trust my spiritual leader
- I trust my parents
- Our own existence
- The order in the universe

These reasons for accepting the claim *God exists* are called supporting material or evidence. For those of you who answered that the assertion *God exists* is an opinion, you probably could list the same reasons. What then is the difference between a **belief** we call a *fact* and a belief we call an *opinion?* The difference between a fact and an opinion is the degree to which an individual believes the evidence that supports the assertion. In other words, an individual forms a belief about the supporting material of an assertion and places this belief on the belief continuum. As a result of how strongly a person believes the supporting material to be true or false, this determines how strongly he/she believes the original assertion to be true or false. The figure below illustrates the difference between facts and opinions with respect to supporting material.

Supporting Material Determines Facts and Opinions

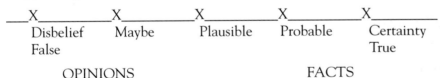

X	X	X	X	X
Disbelief	Maybe	Plausible	Probable	Certainty
False				True

          OPINIONS   FACTS

When you are gathering supporting material you need to be very conscious of your audience. You need to consider how they will view your sources on the belief continuum, as well as what their overall beliefs are about your subject.

Values are concepts people believe to be generally desirable or generally undesirable. Each of us has a set of values that influences, in one way or another, our beliefs, attitudes, and actions. These values serve as guidelines by which we live our lives.

Our beliefs about whether something is good or bad, moral or immoral, or right or wrong, will influence how we think and what we do.

Belief
A non-evaluative assertion that individuals believe to be true or false

Fact
Based on reality/truth

Opinion
Held with confidence, but not substantiated by proof

Values
Concepts individuals believe to be generally desirable or undesirable

If you believe something to be immoral you are more likely not to engage in the activity. If you believe something to be useful or good, you are more likely to engage in the activity.

Just as beliefs are best thought of in terms of a continuum, so are our values. Our value system may range from strongly undesirable to strongly desirable. For instance, how do you value money and personal success? What if you had to weigh your value of money and success verses human kindness and support? Which would you place higher on the continuum?

Value Continuum

___X_____X_____X_____X_____X_____
Strongly   Somewhat   Neutral   Somewhat   Strongly
Undesirable   Undesirable Desirable   Desirable   Desirable

Attitudes
Govern or predispositions towards others and things

As mentioned earlier, an **attitude** is an evaluative assertion that is based on numerous other beliefs and resulting attitudes. "An attitude refers to the thoughts, feelings, and behavioral intentions that govern our predispositions toward people, situations, events, and things."[1] For that reason attitudes are very difficult to measure in other people.

In an attempt to measure a person's attitude about a subject, researchers have developed an attitude continuum similar to the continuum for beliefs and values. The only difference is the assignment of numerical values to points on the continuum.

Attitudinal Continuum

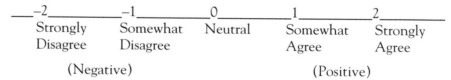

___-2_____-1_____0_____1_____2_____
Strongly   Somewhat   Neutral   Somewhat   Strongly
Disagree   Disagree   Agree   Agree

        (Negative)   (Positive)

When asked a series of related questions about a subject, a final numerical value is the result. This number is then placed on the scale to determine what the general attitude of the person may be on the subject. For instance, take the example of attempting to determine an audience's attitude about welfare reform.

Place your answers to the following questions on the scale above.

- People on welfare are lazy.
- People on welfare do not want to work.
- The welfare system is too generous.
- People take advantage of the welfare system.

Obviously you cannot conduct an actual survey of every audience you speak to; however, you will want to make some general assumptions about their attitudes towards your speech subject. After hypothesizing about what attitudes they hold about the subject, you should hypothesize as to why and how they formulated these attitudes. You will need to ask yourself, "Based on what beliefs have they formed these attitudes?" The answers to these questions will help you formulate a persuasive/organizational strategy in the speech.

The Speaker
The audience will also form an attitude about you, the speaker. As discussed in Chapter Five, in order to enhance your credibility in the introduction of a presentation, you must consider what your audience thinks about you. Aristotle defines the speakers **credibility** as **ethos.** There are three tests for establishing ethos:

- Does your audience believe you have good sense?
- Does the audience believe you have good will?
- Does the audience believe you have moral character?

The first test is that of **good sense.** The audience will form an attitude about your knowledge of the topic. They will ask themselves, "How much do you know about the subject?" and "How well have you researched the subject?" If they believe you are an intelligent, reasonable person who is well-versed in the topic, the audience members are more likely to form a positive attitude about you.

The second test is that of **good will.** How sincere are you? Audiences—and rightfully so—do not trust people who insult their listeners, speak down to them, treat them as if they were inferior, and downplay logical opposing viewpoints.

The third and final test is that of **good moral character.** How virtuous are you? Do you have a high moral purpose? Audiences trust people who do not distort the truth or mislead them. Research has indicated that audiences are most concerned with the following virtues:[2]

Credibility
States the speaker's qualifications on the subject matter, their physical appearance, and their composure

Ethos
Aristotle's term for credibility

Good Sense
Audience's attitude of how well the speaker knows the topic

Good Will
Audience's attitude of how sincere the speaker is

Good Moral Character
Audience's attitude of how trustworthy the speaker is

Houser's Virtues

■ Justice	Is the person concerned about what is right?
■ Courage	Does the person believe in his/her convictions?
■ Temperance	Does the person use self-restraint in his/her conduct?
■ Generosity	Is the person selfless and giving if necessary?
■ Magnanimity	Is the person noble in thought and forgiving?
■ Magnificence	Is the person committed to the highest quality of life?
■ Prudence	Does the person use sound judgment and take sound advice?

Ethos
Aristotle's term for credibility

To demonstrate the importance advertisers place on **ethos** and persuasion, consider the number of products that use spokespersons. Advertisers select people they feel a particular target audience will trust or wish to emulate. If the products are being marketed for a younger generation, the spokespersons may be sports stars such as Shaquille O'Neil, Michael Jordan, or Deon Sanders. Please note that other popular stars, such as Michael Jackson and O.J. Simpson, no longer appear in advertisements because the advertisers believe the public does not perceive either as having much ethos.

The Message

Logos
Aristotle's term related to the logic of the argument that is being made

After conducting an analysis of your audience's beliefs, values, and attitudes, you are now prepared to begin thinking about various persuasive strategies. The appeal to reason or logic is what Aristotle called **logos.** Logos is the logical order of proofs, good reasons, and supporting material a speaker uses in order to persuade an audience to accept the original claim. In short, logos is the arguments a speaker uses to support the presentation's thesis statement.

Thesis Statement
A sentence that clearly tells the audience what the speaker will be discussing

As a speaker you will be constructing arguments in support of your **thesis statement** and presenting these arguments orally. You will be attempting to provide sufficient reasons why the audience should accept your original claim. For a review of the different types of supporting material, review Chapter Five, Informative Speeches.

Organizing a Claim of Policy Presentation

One of the most widely used organizational techniques for persuasive speaking was developed by speech instructor Alan Monroe (1903–1975). Combining his knowledge of sales training and a keen understanding of human motivation he developed an organizational pattern that is easily adopted by public speakers that are attempting to persuade an audience to take or avoid a physical action.

Motivated Sequence
An organizational pattern used in a claim of policy speech

Barriers to Listening
Obstacles that prevent a person from listening to a message even though they hear the message

Based on the expectations of the listeners, the **motivated sequence** organizes a speaker's material so that the listener is anticipating what the speaker will (ought to) say next in the presentation. That is to say, if the speaker conducts a proper situational and audience analysis, the speaker will address the listener's expectations and questions as they might naturally arise in the presentation. By anticipating the audience's organizational and thought patterning, the speaker is able to more successfully avoid the natural **barriers to listening.**

There may have been an instance when you were listening to a speaker and you had trouble following the organization of the speech. You may have wondered why the speaker did not say something at a particular moment in a presentation when it seemed logical or appropriate. Or, you may have wondered why the speaker included certain information in the presentation at that particular point, when it may have appeared to you to be more relevant earlier in the speech. In these instances, the speaker probably missed an opportunity to effectively persuade you of his/her **claim** because of how the speaker organized the information in the presentation.

Claim
A type of thesis statement that states a speakers position on an issue; it is used with persuasive speeches

Suppose a speaker wants you to donate blood to the American Red Cross. It is natural for you to expect the speaker to provide sufficient reasons for you to consider donating blood and/or to adequately explain the necessity or urgency of the situation. How much blood is needed? Why is there a shortage of blood?

After establishing why blood is needed, the speaker should explain where you can donate blood. If the speaker had explained where you could donate blood prior to establishing why your blood was needed, you may have been confused or irritated. "Why are you telling me where to donate blood now? I'm not sure I want to!"

This previous instance is an example of how the motivated sequence works. The speaker attempts to organize his/her information based on the logical and reasonable expectations and anticipation of the intended audience.

Reasoning and Monroe's Motivated Sequence

Culture affects the way an individual will reason a point. In fact, what is even considered to be an "issue" will vary from culture to culture. In the United States, individuals debate issues such as: euthanasia, homelessness, equality of the sexes, and gay rights. To some cultures, these topics are not issues at all, but simply a way of life. In the United States, individuals think of these issues as problems and solutions and we employ Monroe's Motivated Sequence; however, Monroe's paradigm does not conform to issues when a culture sees problems as having only one solution. For example, when an individual perceives a bad relationship with the Deities (Gods), no persuasion is necessary in this case because if there is a problem with something, then the collective experiences of the group or the culture tells them what the answer is. There is no other possible solution that needs to be debated. The Deity is upset. Therefore, public speakers from Asian cultures quote from ancient and sacred texts. Rarely are contemporary quotes used. It is historical precedent which has stood the test of time that convinces an audience. Even empirical data can be refuted by a sacred text. As a public speaker, it is important to know that persuasive topics and the means of reasoning vary across cultures.

Monroe's Motivated Sequence

There are five basic steps in *Monroe's Motivated Sequence*. Each step is followed chronologically by the speaker when organizing a persuasive presentation using a claim of policy.

The Attention Step

Just as in an informative presentation a speaker must gain the attention of his/her audience, a speaker attempting to persuade an audience must do the same. This is only logical. If you are attempting to persuade an audience to take or avoid a physical action, you must first have their undivided attention.

Far too often speakers assume that simply because the audience is present they will be interested in the topic. This is not always the case. To prove the point that attendance does not equal attentiveness, recall the last boring lecture you attended. You may have been in attendance, but you were not very attentive. When presenting an informative speech, a speaker gains the audience's attention in the introduction. In a persuasive speech, using the Motivated Sequence, a speaker starts off with the *Attention Step*.

As you recall from Chapter Five, Informative Speeches, there are several techniques for **gaining and maintaining the attention** of your audience. Briefly, these include but are not limited to: a pertinent rhetorical question, a brief illustration, a startling fact, or a pertinent quotation. Please keep in mind there is no magic formula for gaining the audience's attention. Simply using one or more of the attention-getting techniques does not guarantee you success. Other factors to consider are the Aristotelian proofs of **ethos, pathos,** and **logos.** How did you deliver the information? Were your words clear, appropriate, audible, and spoken at an acceptable rate? Did you use appropriate nonverbal communication? Your delivery, word selection, nonverbal communication, speech subject, and the audience's perception of your credibility, knowledgeability, and trustworthiness all may influence in various degrees your ability to gain and maintain the audience's attention.

In an attempt to further gain and maintain the attention of the audience, the speaker should also clearly indicate the **significance** or the general importance of the topic. The basic question, "Why is this topic important to humankind?" should be answered early in the presentation. More specifically, you need to make the connection between your topic and the audience. You need to ask yourself how this topic affects my audience. It may be important to humankind, but how does it relate to my audience.

If you are unable to persuade an audience that your topic is important, how can you possibly hope to persuade an audience to take or avoid a physical action? The answer is obvious, "You cannot."

You do not have to persuade the audience the topic is the most important issue in their lives. However, you must convince the audience the topic is of some level of importance and this level of importance requires their attention.

Be careful not to overstate the significance of your topic. Audiences are not dumb. If the audience feels a speaker is exaggerating the significance of a topic they may question the speaker's credibility. Once the audience questions the credibility (ethos) of the speaker, they begin to question other information in the presentation. If the audience perceives a speaker is not being completely honest with them or exaggerating information, the speaker is probably not going to be successful in the presentation.

There are instances when the significance of a topic is not enough to persuade an audience that the topic is worthy of their attention. Often a listener will concede a topic is of some importance but not relevant to his/her life. For example, the ethnic conflict in the former Yugoslavia is significant. Tens of thousands of people have been killed. However, some audience members may feel the civil war is taking place in a distant country half-way around the world. They may not be members of any of the ethnic groups involved in the conflict nor are any of their immediate friends. The topic does not appear to be relevant to these audience members. What should a speaker do in this instance?

The speaker should find a method for indicating the **relevance** of the topic to the audience. Granted, the former country of Yugoslavia is far away and the audience may not be composed of members of the warring ethnic groups. However, the conflict may be more relevant than you may think. For instance, World War I was the result of ethnic conflict in this very same area. The speaker could describe the atrocities of the conflict. The speaker could explain how the countries of the world are more interdependent and the likelihood of neighboring country's becoming involved may increase. Or, the speaker may want to explain the role the United States could play in the conflict, and in that case United States involvement would immediately increase the relevancy of the topic. Any of these examples, or a combination of the examples, increases the likelihood the listener will not only view the topic as significant, but will also recognize the relevance of the subject.

A speaker should also attempt to increase his/her **credibility** in the introduction. The audience is constantly forming perceptions with respect to a speaker's credibility. Is this person telling the truth? Does this person know what he/she is talking about? A speaker's nonverbal communication is often perceived by the audience as a sign that the speaker is intelligent, honest, and believable. A speaker who mumbles may be perceived by the audience as untrustworthy. A speaker who dresses inappropriately may be perceived by the audience as unknowledgeable on the subject, and so on.

Relevance
Tells the audience why this speech topic is important to them

Credibility
States the speaker's qualifications on the subject matter, their physical appearance, and their composure

Aside from a speaker's nonverbal communication, a speaker should utilize the introduction (Attention Step) to boost his/her credibility with the audience verbally. If you have firsthand experience with a subject you should indicate this experience in the presentation's introduction. If you are attempting to persuade an audience to buy environmentally safe products and you are a member of an environmental organization, the audience may perceive you as being more knowledgeable and trustworthy (i.e., more persuasive) if you acknowledge your experience early in the presentation. When a speaker is introduced his/her accomplishments and expertise are often so noted. If you are not being introduced or the introduction does not completely establish your credibility with the audience, you should use the Attention Step of your presentation to do so.

Clearly state the **claim of policy** in the introduction of the presentation. This single statement may be spoken louder, softer, faster, or slower than the information preceding and following it. In either case, the claim should be clearly recognized by the audience. The audience should never have to guess at your intent in the presentation.

The final step in the Attention Step is to provide the audience with a brief preview of the presentation. In practice, this preview step is slightly different than the **preview statement** used in the introduction of an informative presentation. In an informative presentation the preview statement forecasts the main points of the presentation. In a presentation using a claim of policy, the preview statement forecasts the speaker's strongest arguments in support of the claim.

Your strongest arguments may be primarily in one portion of the presentation, or they may be in various portions. The preview statement is best explained after you are more familiar with the remaining organizational steps in Monroe's Motivated Sequence.

This completes the Attention Step in Monroe's Motivated Sequence where you are attempting to establish the audience's attention as well as indicate the claim of the presentation and the primary reasons why a listener should agree with it.

The Need Step

Before a speaker can convince an audience to adopt a claim of policy, the audience must first be persuaded that a problem actually exists and the problem is serious enough to warrant a physical action by the listener. For instance, assume you want the audience to become organ donors. After gaining the audience's attention you should inform the audience that there is sufficient reason for considering becoming an organ donor. You should define the existing problem in such a way the listeners understand the **scope, nature, seriousness,** and **urgency** of the problem.

Claim of Policy
States a desired course of action

Preview Statements
Forecasts the speaker's strongest arguments for a persuasive speech

Scope
The size of a problem

Nature
The characteristics of a problem

Seriousness
The importance of a problem

Urgency
The immediance of a problem

In the case of organ donation you may explain the shortage of organs and the long lists of patients in need of transplants. This description of the current problem conveys to the listener the **significance** of the problem and creates a sense of urgency for action on the part of the listener.

It is often necessary for you to not only explain the current problem but also to provide sufficient background information about a topic for the audience. For example, if you are trying to convince an audience to support United States military action in Cuba, it would first be necessary for you to inform the audience briefly of the recent history of Cuban-American relations. In this particular case you may want to explain when and how Fidel Castro came to power and what has been the United States' historical role in Cuba. After the audience has sufficient background information, you would then define the current situation with respect to human and civil rights abuses in Cuba.

There are several factors that may mitigate the depth of the *Need Step*. If your analysis of the audience indicates the audience is very knowledgeable about a topic, the background information may not be as detailed or may be deemed to be unnecessary. If the **relevance** of a topic is blatantly obvious, for example you are speaking at a town meeting called specifically because of citizens' concerns for raising taxes, you may not find it necessary to elaborate on the seriousness of the issue. Everyone in attendance is present because they believe the issue is serious enough to discuss possible solutions.

There are many situations where a speaker may elect to modify the contents of the Need Step. However, each example should be predicated on the speaker's analysis of the audience and the situation (**context**) that governs the presentation.

It would be unrealistic to expect a listener to alter a **belief** or **attitude** or to take or avoid a physical action if he/she does not understand the nature, seriousness, urgency, and history of the existing problem. The Need Step's function is to provide a listener with the necessary information he/she needs to consider adopting the speaker's solution to the existing problem. If a speaker is unsuccessful in defining a problem and convincing the audience a problem exists, the speaker will not be successful in the presentation.

The Satisfaction Step

Now that the audience is convinced of the seriousness of the current problem, they are ready to consider adopting a solution to this problem. The solution to this problem is presented in the *Satisfaction Step*. This solution offered by the speaker, must be a solution that solves the problem previously described in the Need Step.

Significance
Tells the audience why this speech topic is important to humankind in general

Need Step
Part of the motivated sequence where the problem is explained

Relevance
Tells the audience why this speech is important to them

Context
Location in which communication is taking place

Belief
A non-evaluative assertion that individuals believe to be true or false

Attitudes
Govern our predispositions

Satisfaction Step
Part of the motivated sequence where a solution to the problem is presented

If a speaker wants a listener to consider supporting the legalization of marijuana in the United States and in the Need Step the speaker has indicated a serious rise in crime and drug abuse in the country, the solution (legalization of marijuana) should solve all facets of the problem. If the legalization of marijuana solves the rise in crime, but does not alleviate drug abuse, the solution has not satisfied the need. In this case, there would not be sufficient reason for the audience to adopt the solution to the current problem as described by the speaker.

Keep the proposed solution to the problem as simple as possible. This does not mean you should attempt to mislead the audience by simplifying a solution to the point that your depiction of the solution is no longer accurate. However, you should clarify the main points of the solution in such a way that the audience understands the nature of the solution.

For example, if you are proposing the audience support reforming the United States tax system, it may be impossible to describe the solution in detail in the time allotted for the presentation. In this instance you should accurately and concisely outline for the audience the proposed solution.

The Visualization Step

After proposing a solution that satisfies the problem described in the Need Step, you will want to visualize for the audience what the future will be if the proposed solution is adopted and/or if the proposed solution is not adopted. Put quite simply, a speaker is saying to the audience, "Let's look into the future and see what is going to happen." This occurs in the *Visualization Step*. There are three possibilities you can use to describe the future:

Visualization Step
Part of the motivated sequence where the audience is asked to visualize what the future will be if the proposed solution is or is not adopted

- ■ *Positive Visualization*
  The speaker describes the future with the proposed solution in place. Obviously the speaker will describe a more positive future than the present detailed earlier in the Need Step. Positive Visualization works best when the speaker's solution is quite simple to understand and clearly alleviates the current problem.
- ■ *Negative Visualization*
  The speaker describes the future without the proposed solution in place. In this case, the speaker will describe what will happen if the proposed solution is not adopted. The depiction of the future in this example would be less desirable than the present situation. Negative Visualization of the future is very effective for speakers who have shown a propensity for the problem to worsen in the

Need Step. If there is a strong likelihood the current situation will worsen if nothing is done to solve the problem, then negative visualization may be more effective than positive visualization.

■ *Negative and Positive Visualization*
The speaker describes the future without the proposed solution in place and then contrasts that future with a future with the proposed solution in place. In this example, the Positive Visualization will be in stark contrast to the possible negative consequences of inaction by the listener. It is generally more effective for a speaker to end by visualizing the future with the solution in place because he/she is urging the audience to adopt this solution to the problem.

The Action Step

The final step in Monroe's Motivated Sequence is the *Action Step*. In this step you indicate the specific action the audience can take to implement the proposed solution you described in the Satisfaction Step.

Suppose you are urging the audience to support United States military action in Cuba. You obviously do not expect the audience to grab their weapons and become mercenaries. However, you can propose a physical action, such as signing a petition or writing letters to the United States Congress. You may even urge inaction, such as boycotting products produced or manufactured in countries that are friendly to the Cuban government.

Regardless of the physical action proposed in the Action Step, the action must be a method for implementing or facilitating the implementation of the proposed solution. If a speaker were attempting to persuade an audience to support welfare reform in the United States, but did not indicate in the presentation who or how to contact the listener's representative in Congress, the speaker has failed to persuade the listener to action. In this case, the speech may have persuaded the listener to be concerned about the current welfare system, but because the speaker did not take the time to explain exactly how a listener could support the proposed solution the speaker has not been completely successful in meeting the stated claim.

It is often advisable to use visual aids, Chapter Four, with names, addresses, and/or phone numbers if you are requesting the audience contact a person or organization. It is also wise to have petitions ready to be signed and/or to provide a letter for the audience to sign. In each of these cases, the speaker has clarified and facilitated the listener's action.

Action Step
Part of the motivated sequence where the speaker indicates a specific action that he/she wants the audience to take

Goals of Monroe's Motivated Sequence

The Attention Step:

    Goals: (1) To gain the audience's attention
              (2) To indicate the significance of the topic to humankind
              (3) To indicate the relevance of the topic to the audience
              (4) To state your credibility
              (5) To clearly state the claim of policy
              (6) To briefly preview the strongest arguments in support of the claim

The Need Step:

    Goals: (1) To explain the background of the problem
              (2) To explain the seriousness of the problem
              (3) To explain the nature of the problem
              (4) To demonstrate the urgency of the problem
              (5) To demonstrate the propensity of the problem

The Satisfaction Step:

    Goals: (1) To outline the solution to the problem
              (2) To explain how the solution satisfies the problem

The Visualization Step:

    Goals: (1) To describe how positive the future would be if the listener adopts the solution
              (2) To describe how negative the future would be if the listener does not adopt the solution
              (3) To compare and contrast what the future would look like if the solution was not adopted by the listener and if the listener did adopt the solution

The Action Step:

    Goals: (1) To cue the audience the presentation is ending
              (2) To restate the presentation's claim of policy
              (3) To request action
              (4) To effectively end the presentation

Outline Format for Monroe's Motivated Sequence

I.   The Attention Step
   A.   Attention getting device
       1.   Significance of topic to humankind
       2.   Relevance of topic to audience
       3.   Speaker's credibility
   B.   Thesis (Claim of Policy)
   C.   Preview Statement
II.   The Need Step
   A.   History of the Problem
       1.   Inherency
       2.   Seriousness
   B.   Define the Problem
       1.   Significance
       2.   Propensity/Urgency
III.   The Satisfaction Step
   A.   Explain the solution
   B.   Explain why the solution will solve the problem
IV.   The Visualization Step
   A.   Positive Visualization
       or
   B.   Negative Visualization
       or
   C.   Negative/Positive Visualization
V.   The Action Step
   A.   Cue ending of speech
   B.   Restate claim of policy from introduction
       1.   Request action
       2.   Facilitate action
   C.   Exit line linked to attention getter in introduction

Sample Outline

Breaking the Cycle of Nursing Home Abuse
Evelyn Jones, Student

The Attention Step:

A. One out of every 25 older Americans residing in a nursing home will be a victim of elder abuse this year; that is roughly one million elders. (Human Services 3).
  1. Americans are living longer and the nation's elderly population is growing at an unprecedented rate, increasing the need for nursing homes.
  2. In 50 years, the majority of us will be in our 70s and will depend on others for our daily care, just like many abused nursing home residents.
  3. After extensive research, I have come to the conclusion that elder abuse in nursing homes is a rampant and increasing problem which must be stopped.
B. Our government should pass stricter regulation laws when it comes to nursing homes.
C. During the course of my speech, I will show you how the elder population's need for elder homes is increasing, shocking statistics on elder abuse in nursing homes, who the perpetrators of elder abuse are, and three solutions which if adapted could stop the inhuman cycle of elder abuse.

The Need Step:

A. Americans are living longer, and the nation's elderly population is growing at an unprecedented rate, particularly as a result of new technologies and medical advances. (Resident Abuse: Respondent1).
  1. There are now 28 million people aged 65 or older; by the year 2030, they will number more than 60 million or 21.2 percent of the total population.
  2. As individuals live longer, their need for nursing home care increases.
B. National abuse statistics are not available because different states vary in how they define abuse and collect statistics. (Resident Abuse: respondent 6).
  1. In a survey conducted on 232 knowledgeable individuals involved directly or indirectly with nursing home care, there were four major findings. (Resident Abuse: Resolving ii).
    a. 95 percent of all respondents indicated abuse is a problem for nursing home residents.
    b. Physical, verbal, and emotional neglect and abuse are perceived as the most prevalent forms of abuse.
    c. Nursing home staff, medical personnel, other patients, and family or visitors all contribute to abuse; however, aides and orderlies are the primary abusers for all kinds of abuse except medical neglect.

        d. Respondents believe nursing home staff lack training to handle stress-ful situations.

  2. There was a survey conducted in 1988 designed to assess the scope and nature of physical and psychological abuse in nursing homes. (Resident Abuse: Respondent 2).

        a. 36 percent of the sampled nurses and nurses aides had seen at least one incident of physical abuse in the previous year.

        b. 10 percent reported that they had committed one or more physically abusive acts.

C. Nursing aides and orderlies have the principal responsibility for the daily care of nursing home residents. (Resident Abuse: Respondent 14).

  1. As the primary caregiver to nursing home residents, most respondents say nursing home staff (specially direct-care staff—aides and orderlies) are responsible for most incidents of abuse except medical neglect.

        a. Direct care nursing home staff frequently must cope with stressful situations. (Resident Abuse: Respondent 16).

        b. Many respondents indicate staff are inadequately trained to deal with the physical, emotional, and psychological aspects of caring for the elderly and disabled. (Resident Abuse: Respondent 16).

  2. There are some reasons why nursing home staff may resort to abuse. (Wolf 9).

        a. Job frustration

        b. High stress

        c. Cultural differences

        d. Inadequate supervision of staff

        e. Staff's personal problems

  3. Inadequate supervision of staff, low staff-to-resident ratios, high staff turnover, and low wages are cited as factors contributing to abuse of nursing home residents. (Resident Abuse: Respondent 19).

        a. Low wages and the absence of employee benefits, recognition, and opportunity for advancement may all contribute to job dissatisfaction and rapid turnover among nurses aides. (Resident Abuse: Respondent 19).

        b. Because of the high turnover rate, there are usually some openings for positions. (Resident Abuse: Respondent 20).

           1. In order to meet State or Federal requirements many nursing home administrations have chosen to use temporary services.

           2. This habit (procedure) seems to be on the rise.

           3. Although temporary employees can fill critical staff shortages, several respondents expressed that temps may not have been adequately screened or trained to care for nursing home residents.

Satisfaction Step

    A. Nursing home staff training
        1. Training should be provided for staff who deal day-to-day with the elderly.
        2. Staff needs training in stress management, the aging process, and how to cope with and avoid confrontational situations.
        3. Training should be a prerequisite to obtain certification.
    B. Inadequate supervision
        1. Supervision in elderly homes must increase to avoid reoccurring abuse.
        2. By increasing supervision, the opportunities for physical abuse and property theft will decrease.
    C. A plan to maintain both staff and patients happiness and safety.
        1. Nursing home staff should organize a union who will represent them.
        2. The union should seek higher pay, a higher ratio of staff to residents, and employee benefits.
            a. This will lower the turnover rate.
            b. Avoid temporary workers who are not trained and are hired just to maintain Federal or State regulations.

Visualization Step

    A. If no action is taken to put an end to abuse in nursing homes, we may end up becoming victims ourselves.
        1. In 50 years, the majority of us will be in need of some help in our daily lives.
        2. Many of us will live in nursing homes.
    B. If government regulations are imposed and strictly followed, our future life as elderly people will be safe and happy.
        1. We will enjoy our last years in a peaceful environment.
        2. As elders, we will feel respected and not violated.
        3. We should not only do this for ourselves but also for upcoming generations.

Action Step

    A. In conclusion, we must realize that elderly abuse in nursing homes is a problem which affects everyone.
    B. Our government should pass stricter regulation laws when it comes to nursing homes. This problem must stop! As future elders we will not allow such behavior to continue without any legal action. Therefore, I am requesting your signature on a petition that I am sending to Congress.
    C. I sincerely hope that we as young Americans can unite and put pressure on government agencies to put an end to elder abuse and that the one million victims who suffer yearly will be able to live out their last days in peace and with dignity.

Bibliography

Wolf, R. S., & Pillemer, K. A. (1989). *Helping Elderly Victims: The Reality of Elder Abuse*. New York: Columbia University Press. FIU HV 6626.3 W65 1989.

United States. Office of Inspector General. (March, 1990). *Resident Abuse In Nursing Home: Respondent Perceptions of Issues*. Washington: Office of Evaluation and Inspections. FIU HE 1.2:N93/8.

United States. Office of Inspector General. (March, 1990). *Resident Abuse In Nursing Homes: Resolving Physical Abuse Complaints*. Washington: Office of Evaluation and Inspections. FIU HE 1.2:N93/8.

Human Services Monograph Series. (September, 1981). *Abuse of the Elderly*. Maryland: A National Clearinghouse for Improving The Management Of Human Services. Number 27. FIU HE 1.53:27.

Stock Issue Approach

Organizing a presentation using the *Stock Issue* approach is similar to organizing a presentation using Monroe's Motivated Sequence. Each organizational pattern attempts to answer a listener's questions as they would naturally arise during the course of the speech. The questions a listener will need answered before agreeing with the speaker's claim are called Stock Issues.

For example, if you want an audience to adopt the claim *There Should be Term Limits for Members of Congress*, there are several questions that an audience may want answered:

- Why should term limits be implemented?
- Have term limits been implemented in other legislative bodies?
- How should term limits be implemented?
- What will the term limits be?
- Is there a more effective way to achieve the same goal of term limits?

There are stock issues for each of the three types of **claims.** As such, a speaker will need to organize each presentation differently in hopes of addressing each of the listener's potential questions. The Stock Issue approach is not always an effective organizational technique for **claims of fact** or **value,** but the issues raised are important. The speaker should answer these issues in the presentation, but the organizational pattern the speaker uses may be varied.

A speaker organizing a claim of fact or value may elect to organize the presentation similar to an informative speech. A speaker may use chronological, topical, magnitudinal, problem-solution, or a cause-and-effect method for organizing the speech. **Claims of policy** are generally more

Stock Issues
An organizational pattern used for persuasive speeches

Claim
A type of thesis statement that states a speaker's position on an issue; it is used with persuasive speeches

Claim of Fact
State's the speaker's opinion as if it were true

Claim of Value
States a value judgment the speaker wants the audience to conclude

Claim of Policy
States a desired course of action

effective when organized using Monroe's Motivated Sequence or the Stock Issue approach.

Claims of Fact

Claim of Fact
State's the speaker's opinion as if it were true

As you recall, a *claim of fact* is a statement that depicts the speaker's view of reality. The speaker is asserting that something is either true or false. For instance, *Mr. Jones Killed Mr. Smith* or *Cigarette Smoking Causes Cancer*. The first stock issue for claims of fact is the criterion for assessing the truth of the resolution. What evidence is the speaker using to support the claim of fact? Is there a sufficient amount of evidence? In the example of *Mr. Jones Killed Mr. Smith*, the listener will ask:

- Is Mr. Smith is actually dead?
- If so, did Mr. Jones have a motive to kill Mr. Smith?
- Did Mr. Jones have the means to kill Mr. Smith?
- And, if so, did Mr. Jones have the opportunity to kill Mr. Smith?

If the speaker does not provide supporting material for each of these questions, the listener may not be persuaded to adopt the claim, *Mr. Jones Killed Mr. Smith*.

The second stock issue for resolving claims of fact is the believability of the supporting material. Is the evidence trustworthy and credible? In the example *Cigarette Smoking Causes Cancer*, the listener may ask if the supporting materials are trustworthy. Listeners will ask themselves the following types of questions:

- Where did the information in the presentation come from?
- Did the speaker use respectable, knowledgeable, and believable sources of information?

If the answers to these questions are "yes" then the listener is more likely to accept the claim as truthful. If not, the listener will not only reject the claim, but may question the speaker's knowledgeability, trustworthiness, and credibility as well.

Claims of Value

Claim of Value
States a value judgment the speaker wants the audience to conclude

Claims of value make a value judgment about a person, place, or thing. Examples of this include *Abortion is Morally Wrong*, *Capital Punishment is More Effective than Prison*, and, *Lincoln Was a Better President than Washington*. In each example the speaker is judging the desirability or worth of something or someone.

The same issues listeners will have for claims of fact will need to be answered for claims of value. Each listener will question what material the speaker has used to support the claim and if the material is credible.

However, there are additional issues raised by listeners when a speaker is asserting a claim of value.

The first question a listener will raise is whether the value being proposed is truly good or bad? For instance, a speaker who asserts that *Abortion is Morally Wrong Because it is Murder,* would first have to convince the listener that murder is morally wrong. This would not be difficult to do if the listener equated murder and abortion. He/she would probably agree that each was morally wrong. If a listener did not equate murder and abortion the speaker would have a much more difficult task of defending his/her choice of value terms, morally wrong.

The second question a listener may raise is how the speaker has defined the value terms being used. In the previous example, *Abraham Lincoln Was a Better President than George Washington,* the listener will ask how the value term better is being defined? The speaker would have to explain to the listener how the term better was being used and based on what criterion the speaker was evaluating the two presidents.

Here better may be defined in terms of leadership, military skill, and popularity. If a listener did not agree with the criteria for evaluating the men, then he/she may not agree with the speaker's definition of better and the speaker's evaluative judgment.

Claims of Policy

The most practical application for the Stock Issues is when a speaker is using a *claim of policy.* As you recall, a claim of policy is a statement that asserts a physical action. *Congress Should Not Adopt the Balanced Budget Amendment* or, *You Should Boycott the Products Manufactured in Countries that do not Adhere to Child Labor Laws* are both claims of policy.

Claim of Policy
States a desired course of action

Aside from the original two issues raised for all claims, (1) the amount of supporting material and (2) the credibility of the material, there are three basic Stock Issues for claims of policy:

- *Justification*
- *Solution*
- *Advantages*

You must first **justify** that a physical action is warranted by the listener. You should explain to the audience why the status quo or present system is either unable or unwilling to solve the problem. By indicating the inability or unwillingness of the present system you are addressing the issue of inherency. For example, a speaker who is asserting that *More Rigorous Standards Should be Used for Admission into Colleges and Universities in the United States,* would have to demonstrate to the audience how colleges and universities are either unwilling or unable to address the problem.

Justify
Demonstrate and/or prove

In addition to indicating the inherency of the problem in the status quo, you should also convince the audience the problem is significant enough to warrant a physical action. This step is equivalent to the Need Step in Monroe's Motivated Sequence. You should indicate the seriousness of the problem, the scope of the problem, the nature of the problem, and the propensity for the problem to continue to worsen. By addressing the issues of inherency and significance you are justifying the listener's attention to the next stock issue, the solution.

In order for a listener to adopt a physical action the speaker must clearly outline the course of action for the listener. As in the Satisfaction Step of Monroe's Motivated Sequence, the speaker should discuss why the **solution** to the stated problem will work and how the plan solves the problem. This is called the solvency of the plan. For example, you may propose that *The Federal Government Should Strengthen Regulation of the Airline Industry*. In this case, you should explain how the plan will strengthen regulation and how these regulations will work in practice.

The final Stock Issue a speaker should consider is the Stock Issue of **advantage.** What advantages will the proposed course of action produce? If there are any disadvantages to the plan, do the advantages outweigh the disadvantages?

Suppose you are proposing *The Food and Drug Administration Should Adopt Federal Standards for Production an Distribution of Seafood*. First you would clearly explain the benefits of such an action: (1) a decrease in the risk of disease and (2) increased consumer satisfaction. The possible disadvantages to the plan may be an increase in the cost of seafood as a result of the federal standards. You should then explain that the disadvantage of rising costs is not as important as the increase in public health. Weighing the potential costs versus the potential benefits is called cost-benefit analysis.

Solution
Process of solving a problem

Advantage
Factor favorable to success

The Stock Issues
Claim of Fact

- Is there sufficient evidence to support the claim?
- Is the supporting material credible?

Claim of Value

- Is there sufficient evidence to support the claim?
- Is the supporting material credible?
- Is the value term truly good or bad?
- How is the value criteria defined?

Claim of Policy

- Is there sufficient evidence to support the claim?
- Is the supporting material credible?
- Is the claim justified?
  a. Is the status quo unable or unwilling to solve the problem?
  b. Is the problem significant enough to warrant action by the listener?
- Will the plan work?
  a. Will the plan solve the problem?
  b. How will the plan be implemented?
- What advantages are there to the plan?
  a. What are the advantages of the plan?
  b. Do the advantages outweigh the disadvantages?

Direct Reason (Topic) Method

The direct reason method is the preferred organizational pattern for a **claim of fact** or a **claim of value** speech. When you use this method you state your claim and then state all the reasons that directly support your initial claim. Your reasons may be organized chronologically or in a form of topical patterning. For instance, a persuasive presentation using the claim of fact, *Affirmative Action is Reverse Discrimination*, may be organized as follows:

Specific Purpose: At the end of my speech, the audience will be able to explain three reasons why affirmative action programs do not work.

Claim of Fact: Affirmative action is reverse discrimination.
Body:
  A. Affirmative action programs have not increased the number of minorities in key management positions.
  B. Affirmative action programs make minorities feel inferior.
  C. Affirmative action programs is reverse discrimination.

A persuasive presentation using the claim of value, *The Distribution of Condoms in High School is Preferred to the Costs of Teenage Pregnancy*, may be organized as follows:

Specific Purpose: At the end of my speech, the audience will be able to list four reasons why distributing condoms in high school is a good idea.

Claim of Value: The distribution of condoms in high school is preferred to the cost of teenage pregnancy.

Claim of Fact
States the speaker's opinion as if it were true

Claim of Value
States a value judgment the speaker wants the audience to conclude

Claim
A type of thesis statement that states a speaker's position on an issue; it is used with persuasive speeches

Thesis Statement
A sentence that clearly tells the audience what the speaker will be discussing

Central Idea
A type of thesis statement used with Informative Speeches; it is a one sentence summary of entire presentation

Body:
A.   Teenage pregnancies are increasing.
B.   Teenage pregnancies cost society money.
C.   Sexually transmitted diseases are increasing among teenagers.
D.   AIDS is fatal.

If you are organizing a persuasive claim of fact or persuasive claim of value, your basic outline format is almost identical to the informative outline. The only differences would be in the introduction and the conclusion. In the persuasive speech you would use a *claim* as your **thesis statement,** rather than a *central idea* in the introduction. In the conclusion it is a good idea to restate your original claim of fact or value for emphasis.

Outline Format for a Claim of Fact or Value Speech

I.   Introduction
    A.   Attention getting device
        1.   Significance of topic to humankind
        2.   Relevance of topic to audience
        3.   Speaker's credibility
    B.   Thesis (Claim of Fact or Claim of Value)
    C.   Preview Statement
II.   Body
    A.   First Main Point
        1.   Subpoint of A
        2.   Subpoint of A
    B.   Second Main Point
        1.   Subpoint of B
        2.   Subpoint of B
III. Conclusion
    A.   Cue ending of speech
    B.   Restate thesis from introduction
        1.   Summarize first main point
        2.   Summarize second main point
    C.   Exit line linked to attention getter in introduction

A Sample Outline of a Claim of Fact

General Purpose:		To Persuade
Specific Purpose:		At the end of my speech, the audience will be able to explain two reasons why the juvenile justice system is ineffective.

I.   Introduction

Attention:	A.	Did you know that the rate of homicide among 14–17-year-olds has increased 124 percent from 1986–1991?
Significance.	1.	The nation appears to be on the verge of a crime wave.
Relevance:	2.	Most of you have probably been affected by crime. In some of these instances, the perpetrator may have been a juvenile.
Credibility:	3.	I fell victim to juvenile crime when my necklace was stolen as I was walking to my car from the mall.
Claim Of Fact:	B.	The juvenile justice system is endangering those it is supposed to help.
Preview:	C.	The juvenile justice system is changing for the worse and the system hurts juveniles.

II. Body

Main Point:	A.	The juvenile system is changing.
	1.	Historically, sentencing in juvenile court emphasized rehabilitation.
Subpoints:	2.	Currently, judges are sentencing juveniles as adults for some crimes.
Main Point:	B.	The current system hurts juveniles.
	1.	Lawmakers are ignoring the immaturity of 15- and 16-year-old children.
Subpoints:	a.	They are not adults physically.
	b.	They are not adults mentally.
	2.	Children are now being placed in prison with adults.
	a.	Some children have been abused.
	b.	Some children have been raped.

III. Conclusion

Cue Ending:	A.	In summary, throwing juveniles in jail is like throwing away America's future.
Claim	B.	Therefore, I conclude the juvenile justice system is endangering those whom it is supposed to help.
	1.	In some cases it recognizes children as adults.
	2.	These children have been abused.
Exit Line	C.	The juvenile justice system is obviously not working since the homicide rate is up 124 percent from 1986–1991.

Endnotes

1. Ross, R. (1990). *Understanding Persuasion*. (p. 46). Englewood Cliffs, New Jersey: Prentice Hall.
2. Hauser, G. (1991). *An Introduction to Rhetorical Theory*. (p. 98). Prospect Heights, IL: Waveland Press.

Bibliography

Bartecchi, M.D., C., MacKenzie, M.D., T., & Schrier, M.D., R. (1994, March 31). The human costs of tobacco use—first two parts. *The New England Journal of Medicine*, pp. 907–912.

Eisenman, R. (1994). Society confronts the hard-core youthful offender. *USA Today*, 122 (2584), pp. 27–28.

Federal Register (1995, August 1). Federal Register via GPO Access. 60(155) pp. 41313–41375.

Institute of Medicine (IOM), (1994). *Report to the FDA*. Washington, DC: U.S. Government Printing Office.

Lisser, E. (1994, July 8). U.S. health costs tied to smoking total $50 billion a year, CDC says. *The Wall Street Journal*, p. B3.

McGinnis, J. & Foege, W. (1993, November 10). Actual causes of death in the United States. *Journal of the American Medical Association*, 270(18), pp. 2207–2212.

Chapter Six
KEY TERMS

Absolute Value
  Claim: _____

_____

_____

Action Step: _____

_____

Attention Step: _____

_____

Attitudes: _____

_____

Belief: _____

_____

Central Idea: _____

_____

Claim: _____

_____

Claim of Fact: _____

_____

Claim of Policy: _____

_____

Claim of Value: _____

_____

Credibility: _____

_____

Ethos: _____

_____

Gaining Attention: _____

_____

Logos: _____

_____

Motivated
  Sequence: _____
Need Step: _____

_____

Preview: _____

_____

Relative Claim
  of Value: _____
Relevance: _____

_____

Satisfaction Step: _____

_____

Significance: _____

_____

Stock Issues: _____

_____

Values: _____

_____

Visualization Step: _____

_____

Chapter Six

EXERCISES

Persuasive Outline Preparation Sheet
Monroe's Motivated Sequence

General Purpose: _____

Specific Purpose: _____

Thesis: _____

I.   The Attention Step

Attention: A. _____

_____

_____

_____

Significance: 1. _____

_____

_____

Relevance: 2. _____

_____

_____

Credibility: 3. _____

_____

_____

Thesis: B. _____

_____

_____

_____

Preview: C. _____
                              _____
                              _____
                              _____
                         1. _____
                              _____
                         2. _____
                              _____
                         3. _____
                              _____

II. The Need Step
First Main Point   A. _____
                              _____
                              _____
                              _____

Subpoint of A   1. _____
                              _____
Subpoint of A   2. _____
                              _____
Subpoint of A   3. _____
                              _____
Second Main Point B. _____
                              _____
                              _____
                              _____
Subpoint of B   1. _____
                              _____

Name: _____   Date: _____

Subpoint of B   2. _____

                                     _____

Subpoint of B   3. _____

                                     _____

Third Main Point   C. _____

                                     _____

                                     _____

                                     _____

Subpoint of C   1. _____

                                     _____

Subpoint of C   2. _____

                                     _____

Subpoint of C   3. _____

                                     _____

III. The Satisfaction Step

First Main Point   A. _____

                                     _____

                                     _____

Subpoint of A   1. _____

                                     _____

Subpoint of A   2. _____

                                     _____

Subpoint of A   3. _____

                                     _____

Second Main Point   B. _____

                                     _____

                                     _____

Subpoint of B   1. _____

                                     _____

Subpoint of B   2. _____

_____

Subpoint of B   3. _____

_____

IV. The Visualization Step

First Main Point   A. _____

_____

_____

Subpoint of A   1. _____

_____

Subpoint of A   2. _____

_____

Subpoint of A   3. _____

_____

Second Main Point   B. _____

_____

Subpoint of B   1. _____

_____

Subpoint of B   2. _____

_____

Subpoint of B   3. _____

_____

V. The Action Step

Brief Summary   A. _____

_____

_____

Name: _____ **Date:** _____

Subpoints of A   1. _____

                                 _____

                            2. _____

                                   _____

                            3. _____

                                   _____

Physical Action   B. _____

                                   _____

                                   _____

Facilitate Action   1. _____

                                   _____

Bibliography

_____

_____

_____

_____

_____

_____

_____

_____

_____

_____

Chapter Six
REVIEW QUESTIONS

1. What are the four possible goals of a persuasive presentation?

   a. _____

   b. _____

   c. _____

   d. _____

2. How does a claim of fact differ from an actual fact?

   _____

   _____

   _____

3. List and define the three possible types of policy claims.

   a. _____

   b. _____

   c. _____

4. What is the definition of a belief?

   _____

   _____

   _____

5. Why is it best to think of beliefs in terms of a continuum?

   _____

   _____

   _____

6. What role does supporting material play in the formulation and classification of beliefs?

   _____

   _____

   _____

7. How do values differ from beliefs?

_____

_____

_____

8. How are attitudes different from beliefs and values?

_____

_____

_____

9. What are the three tests for establishing ethos?

   a. _____

   b. _____

   c. _____

10. How do the goals of a conclusion in a persuasive speech differ from the goals of a con-clusion in an informative speech?

_____

_____

_____

11. How does Monroe's Motivated Sequence address the audience's expectations?

_____

_____

_____

12. List the five basic steps in Monroe's Motivated Sequence.

   a. _____

   b. _____

   c. _____

   d. _____

13. What should the preview statement in an introduction using Monroe's Motivated Sequence forecast for the audience?

_____

_____

_____

14. What are the goals of the Need Step in Monroe's Motivated Sequence?

_____

_____

_____

15. In which step of Monroe's Motivated Sequence should a speaker outline the solution to a problem?

_____

_____

_____

16. What do the authors mean when they say the solution must satisfy the need?

_____

_____

_____

17. List and define the three options a speaker has in the Visualization Step.

a. _____

b. _____

c. _____

Name: _____   Date: _____

Student Critique Sheet—
Persuasive Speech

Speaker's Name: _____
Rate the speaker on each point:

5	4	3	2	1	0
excellent	good	average	fair	poor	not present

_____ Pause

_____ Gained attention of listeners

_____ Significance of topic to humankind

_____ Relevance of topic to our times

_____ Credibility statement

_____ Previewed main points of speech

_____ Need Step clearly explained

_____ Variety of supporting material

_____ Main points fully supported

_____ Satisfaction Step clearly explained

_____ Call for specific action

_____ Details given to adequately solve the need

_____ Visualization Step

_____ Summarized main points of speech

_____ Effective exit line linked to attention getter

_____ Strong eye contact with entire class

_____ Extemporaneous/conversational delivery

_____ Words articulated clearly

_____ Appropriate nonverbal communication

_____ Problem with um's and uh's

_____ Rate of speaking (too fast or too slow)

_____ Visual aids meet five criteria

_____ Visuals strengthen impact of message

Speech Evaluation Form

5	4	3	2	1
excellent	good	average	fair	poor

Time: _____

Attention Step

_____ gained attention and interest

_____ introduced topic clearly

_____ credibility

_____ claim of policy

_____ previewed body of speech

Need Step

_____ need clearly explained

_____ need demonstrated with evidence

Satisfaction Step

_____ plan clearly explained

Visualization Step

_____ negative/positive

Action Step

_____ call for specific action by audience

_____ final summary

_____ vivid concluding appeal

Delivery

_____ maintained eye contact

_____ used voice effectively

_____ used nonverbal communication effectively

_____ Presented visual aids well

Chapter Six
POWERPOINT SLIDES

- Definition of persuasion

- Goals of persuasion

- Persuasive speech types

- Tips for selecting topics

- The persuasion process

- Monroe's Motivated Sequence

- Attention Step

- Need Step

- Satisfaction Step

- Visualization Step

- Action Step

- Stock issues claim of fact

- Stock issues claim of value

- Stock issues claim of policy

DEFINITION OF PERSUASION

Persuasion is the process of changing or reinforcing attitudes, values, or behaviors.

322

GOALS OF PERSUASION

- To change an already existing belief, attitude or value.

- To reinforce an existing belief, attitude, or value.

- To promote a physical action.

- To discourage a physical action.

PERSUASIVE SPEECH TYPES

- Claims of fact
  - Something is true or false.

- Claims of value
  - Something is good, bad...

- Claims of policy
  - Something should or should not be done.

TIPS FOR SELECTING PERSUASIVE SPEECH TOPICS

- Topic must be interesting to you.
- You should have an understanding of the topic.
- Topic must be current and controversial.
- Must be appropriate for the occasion.
- Must be appropriate for audience.
- Must be narrowed down.

PERSUASION PROCESS

- The audience
  - What are their beliefs, attitudes and values?

- The speaker
  - Have I established credibility (ethos)?

- The message
  - Have I used good supporting material?

MONROE'S
MOTIVATED SEQUENCE

- Attention Step

- Need Step

- Satisfaction Step

- Visualization Step

- Action Step

ATTENTION STEP

- Gain the audience's attention
- Indicate the significance of the topic
- Indicate the relevance of the topic
- Establish credibility
- State your claim of policy
- Preview your main points

THE NEED STEP

- The history of the problem

- The nature of the problem

- The seriousness of the problem

- The urgency of the problem

- The propensity for the problem to worsen

THE SATISFACTION STEP

- Does your solution satisfy the problem described in the need step?

- Is your solution clear?

- Is your solution feasible and practical?

- Do the costs of implementing the solution outweigh the benefits?

THE VISUALIZATION STEP

- **Positive:**
  - With the proposed solution implemented.

- **Negative:**
  - If proposed solution is not implemented.

- **Compare/Contrast:**
  - Negative outlook, then positive outlook.

ACTION STEP

- Indicate what the audience can do to implement the solution.

- Summarize your strongest arguments.

- Restate your claim of policy.

- Return to the attention-getting device.

STOCK ISSUE
CLAIM OF FACT

- Is there sufficient evidence to support the claim?

- Is the supporting material credible?

STOCK ISSUES
CLAIM OF VALUE

- Is there sufficient evidence to support the claim?

- Is the supporting material credible?

- Is the value term truly good or bad?

- How are the value and the criteria defined?

STOCK ISSUES
CLAIM OF POLICY

- Is there sufficient evidence to support the claim?

- Is the supporting material credible?

- Is the claim justified?

- Will the plan work?

- What advantages are there to the plan?

PART FOUR

SPECIAL
OCCASION
SPEECHES

CHAPTER 7
Speaking to Entertain

"A speech is poetry; cadence, rhythm, imagery, sweep! A speech reminds us that words, like children, have the power to make dance even the dullest bean-bag of a heart."

Peggy Noonan

There may be a special occasion that requires you to give a public presentation. You may receive an award, be asked to speak at a funeral, introduce another speaker, deliver a toast, or give the commencement address at your graduation, to cite just a few examples. If you recall from Chapter Five, Informative Speeches, we discussed the three general purposes of a presentation. They are to inform, to persuade, and to entertain. Up to this point we have primarily focused on the informative and the persuasive speeches.

In this chapter on special occasion speeches, we will examine the speech to entertain, as well as other special situations where your primary goal may not be to inform or to persuade the audience. These speeches for special occasions are impromptu speeches, speeches of introduction, speeches of presentation, speeches of acceptance, commemorative speeches, and after-dinner speeches.

Impromptu Speeches

This may be the most difficult speech to deliver. As you should recall from Chapter Two, Delivery and Anxiety, the *impromptu* delivery should not be a speaker's first choice of delivery techniques. The impromptu speech, or speaking "off-the-cuff", can be difficult but it is not uncommon. Consider the example of sitting in a meeting and your boss turns to you and says, "Well, what do you think about our new marketing strategy?" Or, as you walk into the office your co-workers shout, "Congratulations! Speech. Speech. Speech." What should you do in these instances where your remarks are not prepared?

Impromptu speeches
Delivering a speech with little or no preparation

The first thing you can do is rely on your previous speaking experiences. By this time you have completed several speeches in class and you have also observed other students give various types of presentations. You have probably overcome much, if not all, of the pre-speech anxiety that you experienced earlier in the semester. However, you may be thinking to yourself, "This situation is different. In my previous speeches I had time to research the topic, prepare an outline, receive feedback from my instructor, and then practice my delivery!"

Despite this being a different occasion you can be confident in the fact that you know how to organize an introduction, body, and conclusion of a speech. You should also keep in mind that most of your everyday conversations are delivered impromptu. You are accustomed to thinking on your feet and organizing your thoughts very quickly. If you should find yourself in a situation that requires an impromptu delivery, follow these basic guidelines:

- **Analyze the occasion**
  In most instances, you have been asked to speak about a topic with which you are familiar. You should consider the occasion and what type of remarks would be appropriate. Quite often you can make reference to the occasion in your introduction.
- **Be brief**
  Regardless of the situation keep your remarks brief. The audience does not expect a lengthy presentation. For most occasions, an impromptu speech should not last more than a few minutes. Remain focused on your main points and do not ramble or try to lengthen the presentation by mentioning irrelevant information.
- **Analyze your audience**
  What does the audience expect you to say? What will they be anticipating given the occasion? Do they have any common characteristics? What do they know about your topic? Can you discuss or make reference to any previous remarks made by a member of the audience or by a previous speaker?
- **Organize your thoughts**
  This is the most important element in preparing an impromptu presentation. The audience will not expect a formal rehearsed presentation. They are aware you are speaking impromptu; therefore, there is no need to apologize for being informal. Simply organize your thoughts into a clear introduction, body, and conclusion.

The introduction, at a minimum, should include an appropriate attention getter (in many instances this is an acknowledgement of the occasion) and

Analyze Occasion
Determine what is appropriate language, topic, and content

Be Brief
Do not ramble

Analyze Audience
What the interest/needs of the audience are

Organize Thoughts
Don't jump around from one idea to the next with no logical connection

a clear thesis statement. The body of the presentation should be limited to no more than two main points. These main points may be supported from your personal experiences or observations. Provide the audience with examples in the body of the speech to support your ideas. The best method for concluding your impromptu speech is to return to your introduction and remind the audience of your thesis statement and main points, same as you would for an informative or persuasive speech. The occasion may also call for a brief "thank you" at the completion of your remarks.

Speeches of Introduction

A *speech of introduction* is a short speech for the purpose of introducing the main speaker. The biggest mistake that individuals make when giving a speech of introduction is that they speak too long and go into too much detail. This situation is exemplified in a speech given by Lord Balfour, the foreign secretary to Great Britain, during World War I. Lord Balfour, was scheduled to speak in the United States. The individual who was charged with introducing Lord Balfour spoke for 45 minutes on the cause of the war and then said, "Now Lord Balfour will give his address." Lord Balfour stepped to the lectern and gave his address—his literal address—his mailing address in London, England. There was nothing left for him to say because the speaker introducing him gave away all the details upon which Lord Balfour was to speak. Guidelines for these speeches (in the correct order) are:

Speech of introduction
The goal is to introduce the main speaker

- Introduce person by their title, not their name.
- Provide information that lends to their credibility.
- Briefly touch upon what they will be discussing in their speech.
- Introduce the person by their name.

Sample Speech of Introduction

Introduction of Modesto Madique
Professor Joann Brown

Board of directors and distinguished guests: It is my privilege to introduce to you today the president of Florida International University, who will address us on where our university is headed in the next decade. Most of you know that he has been the longest running president at this university and has led FIU through more changes than any previous president.

Our president has been lobbying the state legislature for a school of law at our great institution. He has repeatedly made the argument that there is no other university in our region of the state that offers a Juris Doctrin. This of course, provides a great disadvantage to the members of our community who have to choose between traveling great distances to receive a degree in law or paying the high cost of a private college/university education.

His hard work is making a difference because the legislature is taking notice of what he has to say. Today our president is going to tell us how this endeavor has progressed. Please welcome the President of Florida International University, President Modesto Madique.

Speeches of Presentation

Speech of Presentation
Recognize the accomplishments of the recipient

A *speech of presentation* is given when a group or individual recognizes the accomplishments of the recipient. Sometimes these speeches are as short as "the winner is . . ." Usually these speeches praise the achievements of the recipient and inform the audience about the purpose of the award. Guidelines for these speeches (in the correct order) are:

- Discuss the relevant accomplishments.
- State the purpose of the award.
- Mention it was difficult to come to a decision (after all only one person can win).
- Present the award.

Sample Speech of Presentation

Coronado Beautification Award
Major Mary Herron

As you all know, Coronado frequently plays host to presidents and dignitaries, and not to mention a few celebrities, officials, men and women of the Armed Forces, America's Cup racers, and other fascinating people from around the world. As they travel our small town streets, gazing at the mansions, the Victorians, and the cozy cottages, one of the most commonly heard remarks is, "Oh what a beautiful garden!" The world has come to our doorstep and appreciates what it sees. We felt it was time to honor our next-door neighbors for the long hours, great thought, enormous expense, and good old-fashioned toil they've invested to make our island community a blooming paradise.

As mayor of Coronado, California, I am frequently called on to present awards and commendations, but this particular award has great meaning for our community. We have inaugurated the Coronado Beautification Award to recognize the outstanding efforts of our citizens who provide this island community with its memorable elegance, its visual refreshment—in short, some of the most beautiful gardens we've seen anywhere in the world.

This choice was not at all an easy one for our judges to make, as they'll be glad to tell you, but after much study and consideration, our judges have named Brian and Andrea Applegate of 555 "B" Avenue as our first recipients of the Coronado Beautification Award. If you've driven or walked by the Applegates' home, you know that they have not been content to keep their roses, wisteria vines, flowering plums, and exotic annuals well-tended inside the walls of their classic cottage garden. For the passerby who might feel shy about peeking through the arched trellis for a glimpse, the Applegates have extended this floral profusion outside their garden walls. They've planted a colorful abundance or roses, shrubs, annuals, and perennials along the sidewalks of their corner lot, where everyone can enjoy them.

Mr. and Mrs. Applegate, if you'll step up here please . . . I am honored to present you with this plaque, which pays tribute to your selfless toil and investment. You have truly beautified our community, and you richly deserve the first Coronado Beautification Award!

(She presents the plaque, steps aside, and joins the applause for the beaming couple.)

Speeches of Presentation and Cultures

Cultures differ in the extent to which individualism is regarded favorably. The most individualistic cultures in the world speak English. Speakers of English place such great emphasis on the individual that they capitalize the pronoun "I" in writing, but interestingly enough, not the "Y" in the pronoun "you." Thereby, English speakers suggest that "I" am more important than "you". English is the only language that does this. In collective cultures such as Native American, Indonesian, Panamanian, and Pakistani, commitment between individuals in a group is very strong. In fact, Apache Indians do not use a pronoun equivalent to "I" at all in their language. They use "dene," which is equated to mean "we." They are a collective culture. They view everything as happening to the group, not to one particular person.

As far as special occasion speeches are concerned, collective cultures do not like to single out one individual to praise over other members of the group. In New Zealand, they have a saying: "The tall poppy gets mown down." A similar saying exists in Japan, "Deru kugi wa utareru" when translated means: "The nail that sticks up is hit." Compare these sayings to the one used in the United States, "The squeaky wheel gets the grease." In other words, in an individualistic society, if you speak out, you are taken care of—your problem is solved. In a collective culture, if you speak out, there are negative consequences. Consequently, the members of collective cultures feel uncomfortable having their personal characteristics (good or bad) publicly acknowledged. Therefore, speeches, of presentation are most likely to be made to an entire group as opposed to one individual.

Speeches of Acceptance

Speech of Acceptance Expresses gratitude for an award

A *speech of acceptance* is a speech to express gratitude for an award. Your objective is to sincerely convey your appreciation for the recognition of all your hard work, which is why you received the award to begin with. The format (in the correct order) is as follows:

- What this award means to you.
- Thank the people who helped you.
- Thank the people bestowing the award on you.

Sample Speech of Acceptance

Coronado Beautification Award
Mr. Brian Applegate

My wife and I are quite touched by this honor, considering the many beautiful homes and gardens that cover this island. It has always been our joy to fill our garden with new plants, and things just kept expanding, until we have finally run out of room for more. If our joy brings pleasure to others, then so much the better. I would just like to thank our many friends who have given us cuttings from their own gardens; our children, who have always endured our passion for pulling weeds and digging in the manure every spring; my mother, who taught me how to prune a rose; and the committee, for bestowing this honor upon us. We have just been doing what we love to do, and we're glad you've enjoyed it, too. Thank you Mayor Herron, friends, and judges of the committee.

Commemorative Speeches

Commemorative speeches are a group of speeches such as: toasts, tributes, commencement addresses, eulogies, and inaugural addresses.   These speeches pay tribute to someone or something. Commemorative speeches are lengthier than the other special occasion speeches previously discussed in this chapter. They are also serious in nature and are delivered from a **manuscript** as discussed in Chapter Two. When delivering a commemorative speech, your **general purpose** is to entertain your audience with the creative use of language. The old saying "it is not important what you say, but how you say it" is the heart of a commemorative speech. If you think of some of the great speeches in American history, Abraham Lincoln's *Gettysburg Address*, JFK's Inaugural Address, Martin Luther King, Jr.'s *I Have a Dream* speech, Jesse Jackson's *Rainbow Coalition* speech—just to name a few, we bet you will have trouble listing the main points of these speeches, yet you can recall memorable lines from each of these speeches. It is those memorable lines that make these speeches great.

Commemorative Speeches
Pay tribute to a person, place, or idea

Manuscript
Delivering a speech from an essay

General Purpose
Never spoken by the speaker; helps determine the type of research material

Sample Speeches of Commemoration

I Have a Dream
Martin Luther King, Jr.

I am happy to join you today in what will go down in history as the greatest demonstration for freedom in the history of our nation.

Five score years ago, a great American, in whose symbolic shadow we stand today, signed the Emancipation Proclamation. This momentous decree came as a great beacon, light of hope to millions of Negro slaves, who had been seared in the flames of withering injustice. It came as a joyous daybreak to end the long night of their captivity.

But one hundred years later, the Negro is still not free. One hundred years later, the life of the Negro is still sadly crippled by the manacles of segregation and the chains of discrimination. One hundred years later, the Negro lives on a lonely island of poverty in the midst of a vast ocean of material prosperity. One hundred years later, the Negro is still languished in the corners of American society and finds himself an exile in his own land. And so we've come here today to dramatize a shameful condition.

In a sense we've come to our nation's Capitol to cash a check. When the architects of our republic wrote the magnificent words of the Constitution and the Declaration of Independence, they were signing a promissory note to which every American was to fall heir. This note was a promise that all men—yes, black men as well as white men—would be guaranteed the unalienable rights of life, liberty, and the pursuit of happiness.

It is obvious today that America has defaulted on this promissory note insofar as her citizens of color are concerned. Instead of honoring this sacred obligation, America has given the Negro people a bad check—a check which has come back marked "insufficient funds."

But we refuse to believe that the bank of justice is bankrupt. We refuse to believe that there are insufficient funds in the great vaults of opportunity of this nation. And so we've come to cash this check—a check that will give us upon demand the riches of freedom and the security of justice.

We have also come to this hallowed spot to remind America of the fierce urgency of now. This is no time to engage in the luxury of cooling off or to take the tranquilizing drug of gradualism. Now is the time to make the real promises of democracy. Now is the time to rise from the dark and desolate valley of segregation to the sunlit path of racial justice. Now is the time to lift our nation from the quicksands of racial injustice to the solid rock of brotherhood. Now is the time to make justice a reality for all of God's children.

It would be fatal for the nation to overlook the urgency of the moment. This sweltering summer of the Negro's legitimate discontent will not pass until there is an invigorating autumn of freedom and equality. Nineteen sixty-three is not an end, but a beginning. Those who hope that the Negro needed to blow off steam and will not be content will have a rude awakening if the nation returns to business as usual. There will be neither rest nor tranquility in America until the Negro is granted his citizenship rights. The whirlwinds of revolt will continue to shake the foundations of our nation until the bright day of justice emerges.

But there is something that I must say to my people, who stand on the warm threshold, which leads into the palace of justice. In the process of gaining our rightful place, we must not be guilty of wrongful deeds. Let us not seek to satisfy out thirst for freedom by drinking form the cup of bitterness and hatred.

We must forever conduct our struggle on the high plane of dignity and discipline. We must not allow our creative protest to degenerate into physical violence. Again and again we must rise to the majestic heights of meeting physical force with soul force.

The marvelous new militance, which has engulfed the Negro community, must not lead us to a distrust of all white people. For many of our white brothers, as evidenced by their presence here today, have come to realize that their destiny is tied up with our destiny. They have come to realize that their freedom is inextricably bound to our freedom we cannot walk alone.

As we walk, we must make the pledge that we shall always march ahead. We cannot turn back. There are those who are asking the devotees of civil rights, "When will you be satisfied?" we can never be satisfied as long as the Negro is the victim of the unspeakable horrors of police brutality. We can never be satisfied as long as our bodies, heavy with the fatigue of travel, cannot gain lodging in the motels of the highways and hotels of the cities. We cannot be satisfied as long as the Negro's basic mobility is from a smaller ghetto to a larger one. We can never be satisfied as long as our children are stripped of their selfhood and robbed of their dignity by signs stating "For Whites Only." We cannot be satisfied as long as a Negro in Mississippi cannot vote and a Negro in New York believes he has nothing for which to vote. No, no, we are not satisfied, and we will not be satisfied until justice rolls down like waters, and righteousness like a mighty stream.

I am not unmindful that some of you have come here out of great trials and tribulations. Some of you have come fresh from narrow jail cells. Some of you have come from areas where your request for freedom left you battered by the storms of persecution and staggered by the winds of police brutality. You have been the veterans of creative suffering. Continue to work with the faith that unearned suffering is redemptive.

Go back to Mississippi, go back to Alabama, go back to South Carolina, go back to Georgia, go back to Louisiana, go back to the slums and ghettos of our Northern cities, knowing that somehow this situation can and will be changed. Let us not wallow in the valley of despair.

I say to you today, my friends, so even though we face the difficulties of today and tomorrow, I still have a dream. It is a dream deeply rooted in the American dream.

I have a dream that one day this nation will rise up and live out the true meaning of its creed, "We hold these truths to be self-evident that all men are created equal."

I have a dream that one day on the red hills of Georgia the sons of former slaves and the sons of former slave owners will be able to sit down together at the table of brotherhood.

I have a dream that one day even the state of Mississippi, a state sweltering with the heat of injustice, sweltering with the heat of oppression, will be transformed into an oasis of freedom and justice.

I have a dream that my four little children will one day live in a nation where they will not be judged by the color of their skin but by the content of their character. I have a dream today.

I have a dream that one day, down in Alabama, with its vicious racists, with its governor having his lips dripping with the words of interposition and nullification, one day right there in Alabama little black boys and black girls will be able to join hands with little white boys and white girls as sisters and brothers. I have a dream today.

I have a dream that one day every valley shall be exalted, every hill and mountain shall be made low, the rough places will be made plane and the crooked places will be made straight, and the glory of the Lord shall be revealed, and all flesh shall see it together.

This is our hope. This is the faith that I go back to the South with. With this faith we will be able to hew out of the mountain of despair a stone of hope. With this faith we will be able to transform the jangling of discords of our nation into a beautiful symphony of brotherhood. With this faith we will be able to work together, to pray together, to struggle together, to go to jail together, to stand up for freedom together, knowing that we will be free one day.

This will be the day—this will be the day when all of God's children will be able to sing with a new meaning, "My country 'tis of thee, sweet land of liberty, of thee I sing. Land where my fathers died, land of the Pilgrim's pride, from every mountainside, let freedom ring." And if America is to be a great nation, this must become true.

So let freedom ring from the prodigious hilltops of New Hampshire. Let freedom ring from the mighty mountains of New York. Let freedom ring from the heightening Alleghenies of Pennsylvania!

Let freedom ring from the snowcapped Rockies of Colorado! Let freedom ring from the curvaceous slopes of California!

But not only that. Let freedom ring from Stone Mountain of Georgia!

Let freedom ring from Lookout Mountain of Tennessee!

Let freedom ring from every hill and molehill of Mississippi. From every mountainside, let freedom ring.

And when this happens, when we allow freedom to ring—when we let it ring from every village and every hamlet, from every state and every city—we will be able to speed up that day when all God's children, black men and white men, Jews and Gentiles, Protestants and Catholics, will be able to join hands and sing, in the words of the old Negro spiritual, "Free at last! Free at last! Thank God almighty, we are free at last!"

Tribute to JC
Joselle Galis-Menendez, Student

I can still see him, sitting on the back steps that led up to the apartment. A chunk of greasy hair hanging in his eyes, too-long arms wrapped around his wooden lady, as bare feet tap to the melodies only he hears; beautiful songs, spinning in his head, playing hide-and-seek with consciousness. My cousin never went out of his way to be different, he just was. He never went out of his way for much. JC loved music, poetry, worn in Van Halen t-shirts, beautiful women, Peach Schnapps, and me. That was all he needed. It never mattered how much younger I was. I don't think he ever bothered to calculate how many years floated between us, the world saw a little girl blindly following her makeshift older brother, her small sweaty palms clutching the back pockets of his torn corduroys. We never analyzed what brought us together, just appreciated it and went along our business.

I once (suffering from a brief case of self doubt) began questioning. Questioning every thick, summer afternoon I spent listening to him tickle his beloved guitar, memorizing every iridescent string, or every game of pool he let me win again and again. Then I remembered that last summer we spent together. He, as usual, squeezed out the fresh, tangy juice of every moment; passing down to me every obscure theory and tidbit of information he could, and I welcomed each as my own precious heirloom. We spent hours in the den of that tacky apartment, reading articles he'd clipped and collected, poetry he'd never forgotten and stories and lyrics written on crumbled napkins and used envelopes. I folded their words and meanings into the layers of my memory. Some how, even then, I knew the idealistic ranting of a nineteen-year-old dreamer, would be of more use to me than the endless charts and chapter summaries I analyzed during the school year.

He was the piper, playing a hypnotizing tune with one ink-stained hand, and leading me by the heart with the other. We spent days at a time, belly up, legs rested on the wall listening to every CD, tape, 8-track, and record he'd manage to collect from only-God-knows-where. Of course, some could argue JC was a terrible influence. Without him, I may never have lit that first cigarette (or every one after that), drank gallons of Peach Schnapps, or filled dozens of notebooks with pages of irrational banter about the way things should be. But without JC, I would have never been as happy as I was every one of those lazy summers, or as happy as I manage to be now.

At the end of that last summer, I hugged, kissed him, and cried, sending him off to write more songs no one would hear and more poetry no one could understand. Three weeks later, I had left the den, Dickinson, and Dylan buried in the mounds of white sand. In the midst of the dreaded back-to-school preparations, I received a letter and my very first brown paper package tied up with string (these are one of my favorite things). Inside that package I found: books, crumbled napkins and envelopes, videotapes, and a collection of music that could only have belonged to one person. JC had finally decided what to do with himself, he'd boarded a plane for Spain and set off to do everything he did here, except in a different language and with red wine instead of Peach Schnapps.

Now, as I find myself tumbling inside the black hole of coming of age, the anxieties I face every day, instead of new and frightening, appear as old friends I once sung about to the strum of a guitar. They've come to remind me of poems I haven't read in years, songs I'd forgotten the words to, ideas so fresh and unspoiled you want to hide them from the world forever, and a greasy-haired, nineteen-year-old, who plays his guitar from a sandy time capsule in my mind.

After Dinner Speeches

After Dinner Speeches
Festive/light hearted speeches to entertain an audience

Thesis Statement
A sentence that clearly tells the audience what the speaker will be discussing

A presentation delivered after a meal at a banquet or reception is called an *after dinner* speech. These are festive light-hearted occasions where people have gathered to enjoy themselves. If you are asked to present an after dinner speech, your goal should be to make the audience laugh.

Unlike a comic's monologue, a speech to entertain is organized around a central theme. Just as a speech to inform or speech to persuade has a **thesis statement,** the speech to entertain also has a controlling thought. While the speech subject may be serious, such as *Child Raising*, *American Business Practices*, or *Popular Culture*, the speech should not be full of statistics and quotes nor should it be a series of jokes or unconnected funny anecdotes. This speech should have a clear introduction, body, and conclusion.

Samples of After Dinner Speeches

Public Speaking
Michelle Reyes, Student

Good evening ladies and gentlemen. I would like to begin by thanking you for being here tonight. As you all know, we don't have much time left together, and because of that, I would like to take a moment to look back upon some of our monumental accomplishments in the history of the most exciting class at Florida International University. I know by now that most of you have probably guessed what class I am speaking about, but for those of you dozing off, due to internal noise, it would be my pleasure to pronounce with perfect articulation, the name of this wonderful and fulfilling class. You probably know it as SPC 2600, or better yet, public speaking.

Now that I have gained your attention and introduced my topic clearly, let us travel back in time to that first day of class when we all sat here, nervously looking around at each other, wondering what was in store for us. Little did we realize that it was to be one of the most significant and groundbreaking days of our lives. This day, January 8, 2004, to be exact, marked the beginning of our journey together in becoming superior public speakers.

As a member of this class, and an outstanding speaker because of it, I have worked the entire semester, gathering information that you will find interesting. If you can recall, one of our biggest struggles was overcoming the obstacle of delivering a narrative speech. I have to say that I am sorry I did not bring in a videotape of my narrative speech in order to use it as a visual aid today. However, after we worked together to accomplish our goal of delivering outstanding narrative speeches, our next task, the informative speech, if you'll all agree with me was a walk in the park. We all seemed a little more at ease, because at this point in the class, most of us were at the level of, say, a speaker of the White House or a motivational speaker.

I rejoice when I look back upon the tremendous progress we have made in this class. When I first began, I must say I did not even know the meaning of the word extemporaneous. Now, I've made it a part of my everyday vocabulary, as I am sure you all have too. Plus, I've not only learned how to deliver a speech the correct way, but by listening to your speeches, I have gained knowledge on a variety of subjects ranging from art, wars, and diseases.

So you can see that we have really come from the dark ages where we used to hold onto the lectern for dear life while we delivered a speech with more um's and uh's than actual words. We have soared through our narrative and informative speeches like hawks in the sky, overcoming the distance of faraway lands. Finally, we have paved out for ourselves a golden road leading to a better future.

Before I conclude, I would like to give special thanks to the one who made all this possible, and I'm sure you'll all agree, the one who has also made our lives full of anxious moments. We know her as the woman in purple, Professor Joann Brown. Without her, this accomplishment would not have been possible.

In conclusion, I would like to thank each and every one of you, for being part of this group and for helping me to overcome the fear associated with public speaking. The only fear we are left with now is the fact that we must face the dreary days of summer ahead, days without a public speaking class. I know it will be hard, but it will be up to you to keep the memory of this class alive. I would like to leave you with one more thought tonight—if you ever run into a problem with your speech, always remember the phrase, "I don't have that information with me, but I can get back to you on that." I wish you all well. Have a good night.

My True Love
Jorge Rodriguez, Student

There is nothing that I wouldn't do for her. I love her as much as I could love any person. But no matter what I do for her, she never shows any appreciation and never gives me any love back. You may ask yourself, does this creature have a heart? Well, to be honest no, but she does have a six-cylinder engine, a water pump, and a carburetor. Yes, this thing that I love so much is my car.

When I first saw her three long years ago, I knew right away that I had to make her mine. Her beautiful brown interior, her sparkling green paint, and of course her big round tires made her totally irresistible. What can I say, it was love at first sight, at least on my part. But little did I know that she did not feel the same way. Let me explain to you the torture that I have been through during this three-year relationship.

The first time that I realized that my sacrifices were unappreciated was just a few months after we met. I bought her this gorgeous dark green paint job for our four-month anniversary. She looked really good in it, but do you think that I could get a thank you? Of course not, instead I got a dead alternator in the middle of a busy intersection, and let's just say that she was rudely greeted by an oncoming station wagon. This is the first way in which my giving spirit went unappreciated.

Needless to say, after the accident she was feeling pretty bad. I felt that I had to do something to end her misery. So I went out and found a second job, and after a few months I was able to surprise her with a new alternator, quarter panel, and yet another paint job. And for a while after that, our relationship went well. We went everywhere together, to Orlando, New Orleans, even to Baltimore. It seemed as if nothing could stop us now.

Well, maybe something could stop us. She caught me cheating on her with someone else, a new red Maxima to be exact. Because of this, she felt she had to punish me. She figured the best way to make me suffer was to get together with the evil Mr. Median. She met with Mr. Median twice within a period of a week and a half. The second time he gave her a gift, a popped tire and major alignment damage. I realized that I had to act straight away or I would lose her, so I went running to her with four brand new sports tires. This patched things up for a while, but things went downhill quickly.

By this time, my friends were telling me that I should get rid of her. They could see that she was sucking me dry and they thought that I would be better off with something younger. This actually crossed my mind, since she was not nearly as energetic as she used to be. But still I felt very attached to her, and I couldn't just dump her. Boy that was a mistake.

I took her for her annual check up on our second anniversary, and the doctor aid that she was going to need major surgery. If not, she was given 2–3 months. So I took out four thousand dollars, yes four thousand dollars, and brought her to the hospital. She underwent an engine transplant as well as a transmission transplant, and this made her feel better. But do you think she showed any gratitude towards me. I'm sure you know what the answer is.

This previous chapter in our relationship shows how much I sacrificed just to be with her. No one else in their right mind would have spent that kind of money on her. But as I have mentioned several times before, everything I do goes unappreciated. Instead of being good to me for giving her new life, she tried to take her own life just three short months later.

She went and blew up her radiator, and almost killed herself in the process. For me this was the last straw. I knew that I had to end it here. I had to stop tormenting myself. She was sucking my bank account dry, and I wasn't getting anything in return except for stress and irritation. And when the doctor told me that she needed a radiator transplant, I told him to forget about it. And this was the end of our almost three year relationship.

So that's my story. I'm sure you have heard it before. But even though she put me through so much torment and sacrifice without showing any appreciation or love, I still feel that one day we will be together again.

Chapter Seven
KEY TERMS

After Dinner
  Speeches: _____

Commemorative _____
  Speeches: _____

Impromptu _____
  Speeches: _____

Speeches of _____
  Acceptance: _____

Speeches of _____
  Introduction: _____

Speeches of _____
  Presentation: _____

Chapter Seven
REVIEW QUESTIONS

1. What is the key component of a commemorative speech?

    _____

    _____

    _____

    _____

    _____

2. What is the format for delivering an acceptance speech?

    _____

    _____

    _____

    _____

    _____

3. What guidelines should you follow when preparing a speech of introduction?

    _____

    _____

    _____

    _____

    _____

4. How should you organize a presentation to accept an award?

    _____

    _____

    _____

    _____

    _____

5. How does an after dinner speech differ from a comic's monologue?

_____

_____

_____

_____

6. How do you determine the appropriateness of humor in an after dinner speech?

_____

_____

_____

_____

After-Dinner Speech Evaluation Form

Time: _____

	Excellent	Good	Average	Fair	Poor
First Pause	5	4	3	2	1
Introduction Gained Attention	5	4	3	2	1
Um's and Uh's	5	4	3	2	1
Topic Dealt with Creatively	5	4	3	2	1
Language Clear	5	4	3	2	1
Nonverbal Communication	5	4	3	2	1
Supporting Materials Entertaining	5	4	3	2	1
Strong Eye Contact	5	4	3	2	1
Voice Used Expressively	5	4	3	2	1
Speaking Rate	5	4	3	2	1
Speaking Volume	5	4	3	2	1

Commemorative Speech Evaluation Form

Time: _____

	Excellent	Good	Average	Fair	Poor
First Pause	5	4	3	2	1
Introduction Gained Attention	5	4	3	2	1
Um's and Uh's	5	4	3	2	1
Topic Dealt with Creatively	5	4	3	2	1
Language Clear	5	4	3	2	1
Nonverbal Communication	5	4	3	2	1
Supporting Materials Entertaining	5	4	3	2	1
Strong Eye Contact	5	4	3	2	1
Voice Used Expressively	5	4	3	2	1
Speaking Rate	5	4	3	2	1
Speaking Volume	5	4	3	2	1

Chapter Seven
POWERPOINT SLIDES

- Types of Special occasion speeches

- Impromptu speeches

- Speeches of introduction

- Speeches of presentation

- Speeches of acceptance

- Commemorative speeches

- After dinner speeches

TYPES OF SPECIAL OCCASION SPEECHES

- Introduction
- Presentation
- Acceptance
- Commemorative
- After Dinner

IMPROMPTU SPEECHES

- **Analyze the occasion**

- **Be brief**

- **Analyze your audience**

- **Organize your thoughts**

SPEECHES OF INTRODUCTION

- Be brief

- Introduce person by their title

- State the topic of the speech

- Provide information that lends to speaker's credibility

- Save speakers name for last

SPEECHES OF PRESENTATION

- Why this person is receiving award

- Purpose of award

- Qualified pool of candidates

- Present award

367

SPEECHES OF ACCEPTANCE

- Reference of award to life

- Thank people who helped you

- Thank people bestowing award to you

COMMEMORATIVE SPEECHES

- Pay tribute

- Inspire through use of language

AFTER DINNER SPEECHES

- Light hearted

- Contain sense of humor

- Is not a comic routine

FINAL REVIEW

INDEX

Final Review

Define communication.

_____

_____

_____

_____

List and explain the different elements of the communication process.

_____

_____

_____

_____

List and explain the different levels of communication.

_____

_____

_____

_____

Define Symbols.

_____

_____

_____

_____

List and explain the different delivery styles.

_____

_____

_____

_____

List and explain the different ways to prevent anxiety.

_____

_____

_____

_____

List and explain the different criteria for visual aids.

_____

_____

_____

_____

List and explain the different types of visual aids.

_____

_____

_____

_____

List and explain the different general purpose statements.

_____

_____

_____

_____

List and explain the different rules of specific purpose statements.

_____

_____

_____

_____

List and explain the different thesis statements.

_____

_____

_____

_____

List and explain the items of the introduction.

_____

_____

_____

_____

List and explain the items of the conclusion.

_____

_____

_____

_____

List and explain the different types of connectors.

_____

_____

_____

_____

List and explain the different organizational patterns.

_____

_____

_____

_____

List and explain the different types of outlines.

_____

_____

_____

_____

List and explain the different types of attention-getting statements.

_____

_____

_____

_____

List and explain the different types of supporting material.

_____

_____

_____

_____

List and explain the different types of special occasion speeches.

_____

_____

_____

_____

List and explain the goals of a persuasive speech.

_____

_____

_____

_____

List and explain the different types of claims used for persuasive speeches.

_____

_____

_____

_____

Define an attitude, belief, and value.

_____

_____

_____

_____

List and explain the components of Monroe's Motivated Sequence.

_____

_____

_____

_____

INDEX